SPEEDWAY
IN SCOTLAND

GLASGOW NELSON DIRT-TRACK
— MOTOR CYCLE CLUB —

FIRST MEETING

AT THE

WHITE CITY SPORTS GROUND
PAISLEY ROAD WEST, IBROX

On FRIDAY, 29th JUNE,

AT 7 P.M. PROMPT

Official Programme - Price 3d

Stewards—DAVID RAINEY   G. CUMMING   J. EDWARDS
A. W. DRUMMOND

Judge—DAVID RAINEY   Starter—DAVID WRIGHT

Secretary—R. W. DRUMMOND

RIGHT OF ADMISSION RESERVED

REFRESHMENT BUFFET on Ground

DIRT-TRACK MOTOR CYCLE RACING
at these Grounds - - EVERY WEEK

See Daily Press for Date and Starting Time of Next Meeting

SPEEDWAY
IN SCOTLAND

Jim Henry and Ian Moultray

TEMPUS

First published 2001

PUBLISHED IN THE UNITED KINGDOM BY:

Tempus Publishing Ltd
The Mill, Brimscombe Port
Stroud, Gloucestershire GL5 2QG

PUBLISHED IN THE UNITED STATES OF AMERICA BY:

Tempus Publishing Inc.
2A Cumberland Street
Charleston, SC 29401

Tempus books are available in France and Germany from the following
addresses:

Tempus Publishing Group   Tempus Publishing Group
21 Avenue de la République   Gustav-Adolf-Straße 3
37300 Joué-lès-Tours   99084 Erfurt
FRANCE   GERMANY

British Library Cataloguing in Publication Data.
A catalogue record for this book is available from the British Library.

ISBN 0 7524 2229 4

Typesetting and origination by Tempus Publishing.
PRINTED AND BOUND IN GREAT BRITAIN.

Contents

Acknowledgements   6

Introduction   7

1. The Pioneer Year   9

2. Edinburgh   14

3. Glasgow   91

4. Ashfield   169

5. Motherwell   187

6. Linlithgow   201

7. Short-lived venues   217

Acknowledgements

To compile any book on the exciting sport of speedway would be impossible without the help of so many enthusiastic people. So we must thank all of those who, from the birth of the sport in 1928, have put into words, facts and figures all the relevant details of the time which has greatly helped with the compilation of this and many other such books.

For this book, we thank the speedway press, including the *Speedway News*, *Broadsider*, *Speedway Gazette* and *Speedway Star*, along with many others. The local newspapers, including the *Edinburgh Evening News* and *Daily Record*, have also provided a wealth of information.

We would like to thank Mike Hunter and Jimmy McIntyre for their encouragement and help and George Sherridan and David Wardrope for their patient reading of the text – which helped ensure the accuracy of the facts and the flow of the sentences.

For the photographs which appear in this book we thank 'Friends of Edinburgh Speedway', Jimmy Grant, Jack Cupido and the late Drew McLaren (all Edinburgh). The Ashfield photographs all come from the private collection of the late Norrie Isbister. Alex McIntosh, Ian Steel and Jeff Holmes contributed the images for the Glasgow section. We also thank the late Spencer Oliver (Middlesbrough/Newcastle) and Mike Hinves (Eastbourne). Motherwell photographs were supplied by one time Eagle, Bluey Scott. There are also pictures where the photographer is not known – we would like to thank these unknown 'snappers'.

Finally, we would again like to thank our long-suffering spouses Nan Moultray and Anne Henry, who see us from time to time as we work on our speedway histories.

Introduction

The development of motorcycle speedway racing in Australia since 1923 had been chronicled in the British motorcycle press. However, it was not until 1928 that speedway racing arrived in Britain. The first event in Britain, in mid-February, made front page news and set off a mad scramble to present the sport to the British public.

There were hundreds of motorcycle clubs in Scotland, but none seemed interested. The first steps to present the new sport, then called 'dirt-track racing', were taken up by a group of motorcyclists who came together under the name of 'The Glasgow Nelson Dirt Track Motor Cycle Club'. By early March they had a venue, a disused trotting track in the east end of Glasgow known as the Olympic Stadium, and were trying to develop the new skills required to put on dirt track racing.

The Glasgow Nelson boys had made a modest start whilst the newly arrived Australians were searching for venues. By late March 'Dirt Track Speedways Ltd' had tied up the use of Celtic Park in Glasgow, and a professionally backed club in Edinburgh had secured the use of a site at Marine Gardens in the seaside suburb of Portobello. Other venues were secured in Glasgow, but they had all fizzled out by mid-July. Only Marine Gardens was a success.

Scottish speedway saw out the initial boom period, but by mid-1932 it was a dead letter. It had a brief resurgence in both of the major cities just before the Second World War and came back to enjoy the post war boom. At its zenith Scotland had four League tracks, but television and entertainment tax helped kill off the sport in Scotland in the mid-1950s.

You can't keep a good sport down and in 1960 the sport came back to stay. It has its ups and downs, but the sport has been staged north of the border every year since the 1960 watershed.

This book tells the story of speedway racing in Scotland, from the pioneering days of 1928 through to the new millennium. Although not a comprehensive history, it concentrates on the two main venues of Glasgow and Edinburgh, through their many changes of track, and looks at the other main venues of Linlithgow, Ashfield and Motherwell. The border ventures at Berwick have not been included in this book as, despite its very strong Scottish links, the town lies just inside England. The Pioneer Year is singled out for special attention and the many short-lived venues are covered under a single chapter.

The book does not attempt to chronicle grass track activity, nor does it look at sand track racing which often used oval tracks. There is only room for this passing mention of the ice racing ventures of the early 1970s which used trials bikes, and those staged later which used modified speedway bikes at Murryfield Ice Rink.

This book can only give a flavour of Scottish speedway's rich past in the space available. However, it is hoped you can taste the whisky, Irn Bru and haggis amid the smell of the methanol and Castrol 'R' as you read on through from 1928 onwards.

Ian Hoskins, the flamboyant Scottish speedway promoter.

One

The Pioneer Year

Ready for the off at Marine Gardens, 1928.

Speedway has always used that name in Australia, but it was introduced to Britain as dirt-track racing and it took some time to adopt the Australian name. It was as dirt-track racing that the Scottish public were introduced to the sport in 1928.

In early March the Glasgow Nelson Motor Cycle Dirt Track Club was formed and it secured a venue in the eastern end of the city. The practice sessions started almost as soon as the club was formed and the public were welcome to go along and watch. Club members practised using road-going machines and some even tried out using machines which were fitted with sidecars.

The first event for the Scottish paying public was staged on the afternoon of Easter Monday, 9 April 1928. This featured heats and finals of events categorised by the capacity of the machine, that is machines up to 350cc, machines up to 600cc and machines of unlimited capacity. There was also a class for sidecars but this was poorly supported.

The Nelson Club's track was an unusual shape, with bends of differing radii. It had an inside post and rail fence and an outer fence composed of vertical railway sleepers. Thankfully the latter were quite rotten; one sidecar crew crashed through them to emerge at the other side largely unscathed.

John Allan, a well known club road racer, won the opening event watched by 2,000 spectators, while another notable road man, Harry Potts, also took part. The remainder of the racers, including pioneers George Cumming, Jimmie Pinkerton and Norrie Isbister who would go on to become professional speedway racers, were either experienced sand track racers or interested amateurs looking to have fun and make a bob (five pence) or two. Prizes were cash plus a gold medal.

Contemporary photographs show the machines in road-going trim, complete with front number plates mounted on the mudguards, horns and tax discs. The brakes, which were soon to be outlawed, were used to promote skids on the bends. The board hard surface, which did not replicate the deep loose surfaces of the Australian tracks, did not allow a broadside. The broadside, or two-wheeled skid, was to be the trade mark of the pioneer racers and literally thrilled millions.

Glasgow Nelson did not draw huge crowds and staged a total of five meetings between 9 April and 11 May. The Glasgow Nelson Club was not finished on 11 May and thus moved on to stage a meeting at the then recently completed White City Stadium in Glasgow's Paisley Road West. As with their other ventures, the public did not turn out in their droves to the meeting on 29 June and the Club bowed out of the dirt track game.

The Glasgow Nelson venue flickered to life very briefly in 1932 when the Lanarkshire Speedway Club tried a revival. This club staged one known and possibly one other event featuring the then established White City stars Billy Llewellyn and Sam Aitkenhead.

The rise of the professional arm of the new sport led to its introduction at Celtic Park, home of the Glasgow Celtic Football Club. Its arrival was announced in March by the legendary Celtic manager Willie Maley and it opened on 28 April. The promotion used a mix of the established stars like Kiwi Stewie St George,

Celtic Park action – Norrie Isbister leading on a 1926 Rex-Acme 350cc OHV Blackburne. The tax disc was reg. no. GD 23675.

Aussies Paddy Dean and Billy Galloway, and the lanky Yank Lloyd 'Sprouts' Elder. They mixed in the emerging English stars such as Alf Foulds, Harry Lewis and Ivor Creek and, to add a Scottish dimension, drew in the best of the locals from the Nelson venue.

Scot Ralston Dunlop, with a handicap of 14 seconds, made it to the final of the Opening Handicap event, while Norrie Isbister made it to the semi-final of the Golden Gauntlet match race event. Norrie gave Stewie St George, the winner of both main events, a run for his money.

The 3,600 crowd saw what was described as 'real broadsiding' but far too few came back to sustain the professional branch of the sport at Celtic Park. The ranks of Scots grew weekly and the reliance on the visiting stars gradually reduced. The promoters tried hard through advertising and promotional events, such as staging a half-time demonstration for thousands of 'Old Firm' (Celtic and Rangers) fans in May. It wasn't enough. By late July they threw in the towel and speedway in Glasgow was dead for 1928.

An optimistic promotion had started out by staging meetings on Saturdays and Tuesday. This was reduced to one meeting a week and then to one a fortnight. Probably the lamest excuse for postponement was given as the visit of the then Prince of Wales to Glasgow. The 440-yard track which circled the hallowed turf staged twelve meetings and featured many of the stars who were drawing in thousands south of the border. Its failure was attributed by some to its East End location, which was not the most salubrious part of the city.

The Celtic Park venue can, however, claim a few firsts. It probably staged the first meetings where bookmakers were present and it certainly staged the first charity event. The beneficiaries of the charity event were the St Andrews Ambulance Association and 3,000 turned out to swell the fund set up to pay for a new headquarters building. It could probably claim to be the first ever major stadium venue in Britain, but despite this the track lies under stands which have squared off the viewing area.

Glasgow's East End tried hard to capitalise on the new sport. A third venue, the Carntyne Greyhound Stadium, opened on Friday 25 May under the direction of track manager Jack Nixon-Browne. Later to become an eminent politician and Peer of the Realm as Lord Craigton, Jack raced himself on a 350cc AJS. Jack had never seen a track so he constructed it to his own specification. One bend swept the inside of the greyhound track whilst the other was a hairpin bend edged with moss to cushion fallers. The track was likened to a ploughed field and the 600 who did turn up saw lots of falls. A second and final meeting was staged a week later at which Mr Nixon-Browne won the 350cc event, a triumph which he attributed to his unlimited access to practice facilities.

Glasgow had four venues in the space of five months and none of them saw out the season. On the other side of the country a different picture was emerging.

A flurry of possible Edinburgh venues for the new sport were mentioned in the

Drew McQueen, one of the great Scottish Pioneers.

local press but the new promotion settled for constructing a track at the recently built football stadium at Marine Gardens in Portobello. It took until early May to prepare the circuit and Sprouts Elder arrived to try it out. A further demonstration-cum-trial event was staged and then it was public showtime.

Saturday 19 May saw the public turn up in their droves to watch Stewie St George win the Scottish Gold Helmet from Scot Drew McQueen. Fellow Scot Sam Reid won the event for local men from McQueen and an open event was won by Eric Burnett. Stewie went home with £25, while Sam took £10 and Eric £15. Drew McQueen won £25 for his two second places.

A total of 8,000 people turned out for the opening event and the numbers gradually rose, to peak at 27,000 near the end of the season. This big turn-out was prompted by an anticipated visit of Sprouts Elder which did not materialise, but they did see the Frogley Brothers, Roger and Buster. The Edinburgh public, it seems, knew their sport and turned out in great numbers to see the visiting stars. Such was the popularity of the sport that it prompted the promoters to produce one of the first local track magazines – the *Scottish Speedway News*.

There were rumours that speedway might feature in the other major cities of Dundee and Aberdeen but this never happened. The sport did make an attempt to take a foothold between the two main cities when a track was built at the Sports Park in Broxburn, then a shale mining town, ten miles west of Edinburgh. The authorities, the Scottish Auto Cycle Union, refused to licence the venue and it only staged a few practice and demonstration events. So that was 1928. Only Edinburgh had caught the speedway bug.

Two
Edinburgh

Great Monarch Jack 'The Giant Killer' Young leading Aub Lawson (West Ham).

Speedway in Edinburgh can be split into three distinct eras, one for each of the three main venues which have staged the sport in Scotland's capital city. Before the Second World War the dirt track fans watched the racers at the seaside Marine Gardens track. The stadium owners had great plans to turn the site into a giant football stadium, which never materialised. After the war, and up to 1967, the citizens of Edinburgh watched the team called the Monarchs perform at Old Meadowbank Stadium, which was sited on what is now part of the Commonwealth Stadium in London Road. Finally, from the late 1970s to the mid 1990s, fans followed the Monarchs exploits at Powderhall Stadium in Beaverhall Road. Sadly, none of these venues exist any more, having been lost to other uses such as a bus depot, the aforementioned stadium and residential development.

The departure from Old Meadowbank saw Monarchs move west to Coatbridge for two seasons, before the licence was sold to Wembley in 1970. Evicted from Powderhall, the Monarchs became the Scottish Monarchs for 1996, based at Shawfield Stadium in Glasgow, before moving to their current home, the Lothian Arena in Armadale.

The Early Days

The Edinburgh paying public first saw dirt track racing on 19 May 1928 on the

A general view of the Marine Gardens speedway paddock.

Left: Programme cover from 1928. Right: George McKenzie

purpose-built and 'oh so smooth' 440-yard circuit. After another meeting the following Tuesday, the promotion settled down to a fortnightly interval until mid-July, when weekly meetings were introduced. The Edinburgh club was quite forward-thinking, purchasing proper Douglas dirt track bikes for the most promising riders to pay for out of their winnings.

The success of local men, like all-round motorcyclist Drew McQueen, George McKenzie, Harry Duncan and Eric Burnett, probably contributed to the growth in the popularity of the sport. The inaugural 500cc Scottish Championship was won by Glasgow's Jimmy Valente and the 350cc Scottish Championship was won by McQueen. The latter also won the track championship.

The meetings were usually staged in the afternoons but, towards the end of the season, track lighting was installed and night racing was introduced. The racing looked faster under lights but the race times confirmed that this was not the case.

The 1929 season was hours old when speedway came back to Scotland. The New Year's Day meeting was attended by 26,000 who saw McQueen clean up. This was a season which saw the dog fight between the two 'Macs'. It was won by McQueen, but McKenzie could have pipped him had he not spent a long spell in hospital after an accident at West Ham. McQueen, who also had a break due to injury, became 500cc Champion in front of a 34,000 crowd, a record attendance that would stand for nearly

Programme cover from 1939.

MEETING No. 4
Season 1939

Tuesday, 30th May

MARINE GARDENS
SPEEDWAY

PORTOBELLO
EDINBURGH

181.5   PROGRAMME   3ᴰ
PRICE

twenty-five years. Aussie Frank Arthur took the track championship from Jack Parker and Sprouts Elder. Team racing came to Edinburgh in late 1929 and the home side beat Newcastle Gosforth in late September and Glasgow a few weeks later.

Set against the highs of the 1929 season was the tragic death of Walter Brown from Musselburgh. A World War One hero, the dirt tracking wire worker's funeral brought his home town to a halt.

1930 saw Aussies Syd Parsons, Len Stewart and a young lad who had a strong Welsh accent but was reputed to be a Scot, Gordon Spalding, join the two Macs in the Edinburgh league side. They won their share of home matches but could not hold off Belle Vue, White City Manchester or Sheffield, while they won nothing on their trips down south. Strange events included the post-match refereeing decision which caused the wrong result to be published and the 20-4 whitewash of Wombwell because the visitors suggested that the match should end two heats early. The 1930 Scottish Champion and the Track Champion was Harry Whitfield of Wembley. Harry's wins in Scotland earned him the nickname '£100 Harry'.

The crowd numbers fluctuated between 2,000 and 25,000 and the promotion decided to close at the end of July. A rider co-operative promotion was proposed but this never materialised. The Edinburgh promotion agreed to give the sport a run in 1931 but only two of a planned five fixtures were raced. Both meetings featured the old favourites and used the handicap and scratch race formula. A

Mick Murphy, at the point of no return, leading Drew McQueen and Clune Johnstone.

third fell victim to rain.

Six barren years came to an end on 14 May 1938. That season fifteen meetings plus a midget car event were staged up to the end of August. Drew McQueen came back for a short spell but gave up after injury in the Scottish Championship early on in the season. The Championship event was dominated by First Division stars and was won by Bluey Wilkinson from Tommy Croombs, Tiger Stevenson and Arthur Atkinson. Film of the event taken by Wilkinson still survives. Ernie Evans of Sheffield won the Track Championship.

The team was called The Thistles and they were beaten at home quite regularly. The line-up varied but the star signing was Oliver Hart, who would blossom in 1939.

Like Glasgow, Edinburgh was turned down for league entry in 1939 but they raced a variety of scratch and team sides until admitted to the ACU Northern Trophy. The Thistles picked up a draw at Belle Vue but lost elsewhere. Jack Gordon and Laurie Packer were two regulars with Hart in a Thistles side that was rather more successful than in 1938. Wilbur Lamoreaux won the Scottish Championship and Cordy Milne the Track Championship.

The 1939 season came to a premature end, closing after a best pairs event, won by Oliver Hart and Jack Hyland, which was staged just before the outbreak of war. To Hart fell the honour of winning the last ever race at Marine Gardens.

The stadium was requisitioned by the Ministry of Defence and not released until after its successor track, Old Meadowbank, was operational. The site of the stadium is now occupied by the Marine Bus Depot.

Edinburgh Monarchs, 1948-54

Speedway moved into its boom years in the late 1940s and early 1950s. Glasgow had resumed track action at White City in 1945, but were on their own in Scotland with Newcastle the nearest track.

At the end of the 1947 season, Ian Hoskins, the Glasgow promoter, felt that there may be an opportunity for speedway in Edinburgh if a stadium could be found to house a track. The Marine Gardens stadium was no longer available, so Ian chartered a monoplane to fly over Edinburgh in search of a suitable location. His quest was successful when he spotted a stadium situated not far from Portobello. On further enquiry he found that the Old Meadowbank stadium, as it was known, was owned by the Leith Athletic Football Club. The main shareholder and chairman was Bob Rae, a builder by profession.

Agreement was reached, and work started to lay a track around the football pitch. Ian's next problem was to build a team and it was his father, Johnnie, who suggested that he approach promoters Frank Varey (Sheffield) and Alice Hart (Belle Vue) as to the possibility of riders. Little did he know that this was to be his

Left: First Edinburgh team captain Bill Maddern. Right: Programme from the first Old Meadowbank meeting against Glasgow.

last involvement with promoting Edinburgh Speedway until the 1960s. Frank Varey was to take up the role as promoter-manager and a team was born. The team would be known as the (Meadowbank) Monarchs with the colours being blue and gold.

Edinburgh were allocated pre-war riders Bill Maddern, an Australian who had experience with Bristol, and Clem Mitchell. Bill was to become the Monarchs' first team captain. Clem, an Australian and former Crystal Palace and New Cross rider, originally joined the side as team mechanic, but he ended up as a regular in the line-up. In the following years Clem was to prove invaluable to the club with his technical knowledge, producing his own frame (the Mitchell JAP) which would be used by most of the team.

Dick Campbell, a New Zealander with one season's experience with Sheffield in 1947, was touring with a Wall of Death troop when he first witnessed speedway at Belle Vue. He liked what he saw and gave it a go. He was recruited to Monarchs' starting line-up the following year for what was to be a long association with the club. Other additions to the starting line-up were Dennis Parker, the nephew of Belle Vue's Jack Parker, and former Glasgow riders Bill Baird, Bert Shearer, Nobby Downham and Eddie Lack.

Eddie Lack, a Londoner, had enjoyed a reasonable season with Glasgow in 1946, but early in 1947 had crashed and suffered serious injuries – to such an extent that doctors had said he would never race again. Eddie proved them wrong and was a great servant to Edinburgh over the coming years. Australian Keith Cox soon pushed his way into the team, and sitting in the wings was a young English-born rider who was to make a big impact in the coming years, namely Don Cuppleditch. Bobby Baxter, a former footballer with Middlesbrough and a Scottish international, took over the track management in June.

Monarchs were a weak side, winning only nine of their sixteen home league matches to finish bottom of the table. They started their league campaign on the road, racing five away before making their home debut, but they did manage to get some league points in the bag. The Monarchs took to the track for the first time at Bristol on 26 March and were well and truly defeated 64-20. Three more big defeats followed at Birmingham, Sheffield and Norwich. Just for the record, the team's first heat winner was Eddie Lack when he won heat seven at Birmingham.

On 13 April the team were to be the first visitors to the new Fleetwood circuit. On arriving early in Fleetwood, the Edinburgh team were surprised to find that they were allowed to practice in the afternoon before the evening meeting – and they took full advantage. The real surprise was that the Fleetwood team did not turn up until just before the start of the meeting.

The result was Edinburgh's first away win 49-35; after a first heat duck, Eddie Lack went on to win his other three. Dick Campbell was beaten into second place in heat one by Fleetwood's Dick Geary, but thereafter was undefeated by a Fleetwood rider, recording 9 paid 11 points.

On 17 April, the Monarchs made their home debut in front of a 17,000 crowd against their neighbours from the West, the Glasgow Tigers. The first race winner on the new Old Meadowbank track was a Tiger – Will Lowther.

Although Will dropped his only point to Dick Campbell in heat five, he led his Tigers to a convincing 44-39 victory. Two further home defeats were to follow for the Monarchs, against Norwich and then Bristol, before they recorded their first home win, over Sheffield, on 1 May, 47-36. Later in the year they raced one 'home' match (2 October) against Middlesbrough at Sheffield, as the Old Meadowbank stadium was unavailable.

In the Anniversary Cup, the Monarchs also finished at the bottom of the table. Although they defeated Glasgow at Old Meadowbank 62-46 in the first leg of the National Trophy, they went out in this first round tie, suffering defeat at White City 70-38.

On an individual level, Dick Campbell won the Caledonia Cup, and Glasgow's Joe Crowther won The Fifty Guineas Trophy. Joe also won the Speedway Riders' Championship qualifying round (this was the forerunner to the World Championship). A Best Pairs on 24 July went to Dick Campbell and partner Norman Evans of Newcastle, and Sheffield's Bruce Semmens won the Border Cup in September.

Glasgow were the visitors in the final meeting of 1948, but this time they left with their tails between their legs, as Monarchs brought the curtain down with a 52-32 victory. If it was a gamble to introduce speedway to this new venue it

Pre season practice, 1949. From left to right: Don Cuppleditch, Bill Baird, Dick Campbell, Eddie Lack, Danny Lee, Jack Young, Clem Mitchell, Tommy Lack, Dennis Parker.

certainly paid off in a big way, as at times crowds topped 20,000: the promotion could look to 1949 with relish.

Changes were made in 1949, but not just to the team. The track, which measured 368 yards in 1948, proved to be too square because it was situated around a football pitch. It was altered to provide more sweeping bends by eating into the terracing, which gave the banked bends a bit more width. With a new track measurement of 365 yards, Bill Maddern's 1948 track record time of 67.8 would stand forever in the record books.

Leaving the side in 1949 were Bill Maddern and Keith Cox. Dick Campbell was back as a full-time Monarch, after transferring from Belle Vue for a fee of £250. This was something of a bargain as Dick improved his scoring with regular double point returns and gathered 7 full and 4 paid maximums in league matches for an average of 8.51 – not a bad buy!

Others who returned were Clem Mitchell, Eddie Lack, Dennis Parker, Bill Baird and Danny Lee, who joined Edinburgh late on in 1948. Don Cuppleditch, who had a few outings in 1948, claimed his place in the 1949 side and returned a respectable 4.12 average from his 42 league outings.

The new faces included Tommy Lack, brother of Eddie, who had a handful of outing early on in the season, and a twenty-four-year-old Australian, Jack Young, from Adelaide where his home track was Kilburn. Jack suffered illness early on in the season, before an ankle injury slowed him up mid-season, but he still topped the averages with 8.69. He scored 10 full and 2 paid maximums in what was a very satisfactory first season. Harold Fairhurst joined the team at the start of July and made his debut against his old team, the Glasgow Tigers, at White City, scoring 11 points. Thereafter he settled to become a solid middle order man.

Monarchs were a vastly improved side in 1949, finishing fifth in the league and only losing twice at home, to Bristol and Sheffield, in consecutive weeks. They won four times on their travels – twice at newcomers Ashfield, plus Coventry and Fleetwood.

Glasgow now supported two tracks. As well as the Tigers there were now the Giants, and it was the Ashfield Giants who opened the 1949 season at Old Meadowbank on 2 April. Edinburgh won that opener 57-27, with new Monarch Jack Young recording a 12 point maximum and establishing a track record of 67.6 seconds.

Jack was to be missing for the next nine league meetings as he was hospitalised with appendicitis. He returned for the home match against Southampton on 7 May and continued from where he had left off with another unbeaten score. On the individual front, Jack won the World Championship qualifying round and then started a remarkable run by winning the Scottish Riders' Championship. In both he scored an unbeaten 15 points. He also won his first international cap, as he was selected for the Australia as reserve at Odsal on 3 September, scoring one point from his three races.

Ron Johnson of New Cross won the East of Scotland Cup, while Clem Mitchell and Eddie Lack won a Best Pairs on 16 April.

1950 Monarchs team. From left to right: Eddie Lack, Danny Lee, Harold Booth, Tommy Allott, Harold Fairhurst, Dick Campbell, Don Cuppleditch, Jack Young (on bike).

Edinburgh were the winners of a four-team competition on 30 July, when the other teams were Glasgow Tigers, Newcastle and Sheffield. First Division West Ham were beaten $45\frac{1}{2}$-$38\frac{1}{2}$, while a combined Sheffield/Glasgow side lost out 54-30. Although the Monarchs went out of the National Trophy 101-112 on aggregate to Fleetwood, it was a most satisfactory campaign.

There were a few additions to the Monarchs' side in 1950. Tommy Allott transferred from Sheffield for the sum of £300, a new Australian, Ron Phillips, joined the ranks, and Yorkshireman Harold Booth came on a transfer from Halifax mid-season.

The North Shield, which ran as a mini-league, opened the season. With away wins at Sheffield and Ashfield, along with a draw at Hanley (Stoke), the Edinburgh side looked as though they might have been in with a chance of some early silverware, but a shock defeat at the hands of the Giants from Ashfield at Old Meadowbank put paid to that dream. They eventually finished in third spot behind Ashfield.

Forty-one-year-old veteran Tommy Allott had started those North Shield matches with some impressive returns, including a 12 point maximum against Glasgow Tigers at Old Meadowbank, but an injury at Glasgow's White City seemed to knock him back, as thereafter his points return dipped. In August he returned to Sheffield, stating that the travelling was too much for him.

Harold Fairhurst missed the start of the season, as he did not return from New Zealand until the end of May. His season was much the same as the previous one, being a steady middle order rider.

Jack Young was in near-unbeatable form in the North Shield, registering 9 either paid or full maximums from the 14 fixtures. He only once failed to reach double figures, when an engine failure restricted his tally to 8 points at Glasgow White City.

There was to be more disappointment for the Edinburgh side when they went out of the National Trophy in the first round to Southampton, who won both the home and away legs for an aggregate 122-94 victory.

Going into the league, twenty-six-year-old Ron Phillips had to be dropped from the side due to a ruling that Scottish teams were only allowed three Dominions riders. Edinburgh had Jack Young, Dick Campbell, Clem Mitchell and Ron Phillips, and there was a question over the returning Harold Fairhurst (who had spent the majority of his years in New Zealand, even though he was born in Wigan). The Control Board relented and classed Harold as a British subject, but refused to bend the rules any further to allow Ron back into the team.

Clem Mitchell retired from racing at the start of July to become track manager, and then team manager. This allowed Ron Phillips back into the side, along with newcomer Harold Booth.

Eighth in the league table was a drop from the 1949 season. Only Jack Young (with a league average of just below 11) and Dick Campbell were consistently scoring the bulk of the points available. They lost out to Halifax and Coventry at Old Meadowbank, but countered those defeats with away wins at Fleetwood and in their final match at Newcastle in October. They also managed a draw at Plymouth.

Glory did come Edinburgh's way when they won the Border Trophy. After disposing of Newcastle in their qualifying round, 122-94 over two legs, they met Glasgow Tigers in the final, winning both home and away legs for an aggregate score of 133-83.

Challenge matches against First Division sides Wembley (38-46 defeat), Belle Vue (44-40 win) and Birmingham (40-44 defeat) were to prove that both Jack Young and Dick Campbell could live with the big boys. Jack's scores were 10, 11 and 10, while Dick managed 4, 12 maximum, and 10. In heat one of the Belle Vue meeting on 1 May, Ron Mason of Belle Vue fell, and Clem Mitchell (who was right on his back wheel) did well to avoid the stricken rider by turning his bike towards the fence. This resulted in Clem injuring himself so badly that he had to withdraw from the meeting.

For his unselfish action, Clem received a Commendation for Valour from the Speedway Control Board for his heroic action in avoiding what would have been a nasty crash. Ron Mason was able to walk away after receiving attention, but took no further part in the meeting.

Jack Young went all the way to the final of the World Championship in this season. He started his World Championship route by entering the second round with 15 points at Norwich. This was followed by the same unbeaten score at Edinburgh which put him into the next round. At Ashfield, 15 in a one-off third

Clem Mitchell.

round put him into the final stages, where he recorded 15 at Belle Vue, 14 at New Cross and then 10 at Bristol to make the final at Wembley as the highest qualifier.

At Wembley on 21 September, Jack scored a last in his first World Championship outing, but soon settled to score a respectable 7 points to finish in eighth position on the night. Jack was now a regular in the Australian Test side, racing in four of the Tests against England. He also won caps in all the five Overseas *v.* Britain matches. Appearing for Scotland, and scoring 14 points in the 67-41 victory over England at White City Glasgow, Jack completed a fine international season. On 5 October, Jack retained the Scottish Riders' Championship with another unbeaten 15 points, completing what was a remarkable year for 'Jack the Giant Killer'.

1951 was the Monarchs' best season to date with great improvements throughout. Jack Young was just unbeatable in what was to be one of the greatest individual performances in the history of speedway. Apart from engine problems, he only dropped points in the league to Glasgow's Tommy Miller and Junior Bainbridge in September, then to Norwich star Bob Leverenz on 20 October. These few men were the only riders to get the better of Jack. The most remarkable thing about Jack was that most of his wins were from the back, as gating was not a strong point. His league record was 340 points from 116 starts for a remarkable average of 11.72.

The North Shield, as in the previous year, started the 1951 season, and Jack began his *annus mirabilis* by recording full 12 point maximums in all 10 fixtures – although it was as a much improved team overall that the Monarchs collected their first major title. Edinburgh also became the Division Two North Shield champions, losing only once to their arch rivals, Glasgow Tigers.

Dick Campbell was still the main support to Jack at this time, but Don Cuppleditch, who did miss a number of league matches through injury in August and September, was otherwise a solid third-heat leader. The most improved rider in the Monarchs ranks was Bob Mark. Bob also scored as a heat leader, whereas he had been no more that a good reserve in 1950.

Both Eddie Lack and Harold Fairhurst had their best season, and in the reserve berths a number of riders got their chance. Harold Booth filled that position for most of the season before he faded from the scene. Edinburgh-born Jimmy Cox took his chance to hold one of the berths with some steady scores, including an unbeaten 9 in the league victory at Fleetwood.

Jim Turner was another locally-born asset who got his chance early in the season, but an arm injury against Leicester in a National Trophy meeting in May ended his campaign.

Others who had brief outings were Harry Andrews, Edinburgh-born Jackie Campbell and Aussies Vic Sage and Johnny Oram. At the end of August, Burnley-born Johnny Green claimed Harold Booth's reserve spot, and with some solid scores proved to be the missing link.

The loss of Don Cuppleditch in July, August and September was to prove crucial, as the Monarchs lost to Motherwell, Leicester, Norwich, and Coventry at Old Meadowbank without his services. Away from home they were victors at Newcastle, Ashfield, Fleetwood, Motherwell, Yarmouth and Cradley Heath, and, but for Don's injury, they may have bettered their third place finish in the League.

They had an easy 139-75 aggregate win over Leicester in the first round of the National Trophy, but they made their exit in round two when Halifax won a tight encounter by one point, 108-107. It was in the National Trophy that Jack Young dropped his other points – an engine failure at Leicester stopped what would have been an unbeaten score; then, against Halifax, Arthur Forrest beat Jack fair and square. Another, (this time vital) point was lost in a last-race decider when, against the odds, Jack Hughes led Jack to take Halifax through to the final rounds.

The inaugural Scottish Cup was won over two hard-fought legs against the Tigers from Glasgow, 108-106. They raced two challenge matches away from home, winning both. Monarchs won in Dublin in May, 37-35, and then 40-13 in a nine-heat match in the second half of the Cradley Heath meeting at Motherwell on 5 October.

Jack Young retained the Scottish Riders' Championship, again with a full 15 points. He also helped Australia win the test series against England 4-1 and went through all three Great Britain *v.* Overseas matches unbeaten. Scotland won the test match series against England 3-2, with Jack overall top scorer.

1951 World Championship 1-2-3. From left to right: Jack Biggs (3rd), Jack Young (champion), Split Waterman (2nd).

Jack's finest hour came at Wembley on 20 September. He qualified for the final with 23 points and a large contingent of Edinburgh supporters made the long journey to Wembley as support. Jack scored second places in his first two outings and won his next two, before coming second in his last for a total of 12 points. Australian Jack Biggs had won his first four races and looked favourite going into his final race of the night, but he made a poor start and trailed home in last place. This forced a run-off for the World title between Jack Young, Jack Biggs and Harringay's Split Waterman. Jack made no mistake in the run-off, taking the title from Waterman (who finished as runner-up) and Jack Biggs. Jack received a tremendous welcome when he returned home to Old Meadowbank as World Champion.

After his success in 1951, it was inevitable that Jack Young would move up into the First Division. During the close season, rumours linked Jack with a number of clubs. Initially Belle Vue were the favourites to land the World Champion, but Jack preferred a move to London and it was West Ham who finally secured his signature for a (then) record transfer fee of £3,750.

Pre-season press stories linked a Norwegian, Henry Andersen, with the Monarchs, but this move failed to materialise, and it was the same team but without Jack Young who were to take to the track for 1952.

It was a league only season, with a forty-four-match programme. It did not get off to a good start for the Monarchs, who had to go into their early fixtures without Dick Campbell and Don Cuppleditch (who both suffered injury while practising at Newtongrange).

They drew their opening league encounter at Old Meadowbank, 42-42 against Liverpool, but a 10 point defeat the following week meeting against Poole added to their problems. Another drawn match followed against Leicester at the end of April, then a heavy defeat when Coventry were the visitors in July. Thereafter they were unbeaten at home.

Monarchs had three wins and two drawn matches on their travels. Had both Dick Campbell and Don Cuppleditch been in the side from the start, they may have finished higher than their finishing League position of sixth.

In the National Trophy, they won the first leg at Old Meadowbank 67-41, but in the return leg at Liverpool they went down in a heavy 71-37 defeat, which ended their interest in the competition. In the Scottish Cup, Monarchs were held to a 4-point lead over a determined Glasgow Tigers, who in the return at the White City recorded a 26 point victory, for an aggregate 119-97 win.

Also during this season, the fourth in the Great Britain *v.* Overseas test series was raced at Old Meadowbank on 25 August. The host nation won 61-47. Wembley were regular visitors to the stadium for challenge matches, and were victorious in their 1952 visit, 48-36.

Jack Young had made the Scottish Riders' Championship his own personal property over the three previous seasons, but with Jack now not eligible to defend it, a new name appeared on the famous trophy: Dick Campbell was the deserved winner with 14 points.

Don Cuppleditch, even allowing for his early season injury, was the top Monarch of 1952 with 336 league points, Bob Mark, who took over the captain's role, was now a genuine heat leader. Along with Dick Campbell and Don, the trio formed a formidable spearhead to the side. Harold Fairhurst and Eddie Lack were again the backbone of the team, along with reserve Jimmy Cox. Keith Gurtner, the former Ashfield/Motherwell rider, joined the team late in August, but failed to recapture any real form.

By 1953, high entertainment tax on speedway, and television were starting to take their toll. Ashfield had withdrawn from the league, although they did run on an open licence. Then Liverpool, who Edinburgh had beaten both at home and away in the league, also withdrew mid-season with all their completed meetings being deleted from the league records. Clem Mitchell had now left his position as general manager and Frank Varey had returned to fill that role, with Eddie Lack becoming rider/team manager.

The main players were all back for the 1953 season, but, as in past years, the reserve berth always seemed to cause problems. Edinburgh-born Harry Darling and Jock Scott had done a good job when given their chance at the tail-end of the 1952 season, but were to be replaced by ex-Fleetwood man Jeff Crawford and veteran Wilf Jay. Jeff lasted just a few weeks before being himself replaced, while Wilf lasted the season, scoring some steady reserve returns.

The league had been reduced to ten teams, which became nine with Liverpool's departure. Edinburgh finished in fifth place.

Poole seemed to be Edinburgh's bogey team, with a win in what was Edinburgh's second home league match, followed in September by a 42-42 draw. Leicester were the only other team to leave with a league victory. On-the-road wins at Motherwell and Yarmouth helped counter the home defeats.

A South African, Roy Bester, joined the Monarchs in May and became a big favourite with the Edinburgh faithful, but he could not stop them exiting the National Trophy at the first hurdle, Glasgow winning both legs for an aggregate 136-80 victory.

In the Queen's Cup, Edinburgh saw off Leicester and Motherwell, and their round three tie was then cancelled due to Liverpool's closure. This put them in the final against their arch rivals the Glasgow Tigers, and a 117-99 victory saw them take the trophy – sweet revenge after those National Trophy defeats. In the Scottish Cup, Monarchs failed to reach the final, going out when Motherwell overhauled them in the semi-final.

Jack Young returned to thrill the Edinburgh faithful when he won the Red Devil Trophy on 16 May. Glasgow's Tommy Miller won the coveted Scottish Riders' Championship.

Left: Roy Bester. Right: Bob Mark.

1954 turned out to be a terrible year in Scottish speedway. Glasgow closed down after running only two meetings – the last, a North Shield fixture against Edinburgh, resulted in a 45-38 win for the Monarchs. Crowds had fallen dramatically since 1951 and the Edinburgh promotion was starting to feel the effects of the high entertainment tax.

The Edinburgh team for 1954 was much the same as 1953, although Harold Fairhurst had decided to remain in New Zealand and Johnny Greenwood, a former St Austell rider, came in as a replacement. Johnny proved to be an adequate replacement with some exciting moments. Roy Bester was a late recruit from his South African base, but soon settled back into the side who finished third out of five in the North Shield.

In the National Trophy, Edinburgh scored a last heat 5-1 at Old Meadowbank to put Leicester out in a thrilling 108-107 aggregate win. Rayleigh were the next to go out at the hands of the Monarchs (117-98), but Coventry put a stop to what was Edinburgh's best showing in this competition. Coventry won their home leg 56-52, then proceeded to win the Old Meadowbank leg (on a night that Don Cuppleditch was injured) 57-50.

Tommy Miller retained the Scottish Riders' Championship and then, on 10 July, Leicester's Ken McKinlay was the winner of a World Championship qualifying round, a meeting that was to signal the end of an era.

The end came suddenly, with riders and fans alike only finding out in the week leading to that final meeting. In a brief farewell message, Frank Varey said: 'Farewells are never easy to say so, without prolonging the agony, we can only say thanks a lot to those who have helped us in the past and the very best of luck to you all for the future.'

Edinburgh riders soon found new teams: Dick Campbell (Ipswich), Don Cuppleditch (Belle Vue), Bob Mark (Coventry), and Roy Bester (Leicester) all managed to fit in elsewhere, while Eddie Lack made a track appearance in Weymouth colours in 1955.

The Old Meadowbank circuit was to go into virtual hibernation for six years.

A Return to Meadowbank, 1960-67

League speedway did return to the Old Meadowbank circuit six years later when the Provincial League was born, but this was not the first time the roar of the bike was heard at the old track. Ian Hart, an American student studying engineering at Edinburgh University, gained permission to use the track for practice in 1957. He then organised two charity events as part of the Edinburgh Students' Charities Appeal. The first of those was held on 18 April 1959 and featured riders such as Doug Templeton, who won the meeting with 14 points, his brother Willie, George Hunter, Jimmy Cox, Jimmy Tannock, Freddie Greenwell, Gordon Mitchell and Bill Landels – who were to form the 1960 Monarchs.

Ian Hart pulled off a real coup by having Wimbledon's Ronnie Moore support

1959 charities programme.

the charity. He featured in the second half, winning the top scorers' race. A second charity meeting was held on 23 April 1960. This time the field consisted mainly of Bradford riders, with Tommy Roper the winner on this occasion. Again, the guest star came from Wimbledon in the shape of Ron How.

Only one Edinburgh rider competed in this meeting, Bill Landels who failed to score. The reason no other Monarchs were in the field was that the Edinburgh side were away to Stoke for their first Provincial League meeting on the same day, drawing 35-35 with Willie and Doug Templeton, along with Freddie Greenwell, scoring the bulk of the points.

It was Ian Hoskins, the former Glasgow promoter back in the 1950s, who organised the use of the Old Meadowbank stadium for the return of speedway. Ian had promoted team matches at Motherwell in 1958. The bulk of the riders used in the Eagles side were to form the nucleus Monarchs side of 1960.

The new era opened on 7 May at Old Meadowbank, with Liverpool the visitors, and a 39-33 win was a good start. That form was not to maintained as the season progressed, however, and with a number of home loses and a failure to pick up any further points on their travels, the Monarchs finished in eighth spot in the league out of ten teams.

They reached the semi-final of the Knockout Cup, defeating Sheffield and Yarmouth, both at home, before going out to the powerful Bristol Bulldogs in the semi-final.

The Northern-based sides in the league were rather weak in that first year, although Ian Hoskins did try to strengthen the team. At one point former Glasgow rider Don Wilkinson's name was mentioned, but this came to nothing.

The 1960 Monarchs. From left to right: Gordon Mitchell, Ron Johnson, Willie Templeton, Ian Hoskins, Jimmy Cox, George Hunter, Bill Landels, Doug Templeton (on bike).

Former New Cross star Ron Johnson did join the ranks without much success. At the end of July, twenty-two-year-old Reg Luckhurst came into the side from New Cross and proved a big hit, making some big scores.

Doug Templeton won the re-named Scottish Open Provincial Riders' Championship on 3 September with a 15 point maximum and Reg Luckhurst finished runner-up on 14 points. Doug was the top Edinburgh rider by far, reaching the second round of the World Championship, and holding the Silver Sash Match Race Championship for a spell.

The 1960 home season ended on 10 September at Old Meadowbank with a challenge match against Liverpool, then finally on 22 October with an away challenge match at Stoke, in which Yarmouth's Ivor Brown top scored as a guest in a 41-29 defeat.

Changes were made to the Monarchs' line-up for 1961. Out went Freddie Greenwell to Middlesbrough, Reg Luckhurst moved back down South and Gordon Mitchell went out on loan to the re-formed Newcastle Diamonds. Another to miss the 1961 season was Bill Landels, who was called up for National Service.

New faces were introduced in the form of 1950s icon Dick Campbell, who after seven years' absence was returning 'home'. Along with Dick came two New Zealanders, eighteen-year-old Alf Wells and sixteen-year-old Wayne Briggs, the younger brother of double World Champion, Barry.

Despite Doug Templeton and his brother, Willie, continuing from where they left off in 1960, and George Hunter showing vast improvement, it was the early form of Dick Campbell that became the talking point. Dick, in his first race for seven years, broke the Provincial track record with a time of 67.4 seconds. He was unbeaten in the first four fixtures, one of which was at Middlesbrough. He held the Silver Sash Match Race Championship for a while, but unfortunately his health didn't hold out, an ulcer being just one of many problems which slowed him down by causing him to miss matches.

The first four Provincial League matches were won (including the Middlesbrough win). Dick Campbell's first defeat came on 6 May at Old Meadowbank, when Plymouth's brilliant Aussie, Jack Scott, got the better of him. A tough match against Cradley Heath was won 43-34 on 20 May, this meeting counting for both Provincial League and Northern League points.

Rayleigh were the visitors on 10 June. This time the home hero was George Hunter, who won a last-heat decider to give the Monarchs a 40-38 victory.

The Northern League meeting against Wolverhampton on 29 July was raced on the Saturday afternoon to accommodate the TV cameras, when Scottish Television broadcast the meeting live. The result was a massive win for the Monarchs 56-21.

Poole stole a point in a 39-39 draw at Old Meadowbank, while on the road Monarchs were involved in drawn matches at Sheffield and Wolverhampton, both in the Northern League. They finished second to Stoke in that competition, and sixth out of eleven teams in the Provincial League.

Wolverhampton's Trevor Redmond won the Scottish Open Provincial Riders'

1961 Monarchs. From left to right: Wayne Briggs, Doug Templeton, Alf Wells, Willie Templeton, George Hunter, Dick Campbell, Jimmy Tannock.

Championship with a 15 point maximum, with Dick Campbell one point adrift in second place.

In what was a good season, Edinburgh reached the Knockout Cup final. They defeated Rayleigh in the second round, then Plymouth in the semi-final. Both matches raced as one-off matches, and both were at Old Meadowbank.

They met Cradley Heath in the final, but this time it would be over two legs, home and away. They lost the first leg at Cradley Heath by the crushing score of 68-28, which by rights killed off any hopes of a comeback at Old Meadowbank in the second leg. Although going down on aggregate they put on a fantastic display to defeat Cradley Heath on the night 59-34.

The most improved Monarch was George Hunter, who finished with a league average of 7.10, while newcomers Wayne Briggs (5.10) and Alf Wells (3.10) looked promising for the future.

The Provincial League was now going from strength to strength, with thirteen teams in 1962. The only new face in the Monarchs line-up was Australian Dudley McKean, who hailed from Melbourne.

Wayne Briggs missed the start of the season when he had an operation in a Southampton Hospital to rectify a fault in his right eye, which had been damaged in a crash at Old Meadowbank the previous year. He was out of action for the first two months, before returning at the start of June.

Edinburgh salvaged a draw in their opening Northern League meeting against

Left: Dudley McKean. Right: Doug Templeton at speed.

Sheffield with a late rally at Old Meadowbank. Dudley McKean made his debut against Newcastle the following week, but he had suffered an ankle injury while practising on the afternoon of the meeting. Needless to say, Dudley struggled, failed to score and was rested the following week, before returning in the next home match against Bradford, scoring paid 9. Dudley went on to prove himself as a useful lower-end man. Known as 'Cuddly Dudley', he was very popular with the fans.

Apart from the draw against Sheffield, Edinburgh won their other three home Northern League fixtures. A draw at Bradford was their only success away and they finished in third spot out of five teams.

Fifth spot in the league was not bad considering they lost their first three home meetings. The first of those defeats went to Plymouth, in a televised afternoon meeting, despite the fact that for the second year running the Monarchs won in front of Scottish Television cameras, 45-32. This score was amended to a 38-39 defeat after Plymouth successfully protested over the rear tyre used by Doug Templeton. They claimed the tyre was illegal and Doug's points were deducted.

Just prior to the following week's meeting against Wolverhampton, the police served notice on the Monarchs' four-year-old mascot, Ross Campbell. Ross, the son of Dick Campbell, had been noticed leading the side on the pre-match parade, riding his miniature bike. The police chiefs who saw Ross on television considered this was not safe and poor Ross had to sit out the rest of the season after being banned!

Wolverhampton took a 10 point win, before bogey team Poole recorded a 41-37 win a week later. There was more controversy in the Poole meeting when Doug Templeton defeated Tony Lewis (holder of the Silver Sash). Poole appealed against Doug's win, claiming (rightly) that Dick Campbell, as top scorer, should have been the challenger. Dick had been taken unwell after the team match and was unable to race. Doug took his place, but again the protest went against Edinburgh and Tony was reinstated as holder of the Sash.

Wayne Briggs was back in the side for the visit of Newcastle on 2 June and started what was a marvellous year with an 11 paid, 12 maximum return.

For the remainder of the season they were unbeaten at home and had success on their away trips, with a draw at Wolverhampton and wins at Sheffield, Leicester and Bradford, which helped them attain a reasonable league position. A reasonable run in the Knockout Cup saw them defeat Wolverhampton and Middlesbrough before going out to Exeter.

The season may have started late for Wayne Briggs, but this was probably his best, winning the Edinburgh round of the World Championship with 15, then the Best Pairs with partner Alf Wells. Wayne's 14 in the home round of the Provincial Riders' Championship helped him reach the final, staged at Belle Vue, where he finished second to Exeter's Len Silver.

There was a scare in August when it was reported that Wayne had broken his back in the win at Bradford, but the Kiwi star signed himself out of hospital and rode four days later!

Left: The long and the short: Alf Wells and Ken 'Casper' Cameron. Right: Edinburgh v. Belle Vue programme.

First Division Oxford were sent packing by 43-34, with the help of Monarchs' guest Eric Boothroyd. Doug Templeton took the Scottish Open Provincial Riders' Championship for the second time with a 15 point maximum.

The final meeting of the season was the third Britain *v.* Overseas test, which went to the home side, 60-48, with Wayne Briggs (15) top scorer for the Overseas. Doug Templeton then shocked the Edinburgh faithful when he announced that he was going to retire. Fortunately this did not happen and he was to enjoy many more years in the sport.

The 1963 season saw Dick Campbell take up the role of team manager, but he soon resigned, claiming that he wasn't being given enough control. Injuries played a big part in Monarchs' slip down the league table; they were to finish in eighth place. Another Australian, Ken 'Casper' Cameron joined the squad. Ken was a leg trailer and rode in white leathers, but his season was cut short when he crashed at Wolverhampton on 17 May. Ken suffered a fractured skull in the collision, which more or less finished his career.

At Old Meadowbank the week before, and against the same Wolverhampton side, a horrific crash between Alf Wells and Wolves' Ernie Baker had resulted in both men careering through the first/second bend fence onto the terracing. Alf broke an ankle and wrist.

At home, Monarchs were undefeated in both the league and the Northern League, while their only successes away were draws at Newcastle in both competitions. The Northern League consisted of only four teams and Edinburgh finished second.

The highlight of the season came on 22 June when the Provincial Final of the World Championship was held at Old Meadowbank. Newcastle's Ivan Mauger won the meeting with 14, while George Hunter (12) finished third and Doug Templeton (7) just scraped through to the next round. The injury bug had struck again, with Wayne Briggs missing this meeting due to a broken collar bone sustained at Southampton.

After Ken Cameron's injury, and with Wayne injured and Doug Templeton on World Championship duty, Dudley McKean returned to the side after a self-imposed retirement since the start of the season. Along with Jimmy Tannock he gave valuable support to George Hunter to record an against-the-odds home victory over Newcastle the following week.

Wayne Briggs returned to the side for the visit of Sheffield, scoring paid 11 in a close 41-37 win, but in the second half he was involved in a clash with Doug Templeton and was back on the injury list, this time with two broken wrists. Bill Landels made an unexpected return in August and slipped into a second string role which at that point was a much needed boost.

Bogey team Poole put Monarchs out of the Knockout Cup, and Britain beat Overseas 59-49 in the first of the test series. Wolverhampton's Maury Mattingly, who always enjoyed his visits to Old Meadowbank, demonstrated his liking for the track by becoming the 1963 Scottish Open Riders' Champion.

The Monarchs then put their unbeaten home run on the line, when in consecutive weeks they took on the might of Belle Vue and then Wimbledon.

The Belle Vue visit was on Friday 20 September, and a large, enthusiastic crowd attended to catch a glimpse of the two times World Champion Peter Craven. Edinburgh were strengthened with the inclusion of Middlesbrough's Eric Boocock and Exeter's Jimmy Squibb. Going into heat ten, Edinburgh held a 4 point lead. George Hunter, who was without doubt Monarch of the Year, was unbeaten after two races, as was Peter Craven. The pair were to meet each other for the first time in the meeting and it was George who took an early lead only for the majestic Peter Craven, showing all his balance and skill, to pass him for a shared race.

Heat twelve saw George and Peter meet one more time. Once again George took the lead, but tragedy struck when George fell on the first bend of the second lap. Peter was very close and, in trying to avoid the stricken George, he clipped his bike and crashed into the safety fence. This accident entirely took the gloss off what turned out to be a 40-38 win for Edinburgh.

Peter Craven was taken to the Royal Infirmary of Edinburgh, suffering from serious head injuries. On Tuesday 24 September he passed away. This was perhaps the worst single blow that Edinburgh and the whole speedway world had ever suffered. There was no blame attached for the accident. Thankfully, few accidents

Peter Craven – 'The Wizard of Balance.'

have such fatal consequences.

Wimbledon won the following week, with Barry Briggs having a mixed night for the Dons. Apart from the Peter Craven tragedy, and the loss of their unbeaten home record to Wimbledon, it had again been an exciting season of high entertainment and drama for Monarchs.

George Hunter, along with Doug Templeton, represented Edinburgh at Belle Vue in the Provincial Riders' Championship final and, after winning a farcical five-man run-off, George Hunter reached the final. George, sharp from the start, led the final before suffering a disastrous engine failure, which allowed Newcastle's Ivan Mauger to win.

There was little change on the team front in 1964. Dudley McKean, who had married an Edinburgh lass, returned home to Australia. Fellow Australian Kevin Torpie moved into the side from Middlesbrough.

This was the year that the Provincial League went 'black', following demands for reorganisation of the sport by the National League which the Provincial League felt were unreasonable. As a result of this, the decision was made that the league would go their own way.

Apart from Provincial League riders no longer being eligible to take part in the World Championship rounds, there was no difference to the way the Provincial League was operated. George Hunter caused a pre-season scare when he missed the practice. He had slipped a disc trying to lift his car out of a ditch, but recovered in time for the opening Northern League match against Sheffield at Old Meadowbank. It wasn't the start the Monarchs were looking for, going down to a 41-36 defeat.

There were no more home defeats, but they only managed one away success, at short-lived Sunderland, and finished second in the Northern League table. On Saturday 18 April the old enemy from Glasgow, the Tigers, returned to the fold, but went home pointless after a 56-21 defeat.

In the league injuries again played a big part, with George Hunter missing two matches after a knock at Newport, while Doug Templeton suffered a broken wrist in the middle of September, missing the final three fixtures.

Bill Landels missed the bulk of the season after suffering a leg injury during the Scottish Best Pairs in July, which was won by Wayne Briggs and Alf Wells. Although not actually a broken bone, that leg injury kept Bill out for the rest of the season.

Wayne Briggs had not had the best of luck since starting his speedway career and he was the victim of another serious crash at Newport in July while representing the Overseas against Britain. Wayne suffered a smashed thigh in what was described one of the worst crashes seen at the track.

With all these casualties Glaswegian Bert Harkins, who had had only limited outings the previous season, took his chance with an extended run in the team, as did Edinburgh-born Alex Hughson. Middlesbrough heat leader Dave Younghusband was drafted into the side on loan for the last few matches.

Dave Younghusband.

To finish in fifth place out of twelve was not bad in an injury-ravaged season, even if they did go out of the Knockout Cup at the first hurdle to Cradley Heath.

With the return of the Glasgow Tigers, the old rivalry returned. The sides met six times, with the Monarchs winning at White City in the league 41-37 in June, only for the Tigers to take a draw at Old Meadowbank, again in the league in September.

In the reintroduced Scottish Cup, which took place in August, Glasgow won the first leg 52-43 at White City. In the second leg at Old Meadowbank, on the following night, it looked as though their lead would be enough to take the trophy. Going into heat fifteen, the Tigers lined up with Trevor Redmond, who was as yet unbeaten, and Graham Coombes. For the Monarchs, Bert Harkins, who had been scoring steadily, was partnered with Kevin Torpie. Kevin was renowned for his fast gating, and reached the first bend in front of Trevor Redmond, who tried everything he knew, but could not catch the Monarch. The resulting 4-2 score helped the Edinburgh side to a single point aggregate victory.

George Hunter reached the Provincial Riders' Championship final at Belle Vue, where his 4 points saw him finish well down the field, but he did have success in the Scottish Open Championship, winning the coveted trophy after a

George Hunter leading Brian Brett (Swindon) and Barry Briggs (Southampton). (Photograph: Alf Weedon, established 1948.)

run-off with Glasgow's Charlie Monk, after both tied on 14 points. It had been a good season for George, who finished the season as top Monarch.

A new era for speedway dawned in 1965 when the warring Provincial and National Leagues became one. The British League was born and the big names would be seen on a regular basis at Old Meadowbank – although the Northern clubs failed to secure any of the former National League stars as part of their team.

The unlucky Wayne Briggs missed the start of the season, but made a comeback for the away Wimbledon meeting. Still suffering from the effects of his broken thigh, he was far from fit, and only appeared in a handful of early fixtures.

Norwegian Henry Harrfeldt, brother of West Ham's Sverre, and Colin McKee, a New Zealander who lived in London, were the new faces at the start of the season. Willie Templeton moved to Glasgow, and then returned with the Tigers on 17 April to score a sensational 11 points in a 42-36 win for Glasgow.

Monarchs also lost their opening British League meeting at Old Meadowbank to Long Eaton 40-38. As the season went on, a further four home defeats were recorded and a failure to open their account away saw them floundering at the bottom of the table, finishing seventeenth out of eighteen.

Barry Briggs was clearly the top rider in the British League, but Charlie Monk (Glasgow), Ivan Mauger (Newcastle) and Edinburgh's George Hunter had all proved that they could hold their own against the best.

George was in sensational form, challenging Barry Briggs for the Golden Helmet in July. He gained four 'Test Caps' for Great Britain against Russia, but a crash with Doug Templeton in the Scottish Best Pairs in June resulted in both missing the World Championship rounds. It was a nasty-looking incident, but thankfully both escaped any lasting injury.

New riders were tried as the season wore on. The Austrian champion, Alfred Sitzwohl, rode two away meetings at Exeter and Long Eaton in June before returning home; at the end of July Preben Andersen, a Dane who looked talented but a bit wild, rode in one match before injury finished his season.

In mid-August, Swedish side Vargarna were touring and in that team was a teenager, Bernt (Bernie) Persson, who was making promoters sit up and take notice. Ian Hoskins stepped in and snapped up the eighteen-year-old sensation for the final few weeks of the season. Bernie proved to be a revelation and soon became a fans' favourite with his neat style and points-scoring ability.

Henry Harrfeldt was a solid second string, while Colin McKee filled the third heat leader role with some match-saving races. Colin's best night was in the Knockout Cup first round against Hackney Wick at Old Meadowbank, when his 15 point maximum helped the Monarchs progress to the next stage. Their interest in the competition did not last long, however, as Poole put the Monarchs out in the second round.

For the first time the Scottish Open Championship went to a Dane, when Oxford's Arne Pander scored an unbeaten 15 points – two points clear of second-placed George Hunter.

What would have been the biggest attraction of the season, Scotland *v.* Russia, was spoilt by the weather. The Russians arrived on 10 July at Old Meadowbank for a morning practice in what was a sunny day, but the meeting was run in terrible conditions as the heavens opened up. Under normal circumstances the meeting would have been cancelled, but both sides put on a good show with the Russians winning 57-51. The Scotland *v.* England series was won 2-1 by Scotland, with the Edinburgh test going Scotland's way 60-48.

An Edinburgh Select team made a six-match tour of Poland at the end of the season. Long Eaton's Ray Wilson and Norman Storer, along with Newport's Jon Erskine and Geoff Penniket, joined Monarchs Doug Templeton, George Hunter, Henry Harrfeldt, Colin McKee and the sensation of the tour, Bernie Persson. Whilst all six matches were lost, it was an ambitious, but successful exercise.

Changes were made to the team for 1966. The unlucky Wayne Briggs moved down to Poole and was accompanied by Kiwi Colin McKee, who wanted a track nearer his London home. Alf Wells moved to Glasgow and Kevin Torpie retired. Bernie Persson also missed the 1966 season due to his call-up by the Swedish army.

The replacement for Bernie was a 1965 World Finalist, Sweden's Bengt Jansson. Dudley McKean returned after a year out and with Doug Templeton, George Hunter, Bert Harkins, Bill Landels and Henry Harrfeldt all returning, prospects looked reasonable for the season ahead.

The campaign opened with Newcastle on 2 April at Old Meadowbank, with a 41-37 victory. There were so many engine problems in the Edinburgh camp, with only Bengt Jansson (10) getting among the points. A better show at

The unlucky Henry Harrfeldt.

Swede Bengt Jansson (left) and Norwegian Reidar Eide.

Wolverhampton the following Friday saw them go down 40-38.

The same Wolves side were at Old Meadowbank the next night, and a heat seven crash resulted in Henry Harrfeldt breaking his right leg. Henry had two previous breaks to this leg, and this accident finished his speedway career. Wolverhampton went on to win the meeting 35 $\frac{1}{2}$ - 42 $\frac{1}{2}$.

The replacement for Henry was another Swede, Runo Wedin, who scored 6 in his debut against Exeter. Runo's stay was cut short, however, when the Speedway Riders' Association banned all new Swedish riders. In the few meetings he participated in, Runo had shown that he may have developed into a useful team member.

In his search for a further replacement, Ian Hoskins turned to Norway and came back with an unknown prospect in Reidar Eide. Reidar made his debut at King's Lynn on 18 May, scoring 3 points, with a win in his second outing. But just as Reidar came into the side, Bengt Jansson went missing due to a broken ankle sustained in a televised meeting at Glasgow. Bengt was to miss nearly two months of the season and never really reproduced the form he was capable of.

Even with all these injury problems, the Monarchs – after losing those first two meetings – managed to keep a clean sheet at home, but only picked up the one away victory at Exeter, 41-37, in June.

Twelfth in the league table out of eighteen, out of the Knockout Cup in their first round to Long Eaton and the Scottish Cup going to Glasgow, meant it was not the season they had hoped for. The Cradley Heath league match never took place, being rained off twice.

George Hunter had another good year, finishing with a 8.50 average. He reached the European Final of the World Championship at Wembley, but only managed two points on his big night. He also won a new bike in the High Speed Gas Superbike Trophy meetings, which were held over two legs at Edinburgh and Glasgow at the end of June.

Reidar Eide had made rapid strides, and on 6 August he scored a maximum in the defeat of Long Eaton and established a never-to-be-beaten Old Meadowbank track record of 64.2 seconds. However, at the end of August he suddenly, and much to the surprise of the fans, returned home and was then replaced by fellow Norwegian Knut Syrrest, who also disappeared after one meeting.

Bill Landels struggled for most of the season with a new bike. The Matchless engine he was trying proved uncompetitive. This resulted in him being dropped from the side for a time, but near the end of the season a change to the more conventional engine saw him back in the side and scoring vital points.

A Test match against Poland on 30 July was to be dubbed 'The Meadowbank Massacre'. Poland ran riot, winning eleven of the eighteen heats by the maximum 5-1 score and the best the Scots could do was share four. The score was Poland 79 Scotland 29. George Hunter and Ken McKinlay did win two late heats on borrowed Polish bikes!

The prestigious 1966 Scottish Open Championship was twice the victim of the weather, but would start the 1967 season. On 1 April Bill Landels provided what

Scottish Open Champion Bill Landels.

1967 Monarchs. From left to right, back row: Bernie Persson, Oyvind S. Berg, Bill Landels, George Hunter. Front row: Bert Harkins, Doug Templeton, Reidar Eide.

was one of the biggest upsets in the Edinburgh history, by being crowned the 1966 Scottish Open Champion. There was no question that he was a deserved winner, beating such names as Ivan Mauger, Arne Pander, Charlie Monk and Sverre Harrfeld, along with home favourites George Hunter, Doug Templeton and the returning Reidar Eide and Bernie Persson.

Bill was mounted on a bike purchased from George Hunter at the end of the previous year and his winning 15 points boded well for 1967. George Hunter did not have the best of starts, as he fell in his first race, forcing him to withdraw from the meeting, while the returning Reidar Eide lost a run-off for second having tied with Charlie Monk and Ivan Mauger on 13 points. Bernie Persson eased his way back with 7.

Two new additions were made to the team for 1967. One was Oyvind S. Berg ('S' for 'Super', according to Ian Hoskins), a Norwegian who on his debut in the Scottish Open scored an encouraging 10 points. The other new member, taking over the managerial duties, was Tommy Hughson, a former Monarchs team mascot in the 1950s.

This was to be the final season at Old Meadowbank. The Monarchs were ousted from their home at the end of the season to allow the building of a new stadium for the forthcoming Commonwealth Games.

On track, Ian Hoskins had a team with the look of championship contenders, but along came the Tigers from Glasgow to spoil the party. As early as 15 April they came to Old Meadowbank and went home with a 40-38 victory. Then in the second half, George Hunter broke a wrist in a clash with Charlie Monk, which put him out for a few weeks.

The only other point lost at home was to West Ham, who forced a draw. Away from home they drew at Poole and had wins at Belle Vue, King's Lynn, Cradley Heath and Newport and finished in their best position since the revival of 1960 – fourth out of nineteen.

The victory at Cradley Heath in September resulted in injury to Bernie Persson when he clashed with Chris Julian, while Reidar Eide felt that Chris's treatment of Bernie was unfair and exacted his own revenge!

Bernie, after a slow start, soon got back to top form, and reached the World Final at Wembley. A huge contingent of Edinburgh supporters travelled to cheer the young Swede and 6 points was a fine achievement, considering he was the centre of a doubtful exclusion in a clash with Ivan Mauger, which held the meeting up for a while. George Hunter, and Bert Harkins both had good runs in the World Championship, with Bert reaching the British semi-final and George going one better and reaching the British final. Reidar Eide had a terrific season, finishing with a near 9 point average and winning the High Speed Gas Trophy and Johnnie Thomson Trophy, both at Poole, with unbeaten maximums. Bill Landels, however, faded after a bright start.

Brian Collins, a local rider from Edinburgh who had had only occasional outings in 1966, got his chance, but a broken leg sustained in a match at Hackney at the end of April effectively put him out for the season. Brian did make a brief comeback near the end of the season and showed that when injury-free he could have a bright future.

Monarchs went out of the Knockout Cup in the semi-final to Coventry, after seeing off Wolverhampton (at Old Meadowbank) and Long Eaton (away). The Scottish Cup was back in the Edinburgh trophy cabinet, after winning both the home and away legs over the old enemy. Poland made a return visit, but this time faced a Scottish Select side strengthened by the inclusion of Reidar Eide and Bernie Persson, that made sure the Poles went away with a 64-44 defeat this time.

The Scottish Open was one of the best staged and full of drama, with Barry Briggs winning a run-off from Ray Wilson (Long Eaton) and Bernie Persson after all three had tied with 13 points.

Bert Harkins, who had second-half outings since 1961, made steady progress with occasional reserve outings in the team. His progress was such that by 1965 he was a regular team member, eventually moving up from reserve into the main body of the side. In 1967, Bert had a steady season score-wise and in the final league meeting at Old Meadowbank, against Sheffield on 30 September, he scored his first full 12 point maximum.

The final meeting to be held at the Old Meadowbank circuit was a Best Pairs, won by Oyvind Berg and Wayne Briggs. In the second half of that meeting, Brian Collins won the Scottish Junior Riders' Championship.

So speedway at one of the best tracks in Britain came to an end. Fittingly, one of the best-ever Edinburgh Monarchs seasons meant that the sport went out on a high. Now the search began for a new home.

A Move to Coatbridge 1968-69

With the Old Meadowbank stadium being demolished, and Ian Hoskins failing to find an alternative site in the Edinburgh area, the net had to be cast further.

A move to Albion Rovers Football ground at Cliftonhill in Coatbridge was the only available option. Track construction work started and when it was finished the track measured 380 yards. It was steeply banked, but it never produced the same class of racing as Old Meadowbank.

Oyvind Berg, who had enjoyed a good first season in Scotland, moved to Glasgow for the 1968 season. Also missing was Bill Landels, who had emigrated to Australia. Into the side came Brian Collins and Alex Hughson, who were given their chance alongside Reidar Eide, Bernie Persson, George Hunter, Doug Templeton and Bert Harkins.

The season opened with a 'Champagne Derby' challenge defeat by Glasgow at White City 45-51. The second leg, staged the following evening, 6 April, opened the Cliftonhill season with a 54-42 victory for an overall aggregate win.

Only Exeter managed a draw to spoil a winning league run at home, while away wins at Poole and near neighbours Glasgow saw the Monarchs finish mid-table in eighth place out of nineteen teams.

Two teams failed to turn up for league fixtures at Coatbridge. At the end of July, in consecutive weeks, Belle Vue and Leicester riders got held up in traffic on the

Bert Harkins.

Action from the ill-fated meeting of 19 July – Reidar Eide (Monarchs) and Bernie Persson (Belle Vue)!

way north, and hastily rearranged meetings with local riders took place. On 19 July Monarchs faced Northern Aces, which resulted in a home win by 40-38, then on 27 they raced The Rest, again resulting in a close win for the Monarchs, 41-37.

In the Knockout Cup they saw off Glasgow, before going out to Newcastle. The Scottish Cup ended up in the Monarchs trophy cabinet with a 103-89 aggregate victory. The second test between Great Britain and Sweden saw a rare visit of Ove Fundin, who led his side to a convincing 71-37 win.

A 62-46 victory for Scotland over England was a memorable night for Brian Collins, who scored 14 paid 16. Brian had made rapid strides in 1968, but this was his best yet. Alex Hughson, who had only a handful of team outings in 1967, also had a successful '68 season.

Doug Templeton had started his ninth season as team captain – which made him one of the longest-serving team captains in the history of the sport. Doug started well, but by mid-season his scoring had slipped quite a bit by his standards. Bert Harkins was quite the opposite, starting the season slowly, then rattling in some double figure returns from mid-season.

George Hunter, who made no secret of the fact that the Cliftonhill track was not one of his favourites, did make history by scoring a paid 7 ride maximum 20 plus a bonus in the win over Glasgow on the Knockout Cup. George was going well and at White City Glasgow on 17 May had scored 5 from his first two outings, but in heat ten entered a dramatic race with Tiger's Bo Josefsson. The two riders repeatedly passed each other until, when going into the finish, George's bike suddenly reared, swung towards the centre green and hit Bo Josefsson's front wheel, knocking it from under him. Luckily, George parted company with his bike, which careered into the starting gate post, snapping it like a dry carrot. George suffered a dislocated shoulder, which kept him out of the side for a few weeks, after which his form slipped quite dramatically.

Bernie Persson had a great year, reaching his second World Final, as did Reidar Eide, who had a troubled route to reach the final in Sweden. The Norwegian authorities wanted to withdraw their representatives, Sverre Harrfeldt and Reidar, from the European Final which was being run in Poland because of the Russian invasion of Czechoslovakia, but both Reidar and Sverre refused instructions not to ride. In the World Final Reidar scored three points, but Bernie suffered bike trouble, scoring just one point.

Reidar looked as though he had the Scottish Open Championship in the bag going into his last race, after winning his first four outings. The final heats had to be started with a elastic tape stretched across the track, as the normal start gate was out of commission. Reidar reared at the start of his last race and failed to make up the ground on a wet track for the vital point which would have given him a second chance in a run-off with Martin Ashby (Exeter) and Charlie Monk (Sheffield).

Martin Ashby won the run-off to take the 1968 Scottish Open title. Martin had not had a bad meeting at Coatbridge, winning the World Championship round with a full 15 maximum, then top scored for Great Britain in the test against Sweden with 14. His 15 points for England against Scotland and his 12 for Exeter in the drawn match in September suggested that he enjoyed his visits to Cliftonhill.

Rider control came into effect in 1969, with Bernie Persson being allocated to Cradley Heath. Bert Harkins was originally allocated to Newcastle, but refused to go, winning his case to stay a Monarch. A pre-season injury saw Bert miss a few early meetings and it was May before he was back to his best.

The rest of the team remained with the inclusion of former Monarch Wayne Briggs, who returned to the fold. Doug Templeton started his tenth season as team captain, but had a torrid time which resulted in him announcing his retirement at the end of July. Bert Harkins took over as captain for the remainder of the season, but Doug's retirement was short-lived and he was back in the side for the away tour of Swindon and Exeter. In the latter part of the season his form returned, which was a grand sight for the Monarchs' faithful fans.

George Hunter had a poor season, showing only glimpses of his true form, mainly away from Cliftonhill. Brian Collins continued to improve, while Alex Hughson started well with 9 against Swindon and paid 13 when Glasgow visited Coatbridge in April, but lost his form as the season wore on.

Reidar Eide, apart for a brief spell out with injury at the end of June, was the King of Cliftonhill in 1969, powering his way to a 10.00 point league average. Reidar was rarely out of double figure scores home or away. After his slip-up in the Scottish Open Championship the previous year, he made no mistake in '69, winning a run-off against Newcastle's Ole Olsen. Reidar top scored for Norway in meetings at Glasgow's White City and Coatbridge, both of which were won by Scotland. In the meeting against Norway at Coatbridge, an unusual occurrence took place as the pipe band, who had been entertaining the crowd during the interval, were marching off over the track to gain exit through the pits. With the riders at the tapes for the first race after the interval, for some reason the referee let the tapes up and the four riders headed for the first bend, which was occupied by the pipe band. Panic ensued as riders fought with their machines to miss the band members and pipers and drummers scattered in all directions, some leaping the fence to safety. Luckily no one was injured in an incident that after the event was quite comical.

In the league the Monarchs slipped to eleventh out of nineteen teams. They only lost at home on one occasion, to Halifax in September, while Newcastle forced a draw in August. Away from home they were winners at Newport and Swindon. In the Knockout Cup they disposed of Hackney before going out to Poole in a meeting which never finished. With the scores standing at 33-33 and with just two heats to go, George Hunter was excluded for a tapes offence. With this exclusion

Superb action shot of Reidar Eide.

Bert Harkins in full flow. (Both Reidar and Bert were bound for Wembley in 1970.)

and earlier controversies, the team walked out of the meeting, gifting the Pirates the match and Monarchs team manager Tommy Hughson a £50 fine.

Monarchs won the Scottish Cup in a tight contest, 88-87 over the two legs. This was another controversial encounter as Glasgow's promoter Les Whaley claimed that the starting gate tapes were illegal, and that they would not race in the competition again.

On 11 October, in what was to become the final Monarchs meeting at Coatbridge , the visitors were Cradley Heath. This meeting also saw the return of Bernie Persson, who scored 14 in a Monarchs win 42-36. Reidar Eide did not know in that final meeting that he was go into history as track record holder of two defunct Monarchs tracks. He held the all-time record at Old Meadowbank and, as Coatbridge closed to the Monarchs, the Cliftonhill record of 64.0 seconds.

It was during the close season that the shock news broke that the Monarchs' licence was sold to Wembley. So started seven blank years for the Monarchs.

Reidar Eide, Brian Collins, Wayne Briggs and Bert Harkins all moved to Wembley, while George Hunter moved to Newcastle along with Ian Hoskins. Doug Templeton, who had threatened retirement during the 1969 season, moved to Glasgow in '70.

The Powderhall Years, 1977-95

Late in 1976, notices in the press indicated that permission was being sought by the GRA to allow speedway to take place at Powderhall. After a period of council meetings, noise tests, and a few setbacks, permission was granted and track construction began in readiness for the 1977 season.

Neil MacFarlane and local councillor Tom Nisbet were prominent in bringing speedway back to Edinburgh. The new promoter was Mike Parker, who was the main mover in the formation of the Provincial League back in 1960. Mike had help from Bill Bridgett and track guru Ted Flanaghan in the construction of the 306-metre track, which was to prove a bit of a trick course with its tight bends.

Neil MacFarlane took on the role of team manager and had Bert Harkins as team captain. Other team members were former Glasgow icon Charlie Monk, and Alan Bridgett from the defunct Paisley was more than just a useful rider. Jack ('Villain') Millen, the victim of many crashes and a man of many tracks, was to become a valuable team member. Former Boston/Berwick team man Dave Trownson and Wolverhampton junior Alan Morrison were joined by Aussies Neil Webb, Mal Chambers and Des Allen.

Jack 'The Villain' Millen.

The season started on 15 April in front of a massive crowd with a challenge match against Berwick Bandits, which was won 42-36. It was straight into league action the following evening at Berwick, the team going down 43-35, with Charlie Monk and Jack Millen scoring the bulk of the points.

As the season wore on, changes were made to the side. Neil Webb lasted two meetings, then Mal Chambers broke his femur, which finished his speedway season. Des Allen had a short run in the team, before Nigel Wasley came from Cradley Heath and Steve McDermott arrived from Stoke, which helped settle the side. Charlie Monk missed the month of May after injuring his back at Scunthorpe and this injury affected Charlie's scoring ability for the rest of the season. Jack Millen at times carried the team and scored an immaculate 15 point maximum at Mildenhall in May. Steve McDermott came into the side in the middle of June and proved to be a solid team man. He missed a few meetings due to work commitments, but was just the support that Jack Millen needed. Dave Trownson started slowly, but soon became a solid middle-order man and was to go on to better things in a long association with the Monarchs.

Rye House, Newcastle, Ellesmere Port, Eastbourne and Canterbury all won at Powderhall, while wins at Scunthorpe and Stoke left them in fifteenth place in the league table out of nineteen teams. The Monarchs put Scunthorpe out of the Knockout Cup over two legs, before going out themselves to Berwick. The Scottish Cup was the only trophy success, which was won 81-75 on aggregate.

Edinburgh failed to reach the finals of the Four Team Trophy, and in the only open meeting staged at Powderhall, Weymouth's Martin Yeates won the Golden Wonder Olympiad. A four-team tournament involving Edinburgh, Cradley Heath, Hull and White City (London) fell victim of the weather, which was a shame as it would have seen 1960s Monarch Bernie Persson in action at Powderhall.

Bert Harkins ended the 1977 season as track-record holder (65.8 seconds) and was a solid performer throughout, but a fragile side would need to be strengthened in 1978. Changes were made as out went Charlie Monk to Barrow and Jack Millen to Berwick. In came Wolverhampton asset and former Boston heat leader Rob Hollingworth, with a near 10-point average, and Glasgow number one Brian Collins was back with his home town club. Bert Harkins would lead the side, which also included Dave Trownson, Steve McDermott, Alan Bridgett and Alan Morrison.

It was a powerful-looking line-up and so it proved in the early weeks of the season. On 24 March, Glasgow were sent packing 60-17 in a challenge match which opened the 1978 season. Barrow suffered a crushing league defeat 50-28 the following week, then after a win at Mildenhall on 2 April, Boston were decimated 63-14 at Powderhall on 7 April.

But the big wins were not to last. In May, Ellesmere Port, Mildenhall and Eastbourne all recorded convincing wins at Powderhall. Further changes were to be made to the side in June. Steve Lomas (Wolverhampton) came into the team for the meeting against Crayford and scored three wins before suffering an engine

Left: Charlie Monk. Right: Rob Hollingworth.

failure in his final outing.

After a bright start, Steve McDermott had faded by June and rumours linked him with Berwick. He was replaced in the side by English-born Ivan Blacka, who had spent most of his life in America and was another Wolverhampton asset. He made a slow start, but there was never a dull moment when Ivan was on track and his scores soon improved with 10 at Boston, 12 paid 14 against Glasgow at Powderhall and 11 paid 12 at Glasgow.

Seven home defeats, three away wins and a draw found them in fifteenth out of twenty in the National League. They went out of the Knockout Cup to Crayford and lost an Inter-League Challenge to Belle Vue, 56-22 at Powderhall.

In the Four Team Trophy they got through the rounds to reach the semi-finals at Peterborough. Rob Hollingworth and Steve Lomas represented the Monarchs in the National League Pairs at Halifax, but with only 8 points between them, they did not get past the heats.

Two individual meetings took place at Powderhall in 1978: The Strongbow Powderhall Sprint went to Edinburgh's Rob Hollingworth, while Newcastle's Tom Owen won the Golden Wonder Olympiad.

The powerhouse side of '78 turned out to be a flop and, as expected, changes were made for 1979. Long-term supporter George Cummings took up the role of team manager, Rob Hollingworth, who was not altogether happy at Powderhall, moved back to Boston and coming in as a shock replacement was Rob Mouncer, who had been doing his racing in Germany after beginning his career at Boston.

The rest of the side was as in the previous season, although Edinburgh-born Benny Rourke, who had been with Glasgow, finally joined the ranks shortly after the season started.

As in seasons past, the reserve position in the side seemed to be a problem and a number of riders filled this role. Tim Currnock started the season, then Alan Stansfield had an extended run before Aussie Roger Lambert, who had a brief stay at Boston, made his debut for the Monarchs at the end of July.

The injury bug reared it ugly head when Benny Rourke (shoulder) and Steve Lomas (broken scaphoid) were both put out of the match against Weymouth at the end of June and at the same time Ivan Blacka had to return to America as his father was not in the best of health. Steve Lomas missed the whole of July and the loss of Benny Rourke, who did not return until the middle of September, weakened the side considerably. There was more bad news when Dave Trownson missed two meetings at the end of July and then Bert Harkins suffered a shoulder injury which kept him out of the side in August.

Just to add to the injury problems, Rob Mouncer was having licence trouble which saw him miss most of April and he did not return until June. With all the difficulties team manager George Cummings endured, it was no surprise that the 1979 Monarchs finished in seventeenth spot in the league out of nineteen teams,

Captain Bert Harkins welcomes Steve Lomas (left).

although they did get through to the second round of the Knockout Cup by beating Boston before going out to Crayford.

Seven home meetings were lost and Crayford forced a draw. Their only away successes were at Middlesbrough, Workington and a draw at Scunthorpe. In the Scottish Cup, Berwick knocked them out in a qualifying meeting, with the winners going on to meet Glasgow in the final.

Steve Lomas had an up-and-down season. He started well, but had a lull in his scoring on his comeback from injury, before finishing strongly. Dave Trownson upped his average to 7.78 and finished the season as top Monarch. Brian Collins slipped back badly with an average of 6.56, while Ivan Blacka, who always provided entertainment, achieved 5.30.

Powderhall hosted a Scotland *v*. England Test match on 11 May, with British League riders Bobby Beaton and Jimmy McMillan boosting the Scottish side. Scotland won 60-48. Dave Trownson won the Powderhall Sprint after a run-off with Oxford's Les Rumsey, when both had scored 14 points.

It was one of the poorest seasons Edinburgh had ever endured – spoilt by injury, outside problems and, when the chips were down, a lack of team spirit.

After three seasons with a conspicuous lack of success, more changes were made, but this time under the leadership of Alan 'Doc' Bridgett, who had retired from the racing side of the game to don the team manager's jacket. Monarchs moved up from the lower reaches of the league table to sixth.

Missing from the 1979 side were Bert Harkins, who moved to Milton Keynes, Steve Lomas, who got his wish and moved to Boston, and Ivan Blacka, who was recalled by his parent club Wolverhampton just prior to the season starting. This was a blow as Ivan would have fitted in well in what was a very good 1980 side.

George Hunter was back in a Monarchs race jacket, some eleven years on from when the Monarchs had folded at Coatbridge. At forty-one years of age, George was to be the foundation stone of the 1980 side and for most of the year would form a formidable partnership with another new boy, eighteen-year-old Neil Collins.

Neil, the fourth of the famous Collins boys, had previous experience with Nottingham and Workington in 1979 without pulling up any trees, but that was all to change with the experienced head of George Hunter making the gaps which the youthful, but skilful, Neil would exploit. They were a joy to watch with George smooth on the inside and Neil buzzing around the outside. The other new rider was Scot Harry McLean, who came from Milton Keynes and along with Roger Lambert provided stability in the reserve positions.

Dave Trownson put a point on his average, while Brian Collins and Benny Rourke provided middle-order stability. Rob Mouncer started the season, but had moved on by the end of April. The campaign did not start as planned when a challenge match against Middlesbrough at Powderhall ended in a win for the visitors 40-36. By the next week, however, the team got into their stride by winning the Inter City Cup against Glasgow with a home win and followed this with a draw at Blantyre.

Neil Collins.

Neil Collins missed the home match against Crayford on 27 June when on European Junior Championship duty. Bob Humphreys (Milton Keynes) proved a fine replacement at reserve – he not only scored 13 points but broke the track record in heat one with a new time of 64.1 seconds!

All was going well at home in the league until Berwick arrived as visitors on 20 June and forced a draw. They were unbeaten thereafter until the final meeting of the season. With George Hunter missing, Newcastle, who had become a bit of an unlucky team as far as the Monarchs were concerned, won 45-32.

Away wins at Scunthorpe, Workington, Nottingham, Stoke, Crayford and Milton Keynes and a draw at Oxford represented a vast improvement on previous years.

Monarchs knocked Glasgow out of the Knockout Cup, but Berwick drew at Powderhall once again, and then put them out of the competition at Berwick in the return leg.

There were two late-season additions to the side. Veteran Arnold Haley, who had served Sheffield for many years, had a few meetings without much success and Chris Turner, the former Belle Vue and Boston rider, had a run of five meetings. Chris would prove a big hit in 1981.

George Hunter won the Strongbow Powderhall Sprint with a 15 point maximum, and Middlesbrough's Steve Wilcock won the Courage Olympiad.

The successful 1981 Monarchs. From left to right, back row: Neil Collins, Chris Turner, Ivan Blacka, Benny Rourke, Dave Trownson. Front row: George Hunter, Roger Lambert.

Carlo Biagi was a man who would keep himself out of the limelight, preferring to take a back seat to enjoy his speedway. Dr Biagi had been active keeping so many of the stars and lesser lights active in the sport for some twenty-three years, being known as the 'Miracle Doctor'. He would mend the broken bones and have a rider back on track, either fully recovered, or – as has happened to the likes of Ivan Mauger – encase his broken leg in a plaster cast so he could race in some important World Championship qualifying rounds. Carlo, who was born in Maybole, Ayrshire, was resident surgeon at Peel Hospital near Galashiels and had been the Edinburgh track doctor from the 1960s. He was given a special testimonial meeting in recognition of his services to the club, attracting many top stars, which was held on 5 June.

It had been a fine season of entertainment and success. The supporters were happy at last and a memorable year lay ahead in 1981.

Brian Collins was a surprise departure for the 1981 season. He was unable to agree terms and moved to Berwick. Neil Collins was now a full time Monarch after his transfer from parent club Sheffield for £12,000. Neil was now a heat leader and his improvement in 1980 was to be surpassed in 1981. George Hunter started the new season still feeling the effects of an injury sustained at the end of the 1980 season and it took him a few meetings to get anywhere near his best, but his partnership with Benny Rourke was still a potent one. Benny was always a good starter, but tended to lose position as a race wore on, but when paired with George his scores improved dramatically. However, injury was to blight Benny's season once again. A troublesome shoulder was the main problem and it forced him to miss a big chunk of the season.

Roger Lambert was a late starter due to permit problems and did not start until the middle of April. Another late starter was Ivan Blacka, who joined the side at the start of May. Ivan had a great season providing the support for the three heat leaders: Neil Collins, George Hunter and Dave Trownson.

Chris Turner, who had joined the side at the end of 1980, was another anchorman and his partnership with Dave Trownson one of the most potent in the league. Coming in at the reserve berth was Guy Robson, who although at an early stage of his career, did not let himself or anybody else down as he filled the void till Roger Lambert returned to the side.

The season began with a series of challenge matches, the first away to Newcastle resulting in a 53-25 defeat, before taking on Workington at Powderhall for The Caledonia/Cumbria Cup. The home leg was a 63-15 Monarchs whitewash, before they completed the job at Workington, winning 40-35 to land their first trophy of the season.

Glasgow were beaten 47-30 at home in the first leg of the Inter City Cup, but the Tigers reversed the result in the away leg 48-30 to win on aggregate by one point. In the league all was going well for the Monarchs with eight away wins to their credit and going into October they had a clean sheet at home. At that time a top league placing was looking good, but along came Newcastle on 9 October to put a stop to any league aspirations with a 42-36 win. The next week Middlesbrough clinched the title thanks to a last heat 4-2 from Steve Wilcock and Mark Courtney to win 41-37, and Edinburgh had to settle for fourth place.

In 1981 the BSPA allowed National League teams into the British League Knockout Cup, with the Monarch's first round draw taking place on their home track. Edinburgh faced a strong Sheffield side with American ace Shawn Moran leading their attack. The meeting on 8 May was one of the highlights of the Powderhall years with the track record being broken on two occasions, Shawn Moran in heat one and then Dave Trownson in heat four with a time of 64.6.

It was nip and tuck with Sheffield going into heat fourteen two points in front at 38-40. An exchange of 5-1 heat wins over the next two heats saw the Tigers re-establish that two point advantage going into the final heat.

Sheffield had Shawn Moran and Reg Wilson, while Edinburgh had Neil Collins and Chris Turner for the final showdown. After a race-long battle, Shawn Moran came down on the final bend trying to pass Neil Collins. The race was awarded 5-1 to the Monarchs and a final score of 49-47 saw them through to the next round where they met Swindon. The real hero of what was a truly memorable meeting was Dave Trownson – a new track record and a faultless 15 point maximum said it all.

The second round was a two-leg affair and the Monarchs went down to a heavy defeat (69-27) at Blunsdon. The second leg was a tighter encounter, although

Swindon finished the job with a 49-47 win. The Powderhall leg might be remembered not only for the exciting racing, but for the large Swindon support (around 500) who travelled to Edinburgh in a special train which had been organised by Swindon team member Malcolm 'Mad Wellie' Holloway.

Major trophy wins did come the Monarchs' way though, when in July at Peterborough they lifted the Four Team Trophy, beating Newcastle, Middlesbrough and Wolverhampton in the final.

In the National League Knockout Cup they disposed of Exeter, Oxford and Mildenhall to reach the final against Berwick. Berwick were a bit of a nomadic side in 1981, racing home matches at Glasgow and Barrow before finally being excluded from the league, but they were allowed to compete in the Knockout Cup and raced their home leg at Newcastle.

At one point it looked as though the Bandits might build up a healthy lead as, after seven heats, the Monarchs found themselves 14 points down, but inspirational riding from George Hunter, Dave Trownson and Ivan Blacka brought the final first leg score to 49-46.

The Powderhall staging of the second leg fell foul of the weather on 30 October, and permission was granted to run the following week, 6 November. What a final it turned out to be. Berwick drafted in Glasgow's Charlie McKinna to replace the homeward-bound Wayne Brown and Charlie's 14 points were crucial in keeping the Bandits in front mid-way through the meeting. Terrific racing from George Hunter and Neil Collins saw the Monarchs take control in

Knockout Cup winners. From left to right, back row: Chris Turner, George Hunter, Ivan Blacka, Ian Westwell, Dave Trownson. Front row: Neil Collins, Roger Lambert.

Left: Eric Broadbelt. Right: Brett Saunders.

the later part of the meeting and they eventually ran out winners 101-89 on aggregate and 55-40 on the night. Roger Lambert deserves a mention as his 6 paid 10 points from reserve were crucial in the final score.

As darkness fell on the celebrations, changes in the promotion were looming in 1982. Mike Parker, promoter since 1977, sold the rights to Tom Cook, who had formerly been associated with Berwick. 'Big T', as Tom was known, also acquired several of the 1981 riders in the deal, but Neil Collins was not one of them. As expected Neil moved up into the British League with Leicester. However, it was a big surprise to Edinburgh supporters when it was announced that George Hunter would be lining up for Berwick in 1982.

Team manager for the new season was former 1960s Monarch Willie Templeton, with brother Doug looking after the track. Alan Bridgett had moved south to work for Mike Parker. Eric Broadbelt, who had done well at Powderhall when he visited with Sheffield, came in as replacement for Neil Collins, and Tom Cook brought a young Australian, Brett Saunders, with him from Berwick. Brett was a protégé of Doug Wyer (Sheffield) who spotted his potential while touring Down Under.

Chris Turner, Dave Trownson, Ivan Blacka, Benny Rourke and Ian Westwell made up the side that started the season. Roger Lambert came into the side in mid-April, but never found any sort of form and was replaced by junior Sean Courtney, brother of Mark. Sean was given a extended run, but consistent engine problems limited his progress.

Roger Lambert's loss of form ended with him being dropped from the side in

Mark Fiora receives his Edinburgh race jacket from Ian Hoskins (left) and Tom Cook.

June. He moved to Glasgow, but lasted only one match before fighting himself back into the Edinburgh line-up in August when he started to show the sort of scoring ability expected from him. Injury and Benny Rourke seemed inseparable, as again he missed a chunk of the season, but when around he was a valuable member of a weak side. Eric Broadbelt did not become the number one as had been expected. He started well enough, but his form dipped dramatically and then his season was brought to a premature end on Friday 30 July when he was involved in a horrendous crash. He was coming out of the second bend when he lifted and went headlong into a safety fence post. He was back at Powderhall the following week in a wheelchair – which was remarkable considering how bad the crash was.

Mark Fiora joined the side from Sheffield in July, shortly after being photographed being welcomed to Glasgow. Edinburgh won this particular battle, but there was a delay as Mark's points average was sorted out. Mark had been having a poor time at Sheffield and his Edinburgh performances were inconsistent.

While Chris Turner failed to live up to his 1981 season, Dave Trownson took over the role of leader with some brilliant performances both home and away. Undoubtedly his performance of the year came at Peterborough in May when he scored a superb paid maximum and smashed the track record. Young Aussie Brett Saunders was another who could hold his head high in a season that saw the Monarchs slip to fourteenth in the League and go out of the Knockout Cup in the first round to Ellesmere Port.

Ivan Blacka and Benny Rourke were missing in 1983, but back into the side came George Hunter, who received a deserved testimonial meeting in June to celebrate twenty-five years in the sport. Aussie Glyn Taylor was another new face and Glyn showed some spirited performances before being dramatically released from the club at the start of August to accommodate Sean Courtney. Dave Trownson was as reliable as usual, but injury did disrupt his season from time to time. The two Aussies Brett Saunders and Mark Fiora improved, while Chris Turner had another poor season and retired at the start of October.

The meeting at Scunthorpe on 18 July in the League saw the Monarchs walk out following heat nine after an incident between Brett Saunders and Scunthorpe's Kevin Armitage. The meeting finished with Scunthorpe recording 5-0 heat wins in the remaining heats for a 68-21 victory. Ninth place was an improvement in the League, but they again went out of the Knockout Cup in the first round to Middlesbrough.

1984 was a disaster, even with team sponsor Stelrad supporting the Monarchs, and their problems started before the campaign got underway. New regulations regarding Commonwealth riders were to keep Mark Fiora and Brett Saunders out of the side for a time. Even with the help of Ron Brown MP, who arranged for the two Aussies to appear on TV-am to plead their case, it was still a wrangle which went on and on. Mark did get back in to action after marrying his British girlfriend, Julie, in May, but an injury was to sideline him from the middle of June until his return at the start of August. Brett was not so lucky and it was the end of July before he got clearance to continue, but with such a late start found it difficult to get back to full form and fitness.

Dave Trownson was injured against Middlesbrough on 11 May and this kept him out for thee months. Dave was no sooner back when he took another knock at the start of August which finished his 1984 season. Dave Younghusband, the former Middlesbrough rider from the 1960s, came in as team manager and signed the experienced veteran Craig Pendlebury, but his stay proved to be short. Paul McHale, who had been with Newcastle, filled the reserve berth with his best performance (16 points) coming in the abandoned Scottish Cup fixture against Glasgow at Blantyre.

'Big T' pushed the boat out at the start of the season by forking out a reputed £10,000 to Newcastle for Scot Bobby Beaton. Although Bobby was nearing the end of his career he still rattled in the big scores, but even he missed most of July when the dreaded injury bug hit. Other riders who helped out in what was a disaster of a season included Phil Jeffrey, who had his moments in the second string department, Rob Grant of Berwick, who came in for six matches at the end of April, and Edinburgh junior Martin Johnson, a young Australian who also had an extended run due to the injury crisis.

It was no wonder that the Monarchs finished bottom of the league. Surprisingly they progressed through the first round of the Knockout Cup, knocking out Boston before Berwick saw that they went no further. The one success to come Edinburgh's way was beating Glasgow for the Scottish Cup. The Scottish Open Championship was reintroduced, and was staged at Powderhall for first time, with Reading's Mitch Shirra winning with 14 points.

New names in the 1985 promotion were John Campbell and Toni Frankitti, with Frankitti – who was often described by the fans as eccentric – playing a high-profile role. Mark Fiora was transferred to Middlesbrough for a five-figure fee, but the Tony Frankitti-instigated signings of Billy Burton and Alan Mason did not go down well with many of the supporters. Bobby Beaton, Dave Trownson, Brett Saunders, Roger Lambert and Sean Courtney were all back to form in what looked a weak Monarchs side.

The opening night's meeting against Glasgow in the Scottish Triangle was snowed off. The restaging was the following week and the 35-42 Glasgow win was just a hint of what was to come. Barrow were the next visitors to Powderhall for a league match and a huge win 59-19 was rendered meaningless when the north-western club were expelled from the league for being too weak.

Things looked a bit brighter when they held the Gunners to an eight point deficit (43-35) at Ellesmere Port in a Knockout Cup first round tie, but the next night at Powderhall they threw it away when the Gunners forced a draw.

As the season wore on things just went from bad to worse. Bobby Beaton was way below par, suffering many engine problems. Dave Trownson was struggling to get back to full fitness when he suffered another injury, this time an ankle which brought a premature end to his season in the middle of August. Billy Burton and Alan Mason both failed to produce the points, and a succession of riders were used to plug so many gaps: Mark Burrows, Gordon Whitaker, Gary O'Hare and Tony Forward were all used at some point. Scott Lamb and Phil Jeffrey had an extended run after coming to Edinburgh in an exchange for Sean Courtney who went to Berwick. Brett Saunders was the one bright spot in the team, receiving solid support from Steve Finch when the former Ellesmere Port rider joined the side at the end of May. With so many home defeats and only one success on the road, a 40-38 win at Long Eaton, it was no surprise that they retained the bottom slot in the league table.

Ivan Mauger, who had some terrific matches against the Monarchs at Old Meadowbank, staged his Farewell to Scotland meeting, which was a magnificent interlude, in September. Eric Gundersen, Shawn Moran, Peter and Phil Collins and top entertainer American John Cook were just some of the stars who partook in this memorable event.

Wimbledon's Jamie Luckhurst won the second Powderhall staging of the Scottish Open Championship, but this meeting just summed up Edinburgh's

Les Collins leading brother Neil.

season when Bobby Beaton broke his arm in a bad crash. After two years at the bottom, the club was at its lowest ebb and major changes were needed. A new promotional team took over from Tom Cook and Toni Frankitti for the 1986 season.

Delicatessen owner Doug Newlands, together with John Campbell, fronted the seven-man consortium which was to give the club a new lease of life with the signing of former World number two Les Collins from Sheffield for a reputed £20,000 transfer fee. Les was joined by another World Finalist Doug Wyer, which meant there was no place for Bobby Beaton.

The retained riders were Dave Trownson (in his testimonial year), Brett Saunders, Scott Lamb, Phil Jeffrey and Mark 'Buzz' Burrows, with Jamie Young being given a chance.

What a difference a year makes. Les Collins and Doug Wyer led from the front, although first Stoke then Berwick took vital league points away from Powderhall. The only other side who put a blot on the Powderhall record book in 1986 was Eastbourne.

Edinburgh had yet to defeat the powerful Eagles, either at home or away, and in 1986 Eastbourne recorded two wins. The first was in the Knockout Cup, ending the Edinburgh interest in this competition for another year, after the Monarchs had disposed of Glasgow with home and away wins in the first round. Eastbourne returned in the league in September and in a thriller of a meeting again got the better of the Monarchs, winning 40-37.

In May at Berrington Lough, Edinburgh reaped sweet revenge over the

Left: National Best Pairs winners Doug Wyer and Les Collins. Right: Testimonial man Dave Trownson.

Berwick Bandits by winning 43-35 in an all-round team performance, but they had to wait until September before recording their next away success at Hackney, where Dave Trownson was the hero on a night when Doug Wyer was missing. Even so, ninth out of twenty was a respectable league finish.

Les Collins was the true star, being consistent all season (a 10.14 average said it all). He held the Silver Helmet for a long period and on the 13 July brought some silverware back to Powderhall when, along with Doug Wyer, he won the National League Best Pairs at Hackney. Doug Wyer, apart from missing the end of the season with a back injury, had been the solid sparring partner Les required, while Dave Trownson – who had an injury-free season – took half the campaign to get back to near his best. He then received a deserved testimonial for ten years' faithful service to the Monarchs, which was held in October. Brett Saunders, Scott Lamb and Mark Burrows all had their moments during a season that brought a smile back to the supporters' faces.

The National League Fours once again looked a better prospect as far as Edinburgh was concerned, but they went out at the semi-final stages at Peterborough. Les added the Scottish Open Championship to his 1986 collection of trophies with a convincing 15 point maximum. Then, in the National League Riders' Championship, he finished third.

Edinburgh could now look forward to 1987 with a bit more confidence. The 1987 team was much the same as in 1986, with talented Wolverhampton junior

Chris Cobby coming into the side in July when Doug Wyer had to enter hospital for a minor operation. Unfortunately this kept Doug out of action longer than expected, as he did not return until the middle of September.

The Eastbourne bogey continued when in an exciting contest they again went home with a 39-38 victory. Other dropped league points at home were to Mildenhall (draw) and Milton Keynes (44-34 defeat), while on the road the Monarchs were victorious at Newcastle and drew at Glasgow and Exeter to finish tenth out of sixteen teams.

Home and away victories over Glasgow in the Knockout Cup saw them meeting the mighty Eastbourne in the next round, but again the Eagles proved too much of an obstacle, winning both legs to end Edinburgh's interest in the competition.

They were also out of the Fours, but not without controversy. Edinburgh's round at Powderhall on 14 June was abandoned by the referee after Doug Wyer and Middlesbrough's Martin Dixon clashed, but the Edinburgh promotion felt that there was nothing wrong with the track and it was a racing accident. Their point was proved by running an unofficial meeting to keep the supporters happy, but this action cost them a £900 fine!

Les Collins had another good season, maintaining a near 10-point average, winning the Northern Riders' Championship at Middlesbrough and the Hexagon Trophy at Peterborough, but was out of the frame at Coventry in the National League Riders' Championship with 10 points. He also lost his Scottish Open Championship title to Wimbledon's Neville Tatum, finishing third on the night.

All in all, it was a good team, but seemed to have no luck, with Dave Trownson going well until laid low with a kidney infection at the end of August. Around the same time Brett Saunders injured a hand, although this did not seem to affect him too much as he was soon back with a paid maximum against Canterbury.

Scott Lamb proved an exciting prospect with some solid displays, rattling in two unbeaten scores against Middlesbrough and Glasgow. Chris Cobby was a rider who started well, but failed to maintain the same level of scoring throughout. George Wells, who had been around the Edinburgh scene since the late 1960s, caused a major stir by winning The Scottish Junior Championship in the rain – and didn't the rain gods celebrate!

One change that took place in 1987 was that the starting gate was shifted from the stand side of the stadium to the opposite side. The first meeting with the new gate position was a challenge between the Monarchs and Mark Fiora's Kangaroos on 1 May.

Dave Trownson, who had been with the Monarchs since their introduction to Powderhall, moved on to Exeter in 1988. Also on the move were Phil Jeffrey to Glasgow and Chris Cobby to Arena Essex. Les Collins and Doug Wyer were back for their third season in the blue and gold along with Scott Lamb and Brett Saunders. New to the side were brothers Jamie and Jeremy Luckhurst, sons of Reg Luckhurst who had graced the side in 1960. New Australian Darrell Branford was over for his first season of British racing, but found the going tough and moved on to Long Eaton at the end of July.

Former Scunthorpe rider Rob Woffinden came in as a replacement and only occasionally showed what he was capable of. Les Collins was as dependable as ever, but it was Jamie Luckhurst who gave him the fight for the top spot in the team. Doug Wyer had slipped a bit in the scoring and was then involved in a crash that ended his career at Middlesbrough on 9 June.

It was in heat fifteen of a National League Four Team qualifying round that Berwick's Rob Grant and Doug were involved in a horrendous crash which resulted in Doug suffering a serious leg break. It took a number of operations over a period of years for Doug to get over his injury.

As expected, Doug Wyer was sorely missed for the rest of the season, although Brett Saunders did a good job to support Les Collins and Jamie Luckhurst. Monarchs finished in eleventh place out of sixteen in the league. They did, however, have a run in the Knockout Cup, putting out Stoke and Peterborough before losing to Hackney. Les Collins fought his way through to the British Final of the World Championship at Sheffield, but 4 points was not enough to progress any further. In the Scottish Open Championship, Les had to settle for the runners-up spot to Glasgow's Steve Lawson.

The 1989 Monarchs, from left to right: Les Collins, Michael Coles, Scott Lamb, Ray Taafe, Lars Munkedal, Jamie Luckhurst, Brett Saunders (on bike).

Doug Wyer was a big loss, so more team building was required for 1989. Les Collins, Brett Saunders, Scott Lamb and Jamie Luckhurst were all back and Lars Munkedal, a Dane, came via Wolverhampton after two successful seasons in the British League. Michael Coles, son of Bob Coles, was a long distance traveller, making the weekly journey from his home base in Exeter. Michael was an Exeter asset, but had spent 1988 with Mildenhall.

Another new Australian, Mick Powell, was given his chance. Mick came via Poole, who could not fit him into their side, and after a bit of a wild start at Newcastle soon settled as a promising team member. Unfortunately, injury was never far away. A shattered cheek bone in a crash against Berwick at Powderhall in July was followed by a broken left thigh and a fractured right ankle in October at Mildenhall. In between those injuries, Mick produced some thrilling races and respectable returns for the team.

Les Collins, Brett Saunders, Scott Lamb and new boy Michael Coles also all produced the goods, but Jamie Luckhurst lasted only eight meetings before he was sensationally given his marching orders from the club. Jamie failed to turn up for the Powderhall meeting against Wimbledon on 21 April after walking out of the away encounter at Ipswich the previous evening. He claimed that God had told him to stop racing, but John Campbell stated in the programme 'that Jamie Luckhurst took it upon himself to let the promotion, his team mates, his sponsors and the most important people of all, the paying public, down'. He was promptly sacked and after a few week out returned to the sport with Middlesbrough.

Eighth in the league out of eighteen teams was not bad but, as in seasons gone by, the reserve berth gave problems. Peter McNamara from Middlesbrough, local junior Tony Rizzo and Mark Pearce, an Australian, were all given a chance without success.

After defeating Arena Essex, Monarchs went out of the Knockout Cup to Peterborough in a close finish, Peterborough winning 97-95 on aggregate. Monarchs did take the Scottish Cup and Autumn Cup from Glasgow, however. They went out in the first semi-final in the National League Fours finals day at Peterborough, Les Collins and Brett Saunders reached the semi-final stage in the National League Pairs at Hackney.

Wimbledon's Todd Wiltshire won the Scottish Open Championship in October, with Glasgow's Kenny McKinna second. Brett Saunders had one of his best evenings, as he was the only one to defeat Todd Wiltshire on the night and he finished a creditable third.

Danish Monarch Lars Munkedal moved on for the 1990 season. He had suffered one crash too many in 1989 which sapped his confidence and the Edinburgh faithful may not have seen the best of him. Nigel Alderton, a twenty-one-year-old Australian, came into the team, but an early season shoulder injury knocked him back and restricted team chances.

Mark Blackbird, who had been with Mildenhall and Long Eaton, only had a short stay, lasting five meetings. The ironic thing was that his replacement was his brother, Carl, who had enjoyed some terrific meetings at Powderhall in the past with Mildenhall. No sooner had Carl agreed terms with Edinburgh, than he was at the centre of a wrangle with Poole who also wanted the talented rider. Although Carl wanted to go to Poole, the Edinburgh promotion held out for his services – this may explain why Carl's Edinburgh form was so patchy.

Les Collins again led the way; despite a slump in form around August and September he was still the number one. Michael Coles was still making the marathon journey from Exeter each week and his scoring wavered at times causing a drop in his average. Scott Lamb did not show the improvement expected in what was his fifth season with the Monarchs. Mick Powell was returning from serious leg injuries and, as expected, took time to get back to something like his best. A paid maximum against Exeter in September along with some fighting spirit proved that he might be a better prospect in 1991 when fully fit.

Financial problems within the club came to a head in January of 1991 when it was announced that the Edinburgh speedway would be forced to close unless some form of sponsorship could be found to help with the running of the club in the coming season.

A meeting was held at Powderhall, where the promotion outlined the club's difficulties and the response from the gathered supporters on the night was a pledge of £16,000, which was enough for the promotion to announce that it was all go for the 1991 season.

The real hero and saviour of Edinburgh speedway was Mike Hunter. It was Mike who organised the meeting and formed what was a fighting fund. From the

Freddy Schott.

Carl Blackbird.

fighting fund's activities, The Friends of Edinburgh Speedway was organised (and is still in existence to date).

Newcomer of the season was Danish starlet Frede (Freddy) Schott. From his introduction to the Monarchs in a challenge match against Danish Club Slangerup in the middle of April, he improved dramatically, finishing second in the team averages with a figure of 7.88.

Over recent years there seems to have been at least one Edinburgh rider who didn't reach the end of the season without receiving serious injury. The unlucky rider in 1990 was Brett Saunders, who had endured engine problems for most of the early part of the campaign. He had no sooner sorted that out when he was involved in a horrific smash at Ipswich on the 6 September. He crashed through the first bend safety fence and careered across the stock-car track, hitting the concrete outer perimeter fence and sustaining internal injuries which were to keep him out for the remainder of the season.

There were seventeen teams in the league in 1990 and Edinburgh slipped down the table to thirteenth. The Scottish Cup went to Glasgow and the Monarchs failed to make the National League Fours finals. Although Les Collins won all his preliminary heats in the National League Pairs Championship at Shawfield in Glasgow, Carl Blackbird failed to score and so as a team they failed to reach the lattermost stages.

Left: Alan 'Doc' Bridgett track man supreme, back as team manager. Right: Dariusz 'Darek' Fleigert.

Doug Wyer received a benefit meeting in April, which was a success with top division riders showing their respect for the veteran by taking part. The Scottish Open Championship fell foul of the weather twice in October and never took place in 1990.

A change of ownership of Powderhall then took place when Eddie Ramsay, who ran nightclubs in Edinburgh, bought the stadium. It made no difference to the Monarchs, who had a better 1991 season. They finished fourth in the league and third in the Gold Cup (North Division) – the Gold Cup was a mini-league at the start of the season. They got to the final of the Four Team finals at Peterborough and finished second to Arena Essex. Les Collins finished fourth in the Second Division Riders' Championship at Coventry. Then, in unusual circumstances, Les represented the club at Belle Vue in the Division One Riders' Championship (the top three from the division two championship automatically went into the Belle Vue meeting, but Troy Butler, who had qualified, was injured and Les took his place).

This achievements represented the good points. The bad ones included going out of the Knockout Cup to Long Eaton in the first round, Glasgow winning the Scottish Cup and Berwick taking the Autumn Trophy.

Les Collins, Freddy Schott, Michael Coles, Brett Saunders and Nigel Alderton were all back. Twenty-five-year-old Australian Darrin Winkler and Carsten Schott, cousin of Freddy, a twenty-two-year-old Dane were both given early season team outings, but failed to make the grade and were soon replaced. Another Danish newcomer, Johnny Jorgensen, made his debut in May and became an instant hit with his exciting style of riding. Another new face was ex-Cradley Heath rider Justin Walker, who had the occasional good meeting before he too was replaced by Zimbabwean David Steen (who was steady if unspectacular). Alan 'Doc' Bridgett was also back in the fold as track curator and team manager.

Mick Powell, who had suffered such bad luck with injuries, moved to Glasgow. Mick was to have better luck at Shawfield, where he developed into a heat leader with the Tigers and was to have a long association with the Glasgow club. Once the team settled down it was a good year, with Les Collins as dependable as usual and Freddy Schott improving to take over the second heat leader spot. At the end of the season he helped out first division Berwick, such was his progress.

Michael Coles was another rider who improved and had it not been for some irritating engine problems would have finished with a higher points total. Nigel Alderton steered clear of injury and proved himself a solid second string performer. It was a surprise when Scott Lamb moved out on loan to Newcastle, where he moved up into a heat leader position which was good for Edinburgh.

Brett Saunders, had been with the club for ten years and received a deserved testimonial, which took the form of a four-team tournament in September. Cradley Heath's American Greg Hancock won the Scottish Open Championship from Les Collins. The postponed Scottish Open Championship from 1990 took place as a second-half event at the end of May with Les Collins winning from Freddy Schott.

Sponsorship was an important part of the team make-up and it was good news in 1992 when it was announced Gulf Oil (Great Britain) Ltd who came on board in 1991 were to continue. Les Collins, Michael Coles, Brett Saunders and Johnny Jorgensen were back. New to the team were Kenny McKinna, who had been an icon in Glasgow for so many years, Glasgow-born junior Stewart McDonald came in as reserve and local junior Mike McLuskey, who had made the occasional outings over the last few years, got an extended run.

Edinburgh signed their first Polish-born rider, Dariusz Fliegert, who became known as 'Darek' and rode for Rybnik in his home land. Unfortunately, Darek failed to get a grip of the language or the British tracks and was only occasionally able to produce a reasonable points return. He was involved in a spectacular crash with team-mate Kenny McKinna during the meeting against Berwick at Powderhall in April which resulted in Kenny receiving facial injuries. Kenny missed the next five meetings, but he was soon back to his best and proved the perfect leader, along with Les Collins who was as reliable as ever.

Johnny Jorgensen was a bit of disappointment, failing to make the progress that was expected, while Michael Coles, who had increased his average over the past three years as a Monarch, slipped slightly in 1992, but this may have been because he had other things on his mind as the season progressed. In a strange occurrence, Michael was granted a testimonial for ten years' service with Exeter. This was to be held at Powderhall on 2 October, but rain interfered with the proceedings and the meeting was postponed.

However, 2 October was not all bad as Michael married his long-time girlfriend Michelle Kennedy below the main stand at Powderhall, with all supporters invited as guests – a strange day indeed! The testimonial meeting did take place a week later on 11 October.

It had been a bad year altogether as far as the weather was concerned with a total of eleven meetings being postponed due to the conditions.

After the good 1991 season, Edinburgh slipped down to seventh in the league and went out of the Knockout Cup to Peterborough after knocking out Glasgow in the first round. Glasgow exacted revenge by retaining the Scottish Cup. Cradley Heath's Greg Hancock retained the Scottish Open Championship and Kenny McKinna won the Scottish Riders' Championship.

The one highlight of the season was when Edinburgh came so close to winning the Division Two Fours title at Peterborough. Les Collins just failed to catch Mick Poole in the final heat, which was enough to give the home side the championship, but second was not bad. Brett Saunders, a fixture at Powderhall for eleven years, moved out on loan to Sheffield for the start of the season. Brett did not settle with the Steel City club, eventually moving to Middlesbrough (and at times came back to haunt the Monarchs).

Johnny Jorgensen and Dariusz Fliegert did not figure in the 1993 team and were replaced by the returning Scott Lamb, who was out on loan to Newcastle in 1992. Scott had spent the close season racing in South Africa and much was expected after a good year with Newcastle. Another returnee was a Monarch from as far back as 1985, Sean Courtney, who had enjoyed a good season with Rye

Left: Michael Coles. Right: Kenny McKinna.

House in 1992 and was the match winner for Rye House at Powderhall that year. Also arriving at the club was Kevin Little, who had seen action with Berwick, Glasgow and Bradford before coming to Edinburgh via Coventry.

Vesa Ylinen, who hailed from Finland, came into the side with a glowing reputation. Vesa missed the first four meetings due to work permit problems, but when he did take to the track with his quick starts and hard first corners he proved to be a good addition to the side.

Les Collins, Kenny McKinna and Michael Coles all carried out the heat leader roles expected of them and with Vesa Ylinen having such a good season it gave the side a solid top end with Scott Lamb and Kevin Little giving good support. Sean Courtney was inconsistent, however, and not for the first time the reserve position was to cause problems.

Stewart McDonald started the season as reserve, but took being dropped after a series of poor results the wrong way. After a confrontation with the promotion he moved on to Glasgow. His place was filled with a series of riders: Mike Lewthwaite, Paul Gould and then Peter Scully, a Belle Vue junior who proved himself good enough to be given an extended run.

The season started with an aggregate win over Glasgow in the Spring Trophy. The Scottish Cup went to Glasgow, who won both legs by the same 58-50 score line. Brett Saunders, so often the villain at Glasgow when wearing a Monarchs race jacket, was the Tigers' hero at Powderhall when he scored 12 points for the Glasgow club in the first leg.

With only eleven teams in the league, sides met twice home and away. Rye House and Middlesbrough both won at Powderhall, while away the Monarchs had wins at Rye House and Oxford, then a draw at Oxford in their second league visit, finally finishing in fifth place.

The win over Rye House on 6 June was remarkable as Michael Coles missed his first two heats due to his transport breaking down, but when he did arrive to take his place in heat ten, he scored 9 points from the five races he took over the remaining eight heats. The Second Division Fours Trophy was displayed at Powderhall for the second time when Edinburgh went all the way to win the final at Peterborough on 25 July. Michael Coles won the Scottish Open Championship, with Kenny McKinna having to be content with second place ahead of Glasgow's Mick Powell.

1994 was a memorable season, if not in the sense of trophy wins, but for the entertainment served up at Powderhall over the campaign. The league was run on the same basis as in 1993, where clubs met twice home and away and Edinburgh finished third out of ten, losing only the once at home to eventual league title winners Glasgow. On the road they were successful on three occasions, at Sheffield, Swindon and Oxford. They also drew at Long Eaton – which was becoming a favourite hunting ground for the Monarchs.

After putting Newcastle out of the Knockout Cup with home and away wins they did the same to Long Eaton. Middlesbrough were next to go with an Edinburgh aggregate win. This put the Monarchs into the final against arch-rivals

Glasgow Tigers. After plenty of publicity hype, the two sides locked horns in the first leg at Powderhall on 14 October and the meeting opened with one of the most exciting races ever seen at the stadium.

Glasgow's Robert Nagy and Mick Powell shot from the start to lead Les Collins and Lawrence Hare. Les gave chase for three laps before passing first Powell and then Nagy on the last bend for a memorable win. But the Tigers kept this first leg clash close with Edinburgh winning by just 4 points, 50-46. In the second leg at Shawfield two days later, that 4 point lead was not enough as the Monarchs went down 55-41 in a spirited performance against a strong Glasgow side.

The 1994 team was much the same as in 1993, with the addition of a new Danish rider, Jan Andersen, who had made late season outings the previous year, and Lawrence Hare, an Ipswich asset who had been with Rye House the previous year. Lawrence was to become another long distance traveller over the season and, with his leg-trailing style, proved to be an exciting second string in the side. Lawrence had a night of glory in the meeting against Sheffield on 23 September when he became only the second Edinburgh rider to go unbeaten in seven races, recording a paid 21 point maximum. Jan Andersen was another who had the Edinburgh supporters on his side with some spirited displays in first season, his average of 7.12 being well earned.

Les Collins, Kenny McKinna and Scott Lamb took on the role of heat leaders,

Lawrence Hare and Jan Andersen.

with Vesa Ylinen giving solid support. There was not a lot between the top four, with Les boasting an average of 8.40 and Vesa 7.68. However, Vesa sustained a leg injury at Exeter at the start of July which ruled him out for the rest of the season. Michael Coles moved to Belle Vue and Kevin Little only came into the side to help cover for Vesa Ylinen. Peter Scully showed so much promise, but poor machinery and over-enthusiastic riding resulting in too many falls held him back.

As holders of the Second Division Fours, Monarchs again reached the final stages, finishing fourth. They lost both the Easter Trophy and Scottish Cup to Glasgow and Ipswich's Ben Howe became the 1994 Scottish Open Champion.

A cloud hung over Powderhall as the 1995 season approached, as this was to be the final year that both speedway and greyhounds would be seen at the quaint stadium. All the protests and demonstrations made no difference as the developers moved in at the end of the campaign.

Changes were also made to the structure of the league, with the amalgamation of both the First and Second Division teams to form the British Premier League. Ninth place out of twenty-one teams in such a strong league was not bad, considering Edinburgh went with five of the 1994 side – Les Collins, Kenny McKinna, Jan Andersen, Lawrence Hare and Scott Lamb – plus a thirty-eight-year-old American, Mike Faria, who had been with Belle Vue a few years back. The other new face was an unknown Dane, Robert Larsen.

The season opened with the Spring Trophy, which Robert Larsen missed due to work commitments with ex-Monarch Freddy Schott standing in as a guest. Glasgow won both legs to take the trophy.

The first league meeting was against Bradford and ended in a draw. Most of the home matches were won by close scores, which added to the entertainment, with only Eastbourne stealing a close 49-46 win. Long Eaton managed to draw, while on the road the Monarchs pulled off wins at Hull, Exeter and Oxford, as well as draws at Coventry and Swindon to prove that they were capable of matching the ex-First Division sides.

Robert Larsen made a spectacular debut against Swindon on 14 April at Powderhall, scoring a paid 12 points, but he was unable to maintain that form and was replaced by Robert Eriksson, a young Swedish rider who won his debut ride against Oxford at the end of June. Mike Faria proved that age was no barrier with some flamboyant racing and both Les Collins and Kenny McKinna both put their years of experience to good use by providing some exciting wins. Jan Andersen with his sharp starting was a handful for the ex-First Division stars and his partnership with Scott Lamb proved an excellent combination.

King's Lynn's flamboyant American Bobby Ott, always a popular visitor, won the Scottish Open Championship. Hull put Edinburgh out of the Knockout Cup, winning both legs. Edinburgh got through to finals day at Peterborough in the Fours, but went out in the semi-final stages. In the Powderhall staging of the Fours rounds, Hull's Nigel Crabtree received heavy fines from the referee when in heat fourteen he visited the referee's box to complain about a starting infringement. This and his argument with the Start Marshall more or less ended

Ten up – for Testimonal man Les Collins.

his speedway career.

Les Collins received a testimonial for his ten years' service with the Monarchs and on 27 August a Les Collins Select defeated Scott Lamb's All Stars 42-36 in what was a fun day.

Barry Briggs filled the stadium with one of the biggest crowds seen at Powderhall when he brought the Golden Greats, including Ove Fundin, Bengt Jansson, Jimmy McMillan and former Monarchs Doug Templeton, George Hunter, Reg Luckhurst, Bert Harkins and Dave Trownson out of hibernation for the night. All these riders put on a splendid exhibition of racing, while former World Champion Peter Collins showed that he would still be able to hold his own in the league. Former Edinburgh heroes who were on parade in a non-riding capacity were Wayne Briggs, Jimmy Tannock and Gordon Mitchell, while 1960 Monarch Freddie Greenwell – in his original race jacket and JAP bike – was a star on track. Doug Templeton celebrated his sixty-seventh birthday and was presented with a cake by Barry Briggs to end a nostalgic evening.

As the riders walked round the track at the end of the final meeting at Powderhall on 6 October, both the promotion and supporters were left wondering if and where the Edinburgh Monarchs would find a home for the 1996 season.

The Scottish Monarchs at Shawfield, 1996

Having left Powderhall, an application was made for planning permission to run speedway at the Armadale stadium, which is situated some twenty miles along the M8 heading towards Glasgow. The stadium is used for greyhound racing and had previously been used for stock-car events. However, just months before the start of the 1996 season there was a shock in store when planning permission was refused for the Armadale venture.

A team had been formed for 1996, which included Mike Faria, Kenny McKinna, Robert Eriksson and Scott Lamb from the previous year. A new Swede, Robban Johansson, and the first Italian to race for a Scottish side, Stefano Alfonso, were also signed. After ten years Les Collins moved on to join another homeless team, Cradley Heath, who became known as the Cradley/Stoke Heathens.

There were troubles at Glasgow and they did not run in 1996. Glasgow had a track and Edinburgh had a team and no track. Logic seemed to be that the

Scottish Monarchs. From left to right, back row: Scott Lamb, Mike Faria, Robert Eriksson, Robhan Johansson. Front row: Mick Powell, Kenny McKinna (on bike), Stefano Alfonso.

Vesa Ylinen, a late addition to the side.

Monarchs move to Shawfield – giving the Tigers supporters and the travelling Edinburgh fans their weekly fix of speedway. The team was known as the Scottish Monarchs, but the amalgamation turned out to be a disaster.

Only an estimated 250-300 Edinburgh supporters made the weekly pilgrimage to Shawfield and too many of the Tigers faithful refused to watch what was basically an Edinburgh team race in Glasgow. Crowd figures were well below the break-even level.

The only Glasgow connection in the team was Mick Powell, who had an inconsistent year, while Kenny McKinna and Mike Faria both had a reasonable season and exceeded expectations at times. Robert Eriksson started slowly, suffering many machine problems, but finished the year strongly. Stefano Alfonso, with his cheeky smile, became a crowd favourite. He may not have been consistent in the scoring department, but his fence-scraping races certainly livened up some dull meetings. In the Four Team Championship round at Shawfield on 16 June, Stefano was involved in a heat one crash which resulted in a broken arm, putting him out for most of the remainder of the season.

Robban Johansson started off with a storming 15 points at Long Eaton in the opening meeting of the season. He then settled down as a steady team man, but became the victim of cost cutting and moved to Long Eaton at the start of August. His replacement was Edinburgh asset Vesa Ylinen, who did just as well as Robban.

Middlesbrough's Shane Parker won the Scottish Open Championship, in what was a season with little or no atmosphere. It was the year the Lay down engine was introduced and it was after the mauling that Coventry dished out to the Monarchs at Shawfield at the start of June that the Monarchs riders were to waken to that fact and change over.

They went out of the Knockout Cup in the first round to Bradford and finished a dismal season in twelfth spot in the league, with the hope that they may find a new home for 1997.

The Monarchs at Armadale

After the disaster of 1996, there was good news for the Monarchs faithful when an appeal against the refusal of planning permission at Armadale went in the Edinburgh promotion's favour. With planning permission now granted, Alan Bridgett and his team of helpers moved into Armadale to start laying a new track. The finished product was to measure 280 metres – small with tricky bends to encourage close exciting racing.

It was Blair Scott who made history by having the first laps of the new circuit during a pre-season practice. Blair, along with Barry Campbell, was a product of the Heathersfield training track and both men had been team members of the League and Knockout Cup winning Linlithgow side of 1996. Both had cut their teeth in Monarchs colours at Shawfield the previous year and were now ready for an extended run in the Edinburgh team of 1997.

Kenny McKinna captained the team, with only Robert Eriksson remaining

Young guns – Barry Campbell and Blair Scott.

MacRobert Eriksson the flying Swede.

from the 1996 side. Into the revamped Monarchs came Jarno Kosonen, a Finn who had been with Swindon in 1996, and Paul Gould, another product of the Conference League.

Two leagues were formed for the 1997 season, the Elite League and the Premier League. Edinburgh entered the Premier League, which consisted of fourteen teams. They also competed for the Premier League Cup, which was split into two sections, North and South, the top two teams in this competition then going into the elimination stages in the semi-final and final of the Knockout Cup.

Matches were run over fifteen heats with six-man teams in 1997. The Spring Trophy against the resurrected Glasgow Tigers opened the new era, but all did not go to plan as the Tigers – after winning the away leg at Shawfield – came to Armadale on the opening night, 4 April, and won that contest 47-43 for an aggregate Spring Trophy win of 100-78.

Once the team settled they won all their home Premier League Trophy matches and recorded one away success against Glasgow to finish second in the Northern Section table. This put them through to the semi-finals, where they disposed of Reading 93-87 over home and away ties. Oxford were the other semi-final winners and with both stages of the two-leg final resulting in the same score,

47-43 in Edinburgh's favour, the first piece of silverware in the Armadale trophy cabinet.

It became evident that Jarno Kosonen, although having the odd good meeting, was not an out-and-out heat leader and was replaced at the start of May by Peter Carr. Peter, who had been known as the 'B52 Bomber', was a legend at Sheffield before he went into semi-retirement. That was all to change after his debut, when following two falls against his former team he rattled home three wins, to help his new club to a 55-35 victory on 9 May.

Once Peter got his machinery and himself into peak condition, Peter ' The Motor' Carr – as he was christened by Edinburgh mike-man Scott Wilson – provided the perfect spearhead along with Kenny McKinna and Robert Eriksson to lead the younger riders to third place in the league.

All three recorded 9 plus averages: Peter (9.86), Kenny (9.73) and Robert (9.46). Of the younger members of the team, Blair Scott stuttered at the start, was loaned out to Glasgow for a few weeks and then came back twice the rider he was before. Very exciting, but at times unpredictable, Blair improved beyond recognition from the Conference League rider of 1996. Barry Campbell soon found that his

Knockout Cup winners in 1997. From left to right, back row: Peter Carr, Kenny McKinna. Middle row: Paul Gould, Robert Eriksson. Front row: Barry Campbell, Blair Scott.

smooth style was not enough at this level, but once he found some quick starts he produced some outstanding races. It was Paul Gould who gave the heat leaders the steady support that was required and time after time he produced the match-winning ride.

Neil Hewitt came into the side as reserve after some outstanding meetings for Linlithgow early in the season. Neil proved that he was not out of his depth by scoring vital reserve points, but on 30 May in the home meeting against Skegness he was involved in a heat ten crash. It soon became evident that it was serious and this was confirmed some days later when it was revealed that Neil had suffered serious back injuries. Sadly those injuries have confined Neil to a wheelchair ever since.

The Scottish Riders' Championship, won by Kenny McKinna, was run as a successful benefit for Neil. Peter Carr won the Scottish Open Championship and also won the Premier League Riders' Championship, held at Coventry on 13 September. Robert Eriksson was Monarchs' other representative at Coventry and did himself and the club proud by finishing third.

Such was Peter Carr's season that he was voted runner-up in the *Edinburgh Evening News* Sports Personality of the Year contest. It was great to have a fine home venue, which produced some exciting racing, and best of all the atmosphere was back.

The 1998 season was to be Kenny McKinna's twentieth year of racing speedway, and in recognition of this feat was given a special meeting, entitled the 'Gathering', staged on 24 July. Many of the Premier League top stars, including Carl Stonehewer, Martin Dixon and James Grieves, took part along with Elite League

Kenny McKinna's swansong.

king-pin American Sam Ermolenko, to make Kenny's night a memorable one. This was to be Kenny's swansong as he had announced that he would be retiring from racing at the end of the season.

Young guns Blair Scott, Barry Campbell and Paul Gould were back in 1998, along with Kenny and Peter Carr. The dreaded points limit meant there was no place for Robert Eriksson, who at one point was not going to return to Britain for the 1998 season (as it turned out he went to Belle Vue in the Elite League, but returned to Sweden after only a few meetings).

Kevin Little, who had been a Monarch in the Powderhall era, came in for a second time as did Robert Larsen, a Dane. Running in conjunction with the main league was a mini-league for juniors. The Youth Development League was formed and the Armadale side were known as the 'Dale Devils'. They did not win the league, but the youngsters gained experience in team racing.

There were high expectations for the 1998 season after the success of '97 and things looked bright with an aggregate win over Glasgow to take the Spring Trophy. Monarchs then repeated that success by winning the Premiership from Reading. Two trophies in the cabinet in the opening week of the season bode well for the rest of the campaign.

Peter Carr had missed the Spring Trophy meeting with Glasgow due to an ankle injury sustained jumping over a gate. Peter had been a sensation the previous year, although niggling engine problems had held him back in the early part of the season. Once those were sorted out he was back to his best, piling up the points. A fall and engine failure in the Scottish Open Championship stopped Peter making the final and he relinquished his title to Freddy Schott, a Monarch back at Powderhall who now restricted his racing to Scandinavia. Peter also lost his Premier League Riders' title at Sheffield to Peterborough's Glen Cunningham, Peter finished in third place.

Kenny McKinna could always be relied upon to produce the vital win when the pressure was on and even in this, his final year, he still produced the goods, matching Peter Carr point for point around Armadale for a 10.22 home average and a 8.60 overall average. Kevin Little raised his average by over a point and was a model of consistency with his smooth riding style, which was a joy to watch. Kevin held the Silver Helmet Match Race title for a while, having defeated the holder, Nicki Pedersen of Newcastle, at Newcastle in July. He then defended the helmet against Craig Watson of Newport at Armadale, before losing it to Leigh Lanham of Arena Essex at Arena.

Blair Scott and Barry Campbell both had their moments, although most of those were at Armadale and their away form was not what was expected. Barry joined a very exclusive club when he became only the third Edinburgh rider to record an unbeaten seven ride paid maximum (against Newport) on 14 August. This was the same night that Paul Gould was involved in a horrendous crash with Newport's Scott Pegler. Both riders crashed through the safety fence, which resulted in Paul requiring an ambulance journey to hospital. He was to miss a few meetings in what was not a good season for him.

Robert Larsen was another who did not live up to expectations and was replaced in July by Swede Marcus Andersson, a former Poole rider. Sadly, Marcus was not the answer either, and in turn was replaced by 1996 Monarch Stefano Alfonso, who in turn lasted no more than three meetings before vanishing from the scene. It was this position in the team make-up which resulted in the 1998 slide.

Fourth place in the Group B section of the Premier League Cup put Monarchs out of the latter stages and ninth in the League out of thirteen was a severe drop on the previous year's showing. Edinburgh did reach finals day of the Four Team Tournament at Peterborough in August, reaching the final round and finishing joint second with Hull on 19 points, behind home team Peterborough.

The Scotland *v*. England test series was reintroduced, and after winning the first test at Armadale it was England who won the series 3-2 by winning at both Shawfield and Berwick.

1999 was to be a much better year; it was also 'Scottish Year' at Armadale, with six of the seven team members all Scottish-born. The odd man out (but an adopted Scot) was Peter Carr, who had been born in England. James Grieves, Stewart McDonald, Kevin Little, Blair Scott and David McAllan were the true Scots in the side. James Grieves had been with Berwick in 1998, while Stewart McDonald had been with Stoke. David McAllan had come through the Linlithgow training track.

Edinburgh started the season by winning the Spring Trophy, with home and away wins over Workington, and then moved on to the Premier National Trophy rounds. Winning through to the semi-finals, they put out Newcastle to face Newport in a September final, going down 93-87 on aggregate.

After losing out on one major trophy, the Knockout Cup was to end up at Armadale. Newcastle, Newport and then Sheffield in the semi-final all went out to the mighty Monarchs, while Arena Essex were the Edinburgh side's final opponents. A 54-36 Edinburgh win at Armadale in the first leg set them up nicely for the return at Arena. On a night of drama, Arena won 49-41, but it was Edinburgh who were the 1999 Knockout Cup winners.

At one time, the Monarchs were at the top of the league table. With early away wins at Arena Essex, Workington, Glasgow and Berwick, Edinburgh were on a roll. At Armadale their form did not waver except when Newcastle were the league visitors on 13 August. In an exciting encounter in which both sides used Golden Double Tactical Substitutes, (where points counted double for the substitute rider), Newcastle won 50-46 to spoil an unbeaten home run.

Sheffield were the team of the year, winning the league from Newport, and Edinburgh had to settle for third place. They went out of the Young Shield to Exeter 95-84 on aggregate.

Monarchs did reach finals day in the Premier League Fours, but went out early. James Grieves and Kevin Little represented the Monarchs in the Pairs Final at Newport. James was superb on the day, winning five of his six outings,

The All-Scottish Monarchs of 1999. From left to right: James Grieves, Stewart McDonald, Kevin Little (on bike), Peter Carr, David McAllan, Ross Brady, Blair Scott.

but he fell in his other. Kevin was injured in his third outing and had to withdraw from the meeting, leaving the pair well down the field.

The Scotland *v.* England test series was reintroduced the previous year and it was extended to four meetings in 1999. It ended 2-2, with Scotland winning at Berwick and Edinburgh. The contests at Newcastle and Workington went to England.

The only blight on the season were the injuries to Stewart McDonald (neck and back) in August which ended his season. David McAllan also picked up a nasty injury to his leg at Swindon in June and, although he did not regain his team place, was back for Linlithgow in the Conference League by August. He then won the Armadale Junior Championship in October.

Blair Scott had a terrific year at Armadale, although his away form was still suspect. Kevin Little was consistent, as was James Grieves, who filled the second heat leader spot with a 9.12 average. Teenage sensation Ross Brady had come from Peterborough in the Conference League, to the Premier without too much trouble. With his fast starting and fence-scraping races he finished his first senior season with a respectable 6.75 average.

What can be said of Peter Carr? His 11.19 home average makes the point that he was near invincible at Armadale. Away from home he may not be, but an overall average of 9.69 put him up with the best in the league. Peter regained the Scottish Open Championship, and received his own special day to celebrate his twenty years in the sport. 'The Motor Show' was a great success, with main star Joe Screen thrilling the crowd with some spectacular riding.

The 2000 League turned out to be the tightest of finishes for many a year, with Edinburgh finishing in fifth place, only five points adrift of the winners Exeter. Peter Carr was back, as were Blair Scott, Ross Brady and Kevin Little. In came Robert Eriksson, back with the team he always wanted to belong to. Brian Turner, who had been with Glasgow and had come into the Edinburgh side late on in 1999, also returned. Newcomer Christian Henry, an Australian, came in at reserve on a 3.00 average and much was expected of him. Brian Turner only lasted a few meeting before a recurring wrist injury finished his year. Will Beveridge from Newcastle replaced him, but although he lasted the season, he never really got going.

The opening meetings were against Glasgow in the Spring Trophy, which was retained with a 92-85 aggregate victory. The Premiership Trophy against Sheffield went the way of the visitors and their Premier Trophy interest went no further that the rounds. Edinburgh put Arena Essex out of the Knockout Cup, then exited themselves when Workington won both legs in round two. In the Four Team Finals at Peterborough they failed to get through the semi-final rounds.

The British Under-21 final was held at Armadale on 7 April and was won by Peterborough's David Howe after a run-off with Coventry's Lee Richardson. Edinburgh pair Ross Brady and Blair Scott failed to make the cut. Ross Brady and Kevin Little both struggled to find their form in 1999, with Ross missing some meetings due to a foot injury sustained on a moto-cross bike.

Blair Scott was, as always, a thrilling sight at Armadale, but his away performances were no better than in '99 and Christian Henry, after a disaster of a debut when he crashed through the fence in his opening race, settled down as a steady scoring reserve who looks as though he may well improve in a second British season. Robert Eriksson was a model of consistency and could always be depended upon to get the team to a winning start by taking heat one home or away. Along with Peter Carr he saved many a home meeting with last heat 5-1 wins. With Carr himself, it was a case of who would be able to get the better of him around Armadale. Excluding engine failures, only Thomas Topinka (Czech Tourists), Carl Stonehewer (Workington) and Hull's Paul Thorp really bested him. An impressive 9 full and 6 paid maximums for a 10.28 average proved his consistency. He retained his Scottish Open Championship title, then won the *Edinburgh Evening News* Sports Personality of the Year, which finished what was for him a perfect season.

Workington spoilt a home run of wins when they left Armadale after a thriller of a Premier Trophy encounter which resulted in a 50-43 win for the Comets at the end of April. Workington were spoilers again when they knocked the Monarchs out of the Knockout Cup in July, again securing victory at Armadale. They became the only visiting team to record wins on Armadale soil in 2000.

Peter Carr.

Unbeaten at home in the league, it was a case of so near but so far away when on the road. A draw at Isle of Wight, then a win at Hull were the high spots, but there were so many near misses at Glasgow (47-46), Workington (46-44) and Stoke (47-46). With the rub of the green, those near misses may have moved Edinburgh just that bit closer to that elusive league title.

The season finished with a bang, quite literally, when Peter Carr blew an engine while leading Martin Dixon in a run-off after Swindon had finished level on aggregate in the Young Shield quarter-final. Peter's misfortune not only put Edinburgh out of the Young Shield, but closed the Monarchs' season.

Over the years, Edinburgh have won many honours. They have a World Champion in Jack Young, they have won the Pairs, the Knockout Cup and Fours titles, but the one major title they have failed to land since formation of the Edinburgh Monarchs back in 1948 has been the League title. Now, as we enter

Monarchs' Mr Consistency, Peter 'The Motor' Carr.

into a new Millennium, it is the club's ambition to realise this, and it would be particularly appropriate for everyone concerned with Edinburgh speedway for them to land that coveted trophy while Peter Carr – surely the most consistent Monarch since the great Jack Young – is still in full flow.

Three

Glasgow

'Tiger' Steve Lawson.

The story of Glasgow speedway is, in essence, also the story of the White City venue. This was located in the Ibrox area, close to the football ground that is the home of Glasgow Rangers. The track opened its doors in 1928 for one meeting and then staged speedway until 1931 before closing halfway through that season. The Glasgow team raced in the uncompleted 1930 Northern League but failed to complete its fixtures in the following season.

The track reopened in 1939 and team events featuring the Glasgow Lions were a regular bill of fare for the fans. Refused admission to the 1939 Second Division, the team took part in the uncompleted ACU Northern Cup series, but closed down at the outbreak of war in September. The track staged a few meetings in 1940 before the wartime strictures really bit hard and forced closure.

Victory in Europe for the Allies in 1945 signalled a return of speedway and a short open season was staged between August and October. Between 1946 and 1953 the team, now called the Glasgow Tigers, strutted their stuff at Second Division level.

The speedway slump closed the Tigers very early in 1954 and, despite efforts to revive them in 1956, they were in hibernation until 1964. Since 1964, the Tigers have competed in league speedway at a number of different venues – Hampden Park (Glasgow), Cliftonhill Stadium (Coatbridge), Blantyre Greyhound Stadium (Blantyre), Craighead Park (Blantyre), Derwent Park (Workington), Shawfield Stadium (Glasgow) and, finally, at Saracen Park (Glasgow). Only in 1996 did the Tigers fail to roar (their abortive season at Derwent Park in 1987 produced a somewhat muted sound, but the beast was alive for at least a short spell in that season).

The Early Days

The White City Stadium in Paisley Road West was built for greyhound racing in 1928. The site area between the road and the railway dictated the shape of the stadium and the greyhound track. This in turn dictated the shape of the dirt track constructed inside the greyhound track.

A track was built by the Glasgow Nelson club and what was to have been the first of weekly events was staged on 29 June 1928. It followed the Glasgow Nelson format of 350cc, 600cc and unlimited capacity events. The event did not stick to the four-laps per race system, the finals of the last two named events being raced over five instead. Jimmie Pinkerton won the 350cc and unlimited events, taking home £16, while Jimmy Valente, a Glaswegian, won the 600cc prize of £3.

Crowd numbers must have disappointed the promotion and no other events were staged. Jimmie Pinkerton used the track at a motorcycle gymkhana in August to show what dirt-track racing was all about.

The First Years

The sport returned to White City in 1929 with a professional set up under the

Opening meeting in 1929 at Glasgow White City. The riders are, from left to right: Buster Frogley, Alfie Williams, Billy Galloway, Taffy Williams, Ivor Creek.

managerial control of Marine Gardens boss Jimmy Fraser. The track was opened by Sir Iain Colquhoun Bt of Luss on Saturday 20 April. This was the start of a long and successful season of fifty-one meetings. 1929 was Billy Galloway's season. The wee Australian won each of the scratch race trophies in a four meeting unbeaten spell in May and June. In all, he won 20 out of the 100 events raced – and this with a spell away down south! Billy was the star of the white line and few could match him round the circuit with its long straights and tight bends. The big meeting, the White City Championship, was won by Sprouts Elder ahead of George Wigfield and popular local star Jimmie Pinkerton.

A two-event format was usual, but team racing was introduced on Tuesday 10 September when Glasgow drew 14-14 with Newcastle Gosforth. The four-heat match featured the 4-2-1 scoring system. A rematch on Tuesday 24 September produced a 19-9 home win.

The Glaswegian team first met Edinburgh at White City and received their first home defeat, going down 17-10 after using a team without Billy Galloway. Edinburgh used both their stars, Drew McQueen and George McKenzie.

Most of the riders were Scots, who progressed in leaps and bounds. Most of their wins were in the Handicap event, which favoured the men with the generous allowance. The Glasgow lads also had their share of scratch event wins as the season wore on.

Glasgow entered the 1930 Northern League with a team built around Billy Galloway and Col Stewart. Unfortunately, Billy was injured at Marine Gardens early in the campaign and they only managed three wins from eight home events. Glasgow's best home win was over Preston, 20-12, but the worst results included a defeat by Liverpool, 10-26, and a narrow loss to a White City Manchester team that fielded only three riders.

Away from home, Glasgow suffered big defeats, ranging from 13-20 at Rochdale to 9-26 at Preston. Tragically, in the second half of the home Rochdale match, Londoner Eddie Reynolds was fatally injured after falling into the path of another rider.

A busy start to the 1930 season saw two meetings a week – on Tuesday and Friday nights – until early May. Thereafter they raced on Tuesday nights with one Friday night for the White City Championship, which made Wembley's Harry Whitfield £100 richer. The shine was taken off this star-studded meeting, which featured Tom Farndon, Arthur Atkinson, Sprouts Elder and Colin Watson to name just a few of the attending greats, when Sprouts' bike gave up the ghost. The lanky Yank had inadvertently kicked his magneto, effectively killing the motor.

1931 saw Glasgow enter the Northern League. Bolstered by Drew McQueen and George McKenzie, but weakened by the retirement of Billy Galloway, they won only a couple of home meetings. The went out of the National Trophy to Preston, and closed before completing the Northern League tie with Leeds. Drew McQueen and the lads had major bike problems, which did not help their cause. Drew won the White City Championship, progressing to the next round of the World Championship event. He was eliminated by Roy Barrowclough at Leeds.

The novelty of speedway in Glasgow was wearing off, and in early July the track closed down for what would be a break of seven seasons.

The Second Era

Speedway had undergone at lot of changes by the time it returned to White City in 1939. The rolling starts had been replaced by clutch starts from the starting gate and the JAP motor had ousted the Rudge and the other marques. Riding styles had changed from the leg-trailer to the foot-forward men.

Johnnie Hoskins, the man who had started it all in 1923, took the helm and tried to get his new venture a place in the Second Division. This came to nothing, so his makeshift Glasgow Lions faced a mixture of club and scratch sides. Late in the season the Lions entered the ACU Cup, but the outbreak of war brought this uncompleted league to a halt; Glasgow finished down the table.

As the war clouds gathered, Lions introduced Joe Crowther, Gruff Garland and Will Lowther to the side. These men would form the backbone of the post war team.

Jack Milne won the Track Championship from Wilbur Lamoreaux, Cordy Milne and Benny Kaufman in an all First Division, all American, winner-takes-all final – Scots star guest Sir Harry Lauder let everyone know the Milne boys' father was Scottish. Hoskins staged a Scotland *v.* England Test match, which the home side won 45-38, albeit with only one Scot, Leo Lungo. The last pre-war meeting, staged on 26 August, was a best pairs event won by Edinburgh men George Greenwood and Oliver Hart.

No war could phase Johnnie Hoskins, as he staged six meetings in May and June 1940. The Lions faced team opposition and even raced at Belle Vue. Eric Chitty, a Canadian, won the Glasgow Open Championship from Jack Parker, Gruff Garland and Bill Longley. In the end, it was concern about crowd safety rather than petrol problems that closed down White City for the rest of the war.

After The War

Like the rest of Britain, the good citizens of Glasgow had suffered terribly during the war, and with victory secured they made up for lost time. Followers of speedway were no exception; Johnnie Hoskins reintroduced speedway to the White City Stadium on 15 August 1945.

Over 10,000 fans watched a scratch Glasgow side that included Eric Chitty, Ron Johnson, Oliver Hart and Geoff Godwin beat a London side that included Bill Kitchen and Phil 'Tiger' Hart 61-47. The following week, a side billed as

Scots Aussie Ron Johnson.

Scotland, with Scots Ron Johnson and Leo Lungo, beat England 54-53.

On 29 August another scratch Glasgow side beat Newcastle 56-61 and a week later the home side dispatched North London 42-39. For a change the fans were treated to a Best Pairs on 12 September, which was won by Bill Kitchen and Will Lowther who combined to score 21 points. In second place, with 17, were Ron Johnson and Charlie Spinks. Eric Chitty scored a maximum 15, but partner Geoff Godwin failed to score leaving the duo in third position.

The Glasgow side then dispatched The Rest 46-37 before the first encounter between teams captained by Ron Johnson and Bill Kitchen respectively. Bill's team won 50-34 but next time round, on 10 October, the teams drew. Alex Statham switched to join Ron and he was replaced in Bill's team by 'Tiger' Hart.

Glasgow lost their first post-war encounter to The Midlands by 46-37. Will Lowther had a miserable night with three falls in a row while Crowther, Lungo and Frank Varey all managed a fall apiece. To be fair, The Midlands team also had four riders who each took a fall.

The last meeting of the season ended prematurely in a most unusual way – the riders ran out of fuel. The truck carrying the methanol to Glasgow broke down and the riders had to use what they had with them. The Scottish Senior Championship was won by Ron Johnson from Bill Kitchen and Eric Chitty. The

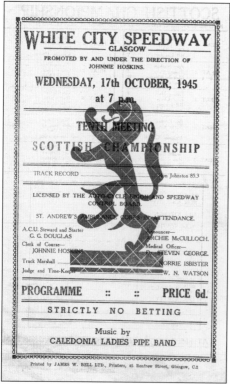

JOE CROWTHER
(Glasgow Tigers)

Left: 1945 programme cover. Right: Joe Crowther.

curtailed Scottish Junior Championship went to Norman Evans from Will Lowther and Wilf Plant. (The other odd thing about this meeting is that forged programmes were produced in the 1960s.)

More tracks opened for 1946 and Glasgow, under the control of Johnnie Hoskins' son, Ian, who was given compassionate leave from the RAF, entered the oddly-named Northern League. This included teams from as far south as Norwich together with Midlanders Birmingham and Northerners Middlesbrough, Newcastle and Sheffield. Teams raced home and away twice to provide twenty fixtures.

The Glasgow season opened on 10 April with Bill Kitchen winning the Glasgow Trophy. The following week the fans saw the Scottish Best Pairs go to Bill Longley and Will Lowther.

The new team were to be called the Lions, but Wembley had booked that name. After some thought, and the rejection of the name Dynamos, the Glasgow Tigers were born. The team had Joe Crowther, and Will Lowther on the books and added Cumbrian Maurice Stobart, Norwich-based Wal Morton, and a young Londoner called Eddie Lack. Stan Beardsall, Ken Tidbury and lad by the name of Dennis Gray completed the line-up that won at Newcastle on 22 April. Tigers took an early lead, lost it then got in front in heat eleven and held on from there, Lack winning heat fourteen to secure the victory. Sadly, the rest of the season did not live up to this great start.

Tigers' home debut on Wednesday 24 April 1946 saw them beat Sheffield 61-47 in the first leg of the National Trophy first round. The following night the Sheffield side turned the tables to draw the tie – Joe Crowther put up a great fight but could not get past Tommy Bateman for the vital extra point. The rematch staged in early May was also a closely fought tussle, with Glasgow winning 62-45 at White City and losing 63-44 at Owlerton: Tigers only needed a couple of points in the last race but Morton and pre-war Glasgow Lion, Gruff Garland, both fell, gifting the tie to Sheffield.

Tigers' league debut on 1 May against Newcastle went 40-44 to the visitors despite Garland's return and Tigers went down by the same score at Newcastle the following Monday. The next league opponents were Birmingham and, despite a better show, the Brummies took the match 40-42.

22 May 1946 was a red letter day for Tigers fans as they won their first ever league encounter 44-38, sending Norwich and Bert Spencer (who had rejected the chance of riding for Glasgow) home point-less. Three days later the Tigers went down to Norwich and won 43-41, recording their first ever away league victory.

Tigers would record only one other league away win, this time at Birmingham. The 45-39 result was a coup for the Tigers, but the local reporters did not give them the credit they deserved, claiming a poor display by the Brummies rather than a good win by Tigers.

At home the Tigers struggled. They could be brilliant one minute and poor the next. Middlesbrough (twice) and Norwich, as well as the aforementioned

Brummies and Diamonds, all took league points away from Glasgow. Not surprisingly, Tigers collected their first league wooden spoon.

As a second league-type event to fill the fixture list, the Tigers raced in the ACU (Auto Cycle Union) Cup. This featured all their league opponents and they raced against them once home and once away. The sixteen-heat match format differed from the fourteen-heat Northern League events – except when the programme compilers forgot which competition was which!

Tigers lost at home to Middlesbrough and Norwich in the ACU Cup and won nothing on the road. When the dust of the competition had settled they were in second last place in the tournament.

Tigers also took part in the 1946 Northern Trophy tournament. They knocked Newcastle out of the competition in the first round, thanks to a 48-48 draw at Brough Park and a 50-46 win at White City: Diamonds went into the last heat needing a 5-1 to win the tie but Garland and Lack secured the match and the tie, winning 4-2 over Syd Littlewood and Norman Evans. Later in the season, Tigers faced Norwich in the final. A respectable 54-24 Tigers win at White City, which featured an unusual dead heat for first place by the home duo of Lowther and Crowther, wasn't quite enough. At Norwich the home team won 59-36, taking a couple of late 5-1 heat wins to seal Tigers' fate. The Northern Trophy went to the southernmost track in the tournament.

Team changes were tried throughout the season to strengthen the side. By the end of May the reserve pairing of Tidbury and Beardsall had been replaced by John Lockley and Charlie Oates. Lockley, in turn, was briefly moved out by Wallie Thomson. Bill Baird joined the team in July, pushing out Oates, and by August Lockley was finally ousted to include Bert Shearer. Lockley and Thomson stayed on in the wings, gaining outings only when needed.

Towards the end of the season the Tigers fans were rewarded by a look at the men from the top division. They added Bill Kitchen and Eric Chitty to take on and beat Bradford, but the help of Eric Langton and Oliver Hart wasn't enough to repulse Wembley. The London team rolled into Glasgow the day before and set up shop showing they took the challenge earnestly.

In 1946, the British Riders' Championship was the main event. Glasgow staged two qualifiers, the first being won by Tommy Allott of Sheffield and the second by the man they nearly had on their books, Bert Spencer. Fans also saw the Sealed Handicap Trophy event which went to a run-off between Jack Parker on 15 race points plus 0 handicap points and Newcastle's Jeff Lloyd on 13 race points plus 2 handicap points. Jack won the decider.

A best pairs event was won after two run-offs, while the first four-man event was tied before Frank Hodgson beat Stan Williams to give himself and his partner Kid Curtis the trophy.

Britain raced and lost 50-58 to an Overseas Select. Jack Parker, Jeff Lloyd and Ron Clarke joined Crowther, Lowther and Morton, but Garland's lads did the business. Englishman 'Tiger' Hart, who had been in Australia when speedway started, also raced for Overseas.

Left: Wal Morton. Right: Bernard 'Bat' Byrnes.

1947 saw the Northern League enlarged and renamed the National League Second Division. The new teams were Bristol and Wigan. In addition to this league, Tigers raced in the British Speedway Cup and the knockout National Trophy competition.

Glasgow lost Wal Morton, who had been transferred. They introduced Bruce Vennier, a Canadian, but he had a torrid opening meeting and, after an even worse second meeting, retired. They also introduced their Scottish find, Angus McGuire. Eddie Lack suffered serious injury in the second meeting so Tigers recalled Maurice Stobart from his retirement and introduced Harold Sharpe for their third meeting. Garland was injured in this event and was to be out for a few weeks. Stobart then immediately retired again and Glasgow borrowed Jack Lloyd and Fred Rogers.

By the end of April, with problems piling up, Tigers signed two young Aussies, Keith 'Buck' Ryan and Ron 'Junior' Bainbridge. They duly won their first league fixture at home against Wigan. The following week, Tigers added Scot Billie Bates to replace McGuire and won a bit more convincingly at home against Bristol.

Garland returned the following week but immediately suffered injury in another home defeat and Sharpe was recalled for one away meeting. Garland came back to displace Sharpe away at Norwich, but was far from fit. Gruff and

Eddie Lack.

Sharpe were in the side without Bainbridge (who had been injured at Norwich) which was swept aside in the opening British Speedway Cup match by Middlesbrough, a side. This encounter also saw the introduction of yet another new Aussie, Bernard 'Bat' Byrnes, and an injury to stalwart Joe Crowther.

Glasgow were still struggling and by the end of May the side, ever in a state of flux, were still taking it on the chin almost everywhere, including White City.

Just before the end of May, Tigers introduced yet another new face, New Zealander Harold Fairhurst. Harold was a reserve rather than a star, however, and, despite a valiant fight, by early June Tigers were out of the National Trophy thanks to a narrow aggregate defeat by Newcastle. Following this result, a big home win against the Diamonds was a boost the Tigers fans had been looking for. It was also an indication that the youngsters introduced into the side were improving, especially at White City.

This did not deter Ian Hoskins from looking around for additional firepower, and for the league match at Newcastle in mid-June they added yet another Aussie, Norman Lindsay.

Tigers now had five Australians, one New Zealander, a Scot and an Englishman in their side. Normally, teams were only allowed two Australians but Tigers were given a dispensation as many English riders were reluctant to travel north to race on a weekly basis.

A settled side saw out June and, at the start of July, Crowther returned to displace the only Scot in the side. Tigers then defeated a side representing First Division Bradford that had only two recognised top league heat leaders, but unfortunately lost Garland for the rest of the season. Despite this setback, the Tigers bogie was back on the rails.

The settling side with its improving Anzac contingent could now withstand a match in which Crowther crashed out and another when Will Lowther – usually Mr Reliable himself – suffered a string of engine failures.

Was manager Hoskins happy? Obviously the lack of a rising Scot was troubling him. In mid-August he gave a debut to Dunfermline-born Gordon McGregor, but after a pointless outing at Birmingham, Hoskins speedily reinstated fellow Scot Bert Shearer.

You can't keep a good man down, and by the middle of September McGregor was back in, filling a space vacated by Ryan (who went back home to Australia, followed a week later by Byrnes). Nobby Downham joined the Tigers' ranks and stayed on to the end of the season.

The top two Tigers were paired together in the Britain side that beat Overseas

Left: Gordon McGregor. Right: Norman Lindsay.

1948 Glasgow team.

68-52, while Bainbridge and Byrnes rode for Overseas. Lowther progressed to the second round of the British Riders' Championship but did not make it to Wembley after a string of low scores.

The new Aussies had been the finds of 1947, but the Tigers had been forced to wait for them to mature. Will Lowther was the true star and Joe Crowther wasn't far behind when he was in the team. How well Tigers would have done had they put out a steady side all season; as it was, they ended up in the wooden spoon position, just below Wigan on points difference.

Up until 1948, the Tigers were the only team in Scotland. Their nearest rivals were in Newcastle, but things were about to change. Speedway returned to the capital city and one of the greatest speedway rivalries was born – the Tigers versus Monarchs fixture.

The Edinburgh team increased the ranks of the Second Division by one and Fleetwood replaced Wigan. Garland and Byrnes did not start back at the beginning of the season and Jack Martin was drafted in for a few meetings before he was replaced by Angus McGuire, who had a run at reserve until Garland came back towards the end of May.

Ex-road racer Byrnes arrived back in mid-June, resulting in Gordon McGregor, known to one and all as 'The Tash' because of his flamboyant facial hair, dropping down to the second half.

For the first time in years Tigers had a settled line up of eight first-team regulars with a few lads in reserve if problems blew up. In addition to Martin, McGuire and McGregor, a third 'Mac', Alf McIntosh, was developing well.

Garland was starting to struggle and surprisingly asked for a transfer to help Division One Bradford. It was McGregor who was given the call up to replace him and Gordon kept his place to the end of the season. The departure to Australia of Buck Ryan in late September saw Tigers recall Nobby Downham to fill a reserve berth and he stayed on until the end of the season.

Billie Bates was given a couple of outings after Bainbridge went home and Bert Shearer and Alf McIntosh were called in to the line-up for the last meeting of the season. Top man this year was Joe Crowther, who had narrowly beaten Will Lowther for the honour. Joe had such a good season that his wife almost ran out of polish keeping his vast collection of second-half trophies clean. Bat Byrnes was also there in the top echelon of the division.

Tigers rose to sixth spot in the league competition and were in third place in the Anniversary Cup competition. In the league they won four away from home but lost four and drew one at home. In cup competition they won one away but lost one at home. For the first time Tigers progressed beyond the opening round of the National Trophy. Edinburgh were their victims with a 70-38 win nullifying Monarchs' 62-46 win in Edinburgh. Unfortunately, a week later Tigers ran into Birmingham in the next round and lost $61\frac{1}{2}$ - $45\frac{1}{2}$ at home and took an 80-28 demolition at Perry Barr.

Glasgow staged one of the Scotland *v*. England internationals and provided four of the home side, who won 59-49. However, Ron Johnson was the only *bona fide* Scot in the line-up, which had England's Lowther and Crowther and Australia's Byrnes and Bainbridge alongside New Zealand's Dick Campbell (an

Les Beaumont (Cradley Heath) leading Will Lowther.

Edinburgh rider).

The Second Division for 1949 was enlarged to include Coventry, Cradley Heath, Southampton, Walthamstow and new Glasgow rivals, Ashfield Giants. The powerful Middlesbrough team moved to Newcastle, a venue that had lost its riders to Ashfield and Birmingham moved up to the First Division.

Garland moved on to Ashfield and Tigers started the season without two Aussies, Byrnes and Ryan, and their Kiwi, Fairhurst, instead using Downham, Bates and (new introduction) Dick Seers. Lowther, Crowther, McGregor, Lindsay and Bainbridge completed the opening line-up. Ryan was soon back, replacing Seers, and Fairhurst, who had won the New Zealand championship in the winter, returned to displace Bates. Bates covered for Ryan when Buck fell foul of the Speedway Riders' Association ban on more than three Aussies per Scottish track but, by the start of June, Bates was displaced by Byrnes.

In mid-July Ryan came back and Tigers transferred Harold Fairhurst to Edinburgh. They had a few useful lads in the second half – Bates, Alf McIntosh, Ken McKinlay and the ever-entertaining Joe 'Whaler' Ferguson. Without Byrnes and Downham, Tigers blooded McKinlay and McIntosh in quick succession. They alternated the two 'Macs', but once Byrnes came back in early August, Alf got the place on a more permanent basis.

By the end of August, however, Crowther's injury gave Ken another chance. Crowther's return in September saw the end of Will Lowther's career as a Tiger after a disappointing run of low scores and the ever-improving youngsters holding

Edinburgh v. Glasgow at Ashfield. From left to right: Dick Campbell, Norman Lindsay, Danny Lee.

Joe 'Whaler' Ferguson.

on in the team. Byrnes departed for home for the last time, never again to be a Tiger.

Manager Hoskins was not prepared to let Tigers drift and signed Jack Hodgson in a swap deal that saw Will move to his favourite Brough Park in Newcastle. McKinlay and Crowther were injured on 19 September at White City and Tigers brought in Ivor Smith and Ferguson for a run to the end of the season. That night saw the debut of a man who would be a sensation in the coming seasons – Tommy Miller. Tommy finished third in his debut ride behind Ivor Smith and Joe Ferguson. McKinlay came back for the end of season and was joined by Eric Liddell as the young Scots replaced Ryan and Bainbridge.

7 October 1949 was a black day for the weakened Tigers side. They were savaged by the Bulldogs, losing each of the fourteen heats 1-5 as Bristol set a record victory. The same team was beaten 49-35 by Coventry at White City as they brought down the shutters on the 1949 season, Glasgow finishing eighth out of twelve teams in the league. They crashed out of the National Trophy in their opening tie – the 67-41 home win made Norwich go for it at the Firs Stadium, where they salvaged the tie with a 71-36 win over Tigers.

No Tiger went beyond the Second Division stage of the reintroduced World Championship. The 1949 Scotland *v*. England international went 52-55 to the visitors, who were led by Norman Parker. McGregor was the only Scot in a side fronted by Jack Young and Ken Le Breton with fellow Aussies Byrnes and

Bainbridge, Kiwi Campbell and Englishman Crowther.

The Second Division was even bigger in 1950, with newcomers Halifax, Stoke, Yarmouth and Plymouth from the 1949 Third Division more than compensating for the loss of Bristol. 1950 was to be Glasgow's best year so far. A single point separated them from the top spot held by Norwich. Tigers kept a clean sheet at home and won four away in what was a fairly close-run race for the title. Wins were recorded at Fleetwood, Newcastle, Ashfield and Stoke.

Teams from Stoke northwards opened the season with a mini-league – the Northern Trophy. The Tigers opened with McGregor, Crowther, Hodgson and Bainbridge, along with new signings Peter Dykes, Johnny Green, Tommy Miller and Bill Gordon. They lost out to Newcastle in the new Northern Trophy. Gordon moved on when Lindsay came back for the second meeting and Tigers blew hot and cold.

As the season progressed, Miller got better and better and by the time Tigers visited Ashfield in early May, Tommy was in the team proper. His elevation coincided with a downturn in form of both Crowther and Green. Green left after the home defeat by Ashfield in May to be replaced by Ken McKinlay.

Glasgow stuck with Joe, who rode himself out the doldrums. The improvement did not last long, however, as further poor displays saw him ride his last race as a Tiger at Stoke on 2 September. This long-term Tiger had gone after a promising start to the season, which saw him win the Glasgow Gala Cup in May.

Gordon McGregor leading Ken Le Breton (Ashfield).

Left: Alf McIntosh. Right: Ken McKinlay

Alf McIntosh came in to take Joe's place, lost it, won it back, then lost it again … so it went on. McKinlay also suffered in this way, dropping out briefly at the end of the season. Change was the one certainty and Junior Bainbridge's injury in early August prompted Tigers to sign Frank Hodgson. However, Junior was soon back and the youngsters were ousted, although not for long.

The start of the league campaign on 21 June saw Miller a heat leader and riding undefeated by a Stoke rider. His tally would, today, be called a paid maximum, but in 1950 bonus points did not exist. Tommy scored his first full maximum a few weeks later and banged in big figures home and away for the rest of the season. He rounded off his meteoric rise by being selected to go to Australia with the Lions.

In the National Trophy, after an aggregate win over Stoke in the first round, Tigers again foundered on the rock that was Norwich in the second round. Glasgow also took part in the Border Trophy and put out Ashfield in the first round. Edinburgh ousted Newcastle and the old rivals met in the final. Monarchs won 62-46 at White City and 71-37 in Edinburgh. Glasgow raced in Ireland in both Dublin and Belfast, losing to both Shelbourne Tigers and Dunmore Bees.

In the World Championship both Bainbridge and Miller progressed the hard way from the first to the fourth round, riding only on away tracks, but neither

Joe Crowther leads team-mate Norman Lindsay and Giants' Keith Gurtner.

made it to Wembley.

Glasgow ended their best season to date with the Lord Provost's Gold Medallion individual event, which was won by Dick Campbell with Miller second. Heartened by Ian Hoskins' Christmas card poetry – 'If you press on regardless and are full of good cheer, you may like the Tigers be on top next year' – the Glasgow fans looked forward to 1951.

The new season lined up with the Hodgson brothers, Bainbridge, McKinlay, Miller, Lindsay, McIntosh and Eric Davies. Jim Blyth was added to strengthen the tail-end. Gordon McGregor had moved on to the new Motherwell side to ride alongside Lowther and Crowther.

Tigers signed Northumbrian Len Nicholson mid-season to replace Blyth, but an injury to Bainbridge allowed Jim to have other runs in the team covering for injured colleagues and he ended the season winning the Novice Championships.

Tigers now had three Scottish rivals as the division grew again, adding the aforementioned Motherwell, as well as Leicester, Liverpool and Oxford. Only Plymouth dropped out of the division.

Tommy Miller was a tower of strength in 1951, scoring a pile of points in the Northern Trophy and league competitions. The wee man from Blantyre won the World Championship qualifier but failed to make it to Wembley. He won the Festival of Britain Trophy at Glasgow, the Skelly Trophy at Motherwell and was runner-up in the Scottish Championship. Miller also won the Second Division Match Race Championship from Jack Young in July/August and the Regent £100 Casket match race series. He was capped by England against Australia, scoring

9 in his only international outing at Birmingham in August.

In the opening Northern Trophy mini-league, Tigers had held their own at home but lost everywhere except Fleetwood. In the 1951 tournament, the Glasgow team won all but one home match and lost all their away matches. They did manage a draw at Coventry but their efforts only earned them tenth place in the league.

The home defeat came from Motherwell – a side with three ex-Tigers who had an old score or two to settle. The contributions of McGregor (9), Lowther (7) and Crowther (2) helped the Eagles, as did uncharacteristically poor displays by Lindsay and Frank Hodgson. Tigers put the Eagles out the Scottish Cup, winning home and away, but losing narrowly to Edinburgh in the final. The single tie Lanarkshire Cup went to the Eagles in a 46-38 defeat at The Stadium in Motherwell.

In the National Trophy a respectable 64-44 home win over Norwich was set aside by a crushing 81-27 defeat in East Anglia on a night in which Tommy Miller did nothing.

The 1951 Scotland *v.* England Test was won by England. The Scots drew with a New Zealand side called the Kiwis and the Rest of Scotland beat the Scots Australians. Tigers closed down with a league win against Edinburgh before the end of September, suggesting something was amiss.

Trophy time for Tommy Miller.

1952 dawned with Tigers lining up Miller, McIntosh, McKinlay, Jack Hodgson, Bainbridge and Nicholson, along with returnee Peter Dykes and new signing Don Wilkinson from Newcastle. Frank Hodgson came back in late April to displace Nicholson, but Frank was injured before May was out and he didn't return until late July. Tigers gave Stuart Irvine a brief run until mid-July before bringing Nicholson back. Len was given another run when Bainbridge was injured in August and stayed until the season's end. Tigers also introduced a colourful young Aussie, acquired from Ashfield, in July; known as 'Cowboy', Bob Sharp held his place to the end of the season. Bob, who dressed in a Western style, with fancy boots and Stetson, was also known as 'Last Bend Bob' for his late charges for the flag.

Miller raised his average to the best in the division, and won the Scottish Match Race Championship. He also had top level England Test caps against Australia and Division Two level Britain caps *v.* Overseas, but could not annex the Scottish Championship or make it to Wembley. Bainbridge also had Test caps for his native Australia and for the Second Division Overseas team.

The league contracted to twelve teams for this season – Norwich went up, Walthamstow, Halifax, Fleetwood and Newcastle all closed down, but Poole came in from Division Three. Tigers climbed to fourth place, finishing as the best-placed Scottish side. They won five matches away from home, at Motherwell (twice), Ashfield, Oxford and Liverpool. At home they lost three, against Leicester, Cradley Heath, and Coventry, and drew with Ashfield.

Tigers won home and away in the first round of the National Trophy against their city rivals Ashfield. In the next stage, Leicester won at White City but Glasgow pulled it out of the bag at Blackbird Road to progress to meet Poole in the following round. It was the Pirates who won this tie 111-105 on aggregate.

The Scottish Cup ended up in the Tigers' showcase thanks to an aggregate win over Edinburgh in the semi-final and Ashfield in the final. A 58-50 win at Saracen Park was followed by a massive 75-33 win at home. The Lanarkshire Cup, however, stayed with the Eagles.

Scotland won the Test *v.* England 61-48 and had three Scots – Miller, Willie Wilson (Giants) and Bob Mark (Monarchs) in the side.

The season closed on a bit of a sour note when a proposed charity event, Scots *v.* West Ham, was cancelled with riders squabbling over payment.

1953 saw further league contraction with Cradley Heath, Liverpool and Oxford, as well as Glasgow rivals Ashfield, dropping out, although The Midlands' representation was maintained with the addition of Wolverhampton.

The squad of Miller, Wilkinson, McIntosh, McKinlay, Bainbridge, Dykes and Sharp were joined by ex-Giant Larry Lazarus, young Scottish find Douglas Templeton and new Aussie Arthur Malm (pronounced 'Marm'). Templeton was given a brief run when Lazarus was injured in early June. He rode again when McIntosh was out, until Tigers signed Harry Welch in mid-August, and had a few more outings after Sharp left for home towards the end of the season. Malm featured in only a very few matches.

Tigers retained their fourth spot and again were the best Scottish team. A home defeat by Coventry and a draw against Leicester were compensated for with away wins at Motherwell, Liverpool and Wolverhampton and a draw at Stoke.

The Glasgow side had a great start in the National Trophy, thumping rivals Edinburgh 75-33 at home and winning 61-47 away. Wolverhampton were then dispatched by Tigers with a 59-49 win at Monmore Green and 76-26 win at White City. Third Division Rayleigh proved tougher opposition, losing 69-39 in Glasgow but winning 64-44 in Essex. The Tigers run came to an end when First Division Birmingham hammered them 74-38 at Perry Barr and held them to 56-52 in Glasgow.

Coronation year saw the Queen's Cup competition and Tigers moved on after beating Wolverhampton 71-37 to put out Ipswich at Foxhall Heath with a 55-53 win. This earned a tie with Exeter. Glasgow lost 69-39 in the first leg before a 72-36 win at White City gave them a crack at Edinburgh in the final. This time Monarchs won 65-53 in the capital and held Tigers 56-52 in Glasgow to collect the silverware. Tigers also won the Scottish Cup, beating Motherwell in the final.

During the winter of 1953/54, question marks were appearing over the Tigers' future. Entertainment tax and television were taking their toll, but the White City management decided to give it a go for 1954.

The price for continuation was the transfer of Tommy Miller to Motherwell and Junior Bainbridge to Ipswich. Tigers started off with Lazarus, McKinlay, McIntosh, Doug Templeton, Sharp and Malm from 1953 and added South African Vern McWilliams and new Scottish finds Douglas Craig and Willie Templeton. The side raced two home and four away fixtures, the last at Motherwell on 23 April, and lost the lot.

The management pulled the plug. Tigers were gone and the riders were cast to the four winds: McKinlay went to Leicester, Sharp to Ipswich, Lazarus and Doug Templeton to Motherwell, McIntosh and Willie Templeton to Edinburgh. Vern McWiliams went to Wolverhampton (which also closed) and then to Poole.

White City lay dormant until 1956, when Miller and Bainbridge decided to try and revive the Tigers' fortunes. Opening in mid-May with an England *v.* Scotland international featuring World Champion Peter Craven, they used old favourites to staff the Scotland side. Scotland lost 57-49.

Fortnightly fixtures saw Tigers race against teams representing Birmingham, Bradford and Norwich in a competition called the Anglo Scottish Cup. The opener was a draw, but Tigers won the other two. Tigers used Miller, Bainbridge, McGregor, Sharp, Lazarus, ex-Giant Willie Wilson, ex- Eagle Ron Phillips and gave odd outings to Doug Templeton and Jack 'Red' Monteith. In between the first two Tigers fixtures, the promotion staged a Britain *v.* Overseas match, which was won by Britain 56-52.

This speedway revival in Glasgow proved to be a false dawn. The crowds did not flock back and the venue fell silent until another attempt was made to

Ready for the off. From left to right: Peter Dykes, Larry Lazarus, Alf McIntosh, Don Wilkinson, Bob Sharp, Tommy Miller.

resurrect the sport.

The 1960s Revival

Speedway had returned to Scotland in 1960 with the rebirth of the Edinburgh Monarchs and Glasgow-based fans did travel through to watch their favourite sport. It was not the same as having their own team, however, and many wanted speedway back in Glasgow. Despite rumours almost every winter, including talk of Trevor Redmond, rider turned rider-promoter, seeking a return to Celtic Park, nothing happened until 1964.

April 1964 saw the return of Glasgow Tigers to the fold. The red and white hoards returned to White City and the circuit, described by one contemporary scribe as 'a feeler and let rip' of a track was once again testing riders. The quote summed up the skills needed on the relatively tight bends and the speed that was required down the long straights.

A promotion, probably heavily financed by the Hoskins family but fronted by Trevor Redmond to distance Monarchs promoter Ian Hoskins from the auld enemy, took the helm. They entered into the 'black' Provincial League and set about building up a team.

Gone were the men from the last generation, although McKinlay and McGregor were still racing in Britain and Sharp was still in action in Australia. Jack Monteith was also still racing and he was among the early Tigers signings. They added another Scot in the shape of Bill McMillan, who had been a reserve at Edinburgh. Like the Tigers of old they looked to the Antipodes for riders.

Glasgow acquired the 'quiet man' of speedway, Charlie Monk, which was a major coup – 'Cha Cha' Charlie said little but did lots on the track. Tigers also signed two relatively unknown New Zealanders, Bruce Ovenden and Joe Hicks, the former blossoming into a real find while the latter struggled at Provincial League level.

Another surprise signing was 1963 Scottish Open Champion, Maury Mattingly. Maury had been with Wolverhampton in 1963 and Glasgow was a long haul from his Southampton home, where he spent his spare time building speedway frames and forks. This proved to be no problem for the Glasgow promotion or Maury, as they flew him up for home meetings.

Two other long distance travellers in the Tigers' opening night squad were Cornishmen Chris Julian and Ray Wickett, who had been part of Trevor

1964 Tigers. From left to right, back row: Bill McMillan, Charlie Monk, Trevor Redmond, Bruce Ovenden, Terry Stone. Front row: Chris Julian, Maury Mattingly, Red Monteith.

Left: Charlie Monk. Right: Terry Stone.

Redmond's set up at St Austell.

Tigers opened on 1 April in a Northern League encounter with Middlesbrough and won 44-34, with Monk scoring his first of many maximums. Mattingly and Julian each scored 11, missing out on their maximums to ex-Motherwell man Bluey Scott. Charlie was the fastest man round White City, setting a new track record in the opening heat of 78.5 seconds.

The Glasgow team were well beaten away at Sheffield the following evening but held on to win the return at home. A defeat at Middlesbrough was followed by a narrow 41-37 over Edinburgh Monarchs in a match which saw the home debut of Essex man Terry Stone. The effervescent Stoney replaced Ray Wickett, who had decided that the travelling was too much and secured a transfer to his local Exeter track.

Going back on the road to Edinburgh saw Tigers on the end of another big defeat. They carried on doing the business at home, however, and wins against Sunderland and Newcastle completed a clean home card in the mini-tournament. Charlie Monk went to his last match unbeaten when Ivan Mauger broke the spell.

As a stop-gap measure, Tigers included the portly shape of Trevor Redmond. Trevor had not intended to ride in 1964 but he appeared in the home event against Sunderland when Julian was ruled out.

Newport Wasps opened Tigers Provincial League season at White City and it went to a last-heat decider before Glasgow claimed the points. They then had a close call against Exeter before dropping a point against Poole and losing a further two against Wolverhampton.

Injuries and a loss of form saw Jack Monteith replaced by Trevor Redmond, who had become a promoter/team manager/rider all rolled into one. Trevor stepped into the side which ousted Sheffield out of the Knockout Cup in the single leg event at White City.

Tigers lost Chris Julian to serious injury in a horrific crash at Sheffield on 18 June. With Jack Monteith still out, they introduced Eric Hanlin to the reserve berth. A week later Tigers lost their first league encounter at home against arch-rivals Edinburgh, when all but Monk had an off night – the thirteenth home fixture of the new Tigers had been very unlucky indeed.

The ship was steadied by a win the following week, when Tigers gave Gordon Mitchell an outing at reserve and introduced another Essex man, Vic Ridgeon, in placed of injured Kiwi Ovenden. Tigers had hoped to included new Cornish signing Chris Bluett, but he had to wait a week before making a nightmare debut – scoring nothing in his only outing against a rampant Newcastle side. Only Redmond scored to form in a night dominated by Tigers' bike problems.

Bruce Ovenden came back but could not stop Newport ousting Tigers from the Knockout Cup in a match which saw yet another Tigers debutant in Kiwi Graham Coombes, who replaced Vic Ridgeon on the night. The changes were not over and the following week it was Vic who took the reserve berth as Stone was

Rider promoter Trevor Redmond with Reg Fearman.

axed. Vic too was dropped when Julian came back and Tigers had him in the line-up for the Scottish Cup home leg against Monarchs. Tigers won this 52-43 but lost 53-43 at Old Meadowbank in a thriller of a meeting that went to the wire. Redmond blamed himself for the defeat when he lost what he considered to be his easiest ride to the fired up Monarchs pair of Bert Harkins and Kevin Torpie after being out-gated at the start.

The run-in to the end of the season saw a settled side and a defeat at home by Middlesbrough close the home league fixture list. Charlie Monk had been magnificent, averaging 11.8, while Trevor Redmond and Maury Mattingly had given him great support. Unfortunately, Tigers ended bottom of the Provincial League. They lost all but one away match, a late season drawn affair at Edinburgh which was a small consolation.

Tigers had staged three internationals. Scotland, boosted by the presence of Charlie Monk, lost to a New Zealand side 57-50. Again assisted by Monk, as well as Mattingly and Redmond with Julian and Ovenden at reserve, they mauled England 73-35. They then took on the Rest of the World at the end of the season but lost, despite including Monk, Redmond, Julian and Ovenden.

Scotland kept Monk in the side when they won a four-team tournament against England, Wales and Overseas. In true speedway fashion, Scots Gordon Mitchell and Jack Monteith occupied the reserve berths for Wales and Overseas respectively.

Redmond and Monk were on the rostrum for the Provincial Riders Championship event separated by George Hunter and it was Julian and

Left: Graham Coombes. Right: Willie Templeton.

Chris Julian (left) and Maury Mattingly.

Monarchs' Willie Templeton who won the Best Pairs from Bluey Scott and Dave Younghusband.

1965 saw the amalgamation of the National and Provincial Leagues and the eighteen-team British League was formed. Tigers added Willie Templeton from Edinburgh and Bluey Scott from Middlesbrough, replacing Redmond and Bill McMillan. The team opened with a big victory over Hackney Wick Hawks – an event that was broadcast by Scottish Television. Willie was a revelation and scored heavily at White City throughout the early season. Team-mate Chris Julian soon moved south to be replaced Nils Paulson, a Norwegian.

The new Tigers did well in their opening fixtures at home and opened their away account with a win at Edinburgh. Their narrow defeat at Sheffield was a fair result. However, there were many stronger sides in the new set up and when Wimbledon came calling, the lack of Mattingly – stranded in London after missing his plane – cost Glasgow their first home league defeat.

They compensated for this loss by winning at Belle Vue, and with a settled side ran up more home wins including a then league record 60-18 whitewash of Long Eaton. Towards the end of May they temporarily lost the services of Mattingly and replaced him with Bill McMillan. An off night for Ovenden's equipment in mid-June cost Tigers the match against Oxford.

The Glasgow side rallied when Maury came back and thereafter they had a good league run – despite spells without Paulsen, Ovenden and Templeton – until their last two fixtures. In these matches they lost to Halifax and Sheffield: Tigers had drafted in Joe Hicks at reserve, but with only Monk and Scott on top form the team slumped and they could not overcome the visitors.

Bluey Scott should have sat out a few meetings after breaking a toe at Newport in late August, but he gamely rode on and piled up the points. Templeton also rode when far from fit suffering the after-effects of flu.

Like many of the former Provincial League teams, Tigers were down in the lower half of the British League table but at least they were well above Edinburgh – who only avoided the wooden spoon thanks to the poor form of fellow strugglers Long Eaton.

Despite two promising away wins near the start of the season and the well-taken draw at Halifax in late May they never came close to winning on their travels after a close run affair at Long Eaton on 1 June.

The single tie Knockout Cup tournament favoured Tigers, who dispatched their Sheffield namesakes in the first encounter before they put Swindon out in a closely contested match. Tigers then faced the powerhouse West Ham team in the semi-final, but with the Hammers on a roll – and including one-time Tiger Ken McKinlay, stoutly backed by Sverre Harrfeldt and Norman Hunter – the Londoners progressed to the final.

The Scottish Cup came west this time as Tigers had the one point aggregate in their favour. It went to a last-heat decider at Old Meadowbank and Tigers held on when Monk and Mattingly shut out Torpie to draw the heat.

The run in to the end of the season was marred by rain and it extended the season to 22 October. Two meetings never started and another ended when Charlie Monk fell in the first attempt to stage heat nine.

On the individual front, Charlie Monk again had a brilliant year when he started out the season winning the high profile Internationale at Wimbledon. He won his home round of the World Championship qualifier and on 30 July he scored another maximum to win the White City semi-final event to qualify for the British Final. Unfortunately, Charlie failed to progress to Wembley, falling at the last hurdle. He was the victim of a last-heat exclusion, which many considered to be unfair, when Ken McKinlay fell. Monk won an appeal but it did not secure a Wembley place because it was considered there was insufficient time to hold a rerun of the heat before the final.

Charlie challenged Barry Briggs, the man who set the absolute White City track record in 1966, for the Golden Helmet. He took the Kiwi to a decider but lost out in a contest that was fraught with bike problems. He also took on George Hunter for the Scottish Match Race Championship. The quiet man lost out in the Scottish Open at Edinburgh and controversially failed to show for the late season Glasgow Championship, which was won by Briggs from Sverre Harrfeldt and Swede Olle Nygren. However, his league form spoke volumes for the quiet Aussie with a massive 10.2 league average (almost three points above Bluey Scott on 7.46 and more that three above Willie Templeton on 7.06).

The Tigers' top Aussie, with the stand-up style, was capped for Great Britain against Russia and was a regular in the Scotland squad that raced against England. He chipped in 17 in the match won by the Scotland side at White City.

The 1966 Tigers added another ex-Monarch to their squad. Tall Kiwi Alf Wells had a great start to his season with 9 points as Tigers took revenge on Sheffield. It was just as well Alf performed, as Monk, trying to get the hang of his new Eso motor, stopped three times in four races. Without Paulsen, Ovenden and Coombes, Tigers used Hicks at reserve. Tucked away in the reserves' race of that opening meeting was the name of a youngster who would progress to be a future Tigers star, Jim McMillan. Jim managed a second place in that historic outing.

By the end of April the home record was intact but the away results were a series of defeats, except for the fixture against Swindon which was snowed off. April also saw Tigers use their first guest rider and the record books will show it was one time Tiger and Monarchs skipper of the day, Doug Templeton. Doug's 3 points helped his team for the night beat Coventry 41-37.

The opening fixture in May saw the arrival of new Norwegian Johnny Faafeng and the departure of Coombes to Newcastle. Tigers again held their own at home, but lost out on the road.

June was a quieter month with few league fixtures, but those that were raced turned out to be big home wins over Long Eaton and Poole. The Pirates limped out of Glasgow having managed only 17 in reply to Tigers 60 on a night when Jim McMillan made his debut as a replacement for Norwegian Faafeng, who had been

Charlie Monk in typical high speed action.

Left: Jim McMillan. Right: Bill McMillan

called up for test match duties. Jim scored 3 points. On the road Tigers were ousted from the Knockout Cup by Halifax at The Shay but they managed a win against a scratch Middlesbrough team at Cleveland Park.

Only one home league fixture was completed in July and the Glasgow Fair trip south saw what was to be their only away league win of 1966 at Newport. The away performances in July saw Tigers run their opponents close, but without Bluey Scott it was a bit of an uphill struggle. Bluey's absence gave Jim McMillan another run in the team, which lasted well into September. Bill's wee brother averaged 3.54 in his thirteen-match stint.

August was a bit of a rollercoaster month with a narrow win over Wolverhampton followed by a big win over King's Lynn and a defeat by Swindon, who were led by Barry Briggs. The zenith for Glasgow fans was the retention of the Scottish Cup thanks mainly to a good win at White City. Tigers did it in style this time, with Monk and Mattingly taking the final heat 5-1 at Edinburgh to keep the record of last-heat deciders in this contest intact. September ended with a good run of home wins, a respectable defeat at Cradley Heath and an absolute thrashing at Halifax, where the league's champions-elect ripped Tigers to bits.

The final fixture was the fourth visit of Cradley Heath, who had turned up three times only to travel home without turning a wheel. The rain came along for this fixture and by the end of heat eleven, with the score standing 36-29 in Tigers favour, the match was called off and the points awarded to the home team. The season ended at Wolverhampton with another defeat and Tigers finished up the league table from the previous season at a respectable eighth position out of nineteen. Had they had the services of Bluey Scott for the whole of the campaign they might have edged a bit higher and taken a few more away points.

The World Championship qualifier went to Ron Mountford of Coventry, the High Speed Gas Superbike round was won by George Hunter and the Glasgow Open was won by Olle Nygren.

Scotland, assisted by Monk and Scott, defeated a strong England side and used the Aussies again to defeat a team from Russia. The Russians took a fair bit of time to settle on the White City track but once they got the hang of the place they gave Scotland a fright – had they had the opportunity to practice, the Scottish side would have been really up against it.

On the individual front, Charlie Monk's average dropped to 9.23 and he failed to progress to the British Final in the World Championship. Charlie's test match outings were restricted to regular selection for Scotland but he showed his class in these fixtures, averaging over 14 points a match.

The 1967 season opened with Tigers under new management. Trevor Redmond moved out and Danny Taylor, a long time speedway fan and Borders farmer, moved in. Tigers introduced a Swede, Nils Ringstrom, to the opening team line-up. They started with a promising away draw at Hackney then a narrow defeat at King's Lynn, but lost their home opener against Newcastle by a 6-point margin.

By the end of April the somewhat Jekyll-and-Hyde Tigers team had taken three narrow home wins and drawn against Poole. Two defeats were compensated for by a narrow win at Edinburgh (an event that always redeemed any failings elsewhere in the eyes of the red-and-white bedecked travellers).

Tigers started their home May fixtures with a win over Sheffield, using Jim McMillan and the then unattached Gordon McGregor in place of their Scandinavians who were away on World Championship business. Ringstrom was back to face Belle Vue, but Tigers lost – mainly because Johnny Faafeng had failed to return. Tigers' form then slumped and they won nothing away from White City. Maury Mattingly's poor form resulted in his resigning the captaincy and Willie Templeton taking the role to emulate his brother at Edinburgh. The upshot of this turn of events was that Faafeng, who was later killed in a car crash in Norway, was sacked and Swede Bo Josefsson added to the squad.

The June form, despite the new line-up, was as before. Two home wins were followed by a big 46-32 defeat by a strong West Ham squad when the Tigers were without Mattingly (who was taking a break for business reasons). This, coupled with engine problems for Templeton and a broken frame for Nils Ringstrom, affected their returns, meaning the home men struggling to come to grips with the Londoners. On the road Tigers went out of the Knockout Cup at the hands of West Ham in London but won the league match at Cradley Heath, thanks to Monk, Templeton and Josefsson plus a good return from young Jim McMillan.

July saw a couple of home wins and a couple of away defeats. Templeton was having a purple patch while Monk was his ever-reliable self, maintaining an average of 10.52 – almost 4 points above the next best among his team-mates.

Tigers lost the services of Bo Josefsson for much of August as the Swede was obliged to compete in domestic fixtures in his home country. His replacement was ex-Diamond Russ Dent, who, although not a heat leader, did his hosts proud with reliable returns at home. The Tigers also raced much of August without Maury Mattingly, who had been injured at Wolverhampton at the end of July. Swindon, the eventual league champions, took the points from the first match in August, but Tigers took the spoils from the other two. On the road they took their third away win at Long Eaton.

September saw the wind down towards the end of the season with a couple of home league wins and an away defeat at Swindon. The league programme was wrapped up with an away defeat at Exeter.

Tigers had finished thirteenth in the league and for the first time they were well below Edinburgh. The Scottish Cup was surrendered to Edinburgh with defeats in both legs of the tournament after a 59-36 defeat in the capital in August was not turned round at White City. Although Tigers had pulled back 10 points of the difference by heat seven, a heat eight 4-2 for Edinburgh sparked off a comeback which pulled the match score level after heat thirteen, with a late Edinburgh surge putting the visitors ahead 50-46 on the night and 106-85 on aggregate. Tigers fans had their revenge a couple of weeks later when Monarchs were downed in the Supporters Trophy.

Charlie Monk was yet again head and shoulders above the rest of the Tigers team with a league average of 10.72. Next best was Swede Josefsson, on 7.24, ahead of Alf Wells on 6.41. Charlie won the World Championship

Newcastle's Ole Olsen leading Russ Dent.

Lars Jansson, Oyvind Berg and Bo Josefsson.

qualifier and the Northern Riders' Championship qualifier. The season closed on 29 September with the Glasgow Open.

What was to be the last season at White City opened with Tigers losing at Hackney and winning at King's Lynn. In the opening meeting against the Coatbridge Monarchs, the home team had a strange look to it. Charlie Monk was absent, transferred to Sheffield at his own request, as was Maury Mattingly, who was in theory transferred to Swindon (but in practice had retired). Alf Wells also moved on to Newcastle.

Jim Airey and Gunnar Malquist were identified as replacements, but both refused to travel up to Scotland. In their places came new Swede Lars Jansson and 1967 Monarch Oyvind S. Berg, who had shown a liking for the White City strip. Les Whaley was now in the promoting chair and his son, Brian, was given a place at reserve for the opening fixtures before being relegated to the second half when Russ Dent returned to the side.

On a track that had been waterlogged a few days before, Tigers won the first leg of the Champagne Trophy but could not spoil Monarchs opening meeting party. The Glasgow side won their two opening league fixtures and ended April with a home draw against Cradley Heath. On the road they lost all of their four fixtures, including a thrashing at Swindon and a mauling at Exeter. April also signalled the end of Tigers' interest in the Knockout Cup as they lost to Monarchs at Cliftonhill.

May was not a good month for Glasgow. A home rain-off was followed by a win and then two defeats, by Monarchs and West Ham. The first loss was a close-run affair in a match that featured a horror smash in which Josefsson and Monarchs' George Hunter demolished the starting gate, but the London team rattled up a big score as they again showed their liking for the Ibrox shale.

The Tigers had not managed to replace the fire power of Monk and only Jim McMillan, who scored his first maximum in April, was consistently piling up big scores. In short, the side lacked the consistency necessary to mount a serious challenge for league honours.

June started with a narrow home win against Wimbledon, but then Halifax and Sheffield took the league points south after Bo Josefsson returned home for domestic action. To their credit the promotion acted fast and added another Swede to the line-up to replace Bill McMillan. Ake Andersson came in after they had been turned down by Gunnar Malmquis t, who did not want to travel to Scotland. Andersson scored four points in his home debut as Tigers defeated the previously hard-to-beat Swindon. The only problem was that the arrival of Andersson meant that Lars Jansson had to be released. On the road, Tigers suffered three fairly heavy defeats.

The poor form displayed at the end of June continued throughout July. There were a series of respectable wins at home, but the performances away were still below par. August started with a home defeat by Hackney and ended with a win over King's Lynn. On their travels, Tigers took a sweet win at West Ham – wreaking some sort of revenge for all these defeats at White City – but lost at Poole.

In between the league fixtures, Tigers defeated the touring team from Prague and Monarchs in the second leg of the Scottish Cup. Unfortunately the latter performance was not enough to secure the silverware on aggregate.

September was up and down with a defeat by Exeter sandwiched between two wins. Tigers' last ever league fixture at White City was a 55-23 win over Newport on 18 September – a meeting which featured the home debut of a youngster who would become a top Tiger, Bobby Beaton. Away from home, Tigers lost both league fixtures, ending the season with the wooden spoon.

The last meeting at White City was staged on 27 September when Nigel Boocock won the Glasgow Open Championship from Charlie Monk.

Tigers' top two were Jim McMillan, who had boosted his average by 3.65 to 8.30, and Oyvind Berg, with an average of 8.15. Most of the rest of the team finished on poor averages in a season to forget which ended an era that had started forty years before.

Glasgow Hampden Park Era

The idea that Hampden Park, home of Queen's Park Football Club – Scotland's only amateur senior league team – and located on the south side of Glasgow could be a home for speedway was mooted in the pioneer days. Even so, the Tigers' move to Hampden Park for the start of the 1969 season must have been a surprise to many people. The stadium had a 420-yard shale track round the national football pitch, but a safety fence had to be constructed and an area set aside for the pits.

The safety fence was built in sections and had to be erected before each meeting and then taken down during the football season, as the terracing extended below the level of the track. Having hosted crowds of up to 120,000, the speedway followers left the stadium feeling a bit empty and for most meetings they were restricted to the home straight-seated stand and back straight terracing.

Tigers, with Charlie Monk and Alf Wells back and Bobby Beaton at second reserve, had planned to open the new track with a match against Coatbridge, but track works caused a delay. Due to Monarchs being unable to change an away fixture, it was King's Lynn who were the opening night visitors on 11 April. Monk won the opening heat in a very fast time and combined with Willie Templeton to record a 5-1 – setting Tigers off to a winning start in their new home.

The fresh venue seemed to help Tigers hold their own through April, with Monk and McMillan making a formidable twin attack, but away from home they failed to win a match. Aussie Jim Crowhurst had an outing in May – perhaps to shake Alf Wells, who duly responded by helping Tigers keep the home record intact to the end of month. Tigers ended the month with a win at Swindon.

June started shakily with a home defeat and a draw, but steadied for a brief spell before another home draw in mid-July. Injuries meant Tigers gave outings to Maury Robinson and Mike Hiftle, the latter staying for most of the season, effectively replacing Alf Wells. Tigers completed their home league season unbeaten but only picked up a draw at West Ham and a win at Wolverhampton to offset home failures. Eighth place in the British League equalled Tigers best performance so far. Tigers went out of the Knockout Cup away to Cradley Heath in June.

In what would be the last Scottish Cup for a few years, Tigers lost on aggregate by a single point when Reidar Eide pegged back McMillan and Berg in the last heat of the tie. Scotland faced England and lost, despite using Monk and Norwegians Eide and Berg. Again with Monk, Scotland beat Norway, who relied heavily on Eide and Berg for the bulk of their points.

On the individual front, Jim McMillan was top Tiger, marginally ahead of Monk. Charlie won the Glasgow World Championship qualifier, but Ivan Mauger of Belle Vue won the Northern Riders qualifier, the Scotianapolis and the Scottish Western Championship, which closed the season.

1970 saw Glasgow as the lone Scottish outpost again after the Coatbridge side moved almost *en bloc* to Wembley. Tigers signed Doug Templeton to replace Mike Hiftle. They also added Alistair Brady, who moved on to Berwick when Bill McMillan returned.

The Tigers had real family connections at this time, with the Templeton

Left: Doug Templeton. Right: Bobby Beaton.

brothers in the same team for the first time since 1964 and McMillan brothers coming together again after a gap of a season. The Templetons are, in fact, the uncles of the McMillans.

Tigers' early season saw reasonable wins at home but by the end of April they had dropped a home point and lost all their away fixtures. Bill McMillan was hardly back before injury laid him low and he was temporarily replaced by Aussie Peter Baldock, who in turn was replaced by Edinburgh-born Brian Murray.

Tigers held an unbeaten home run throughout May and managed a win away at Newport. The same story held at home in June, July and August but away points proved impossible to collect, despite some close run affairs on the road in July. September was completed with league wins but the trips south were fruitless.

Tigers' lost the services of Berg and McMillan to injury in September and used guests to cover. Yet again, they finished eighth in the league. They drew an away fixture in Knockout Cup yet again and their opponents, Sheffield, progressed to the next round. Without the Monarchs to compete against, Tigers resurrected the Border Trophy, losing narrowly on aggregate to nearest rivals Newcastle Diamonds.

Two test matches were staged in 1970. A Scotland side, using only Monk as a guest, lost to England and Great Britain, featuring Monk and Jim McMillan, defeated Sweden. To be fair to Scotland, it must be noted that England's tours to Australia featured Scots in their side from time to time: Tommy Miller had gone Down Under with the team in the early 1950s and Jim McMillan had toured in the England squad, together with ex-Tiger and fellow Scot Ken McKinlay, in the late 1960s and early 1970s.

Jim McMillan raised his average to 10.26 but Monk slipped back to 8.52 and Berg was third heat leader on 7.81. Young Bobby Beaton, yet another rider from that great source of dirt track and speedway riders, Blantyre, raised his average and scored his first maximum.

On the individual front, Monk won the World Championship round while Berg won the Northern Riders qualifier prize. Mauger retained the Scotiapolis and won the Scottish Open Championship, which moved over to the Glasgow promotion. Reidar Eide and Olle Nygren filled the other rostrum places in the Scottish Championship.

Les Whaley was joined in the promotion by the Hoskins family and Blantyre coach operator Jim Beaton, father of Bobby, Jim and George. Les Whaley started the season as the man in charge but he moved on in August to put Ian Hoskins in the limelight once more. Tigers added ex-Monarch George Hunter, who had become homeless with the closure of Newcastle, to the team to replace Oyvind Berg, who moved to Oxford. The team narrowly missed out on a couple of away wins before their opening fixture, which showed a solid rather than spectacular scoring pattern. However, a good win against Cradley followed by an away win there the next day were not to be a taste of things to come.

Yet again the Tigers did not have things their own way at Hampden and when the dust had settled at the end of the season they were looking at a very patchy record indeed. Three home defeats and a home draw, plus a fair few matches that could have gone the other way, were not comforting for fans. The away record, Cradley excepted, was not particularly good although they did run a couple of teams close and an extra couple of race points would have given them the match.

The main players in the side were reasonably settled, with everyone except Jim McMillan, Bobby Beaton, Monk and Hunter taking stints in the reserve berth. However, the tail-end saw Brian Murray, Alan Mackie and Jim Beaton Junior being given chances from time to time. The Tigers finished sixteenth out of nineteen in a strangely polarised league table. Only Bobby Beaton made progress, upping his average by 1.8 to 7.2 in a year that saw all the other Glasgow men slip back. Jim McMillan fell back over 1.2 to 9.03 and Charlie Monk dropped by a similar amount to 7.02.

Tigers had the luxury of a home tie in the Knockout Cup for the first time in years and used the advantage to eject a powerful Leicester side from the competition. Sadly, they drew Cradley away in the next round and lost narrowly.

Glasgow's vast spectator capacity was recognised by the powers that be and it was awarded the European semi-final of the World Championship. Tigers had no competitors but Glasgow and Scottish interest was supplied by Bert Harkins. In a meeting won by Ivan Mauger from Ray Wilson and Nigel Boocock, Bert managed three third places and ended near the bottom of the score sheet. The meeting drew a crowd on 10,000 – which was a great turn out. (Despite this successful test, proposals to use Hampden Park to house the World Final after Wembley was lost in the 1980s were not pursued.)

The domestic round of the World Championship was won by Howard Cole and Ivan Mauger won the Northern Riders' Championship qualifier. Ivan retained his Scottish Open Championship title in the meeting that brought down the 1971 curtains at Hampden. He was pushed all the way by Jim McMillan in a run-off and Anders Michanek took third place from Jim Airey, also after a run-off. Jim had also taken joint second place in the British League Riders Championship, the meeting featuring the top stars of the division.

The strong pair of Jim McMillan and George Hunter won the Scottish Open Best Pairs event from Aussie combination of Airey and Monk, with Swedes Soren Sjosten and Christer Lofqvist in third. McMillan and Hunter could afford the exclusion of the latter in his opening ride as George, yet again, fell foul of the tapes. The only other Scottish interest, the Harkins and Beaton pair, came last.

Les Whaley came back for the start of 1972 and Glasgow Speedway Promotions changed yet again. This time it was long-term team manager Neil McFarlane who replaced the Hoskins interests, thus severing a link that went back to 1939. By the end of August, Whaley's name disappeared from the programme leaving Jimmy Beaton and McFarlane to run the show. A late season change saw farmer Jim Wallace join the board.

Three of the regular 1971 squad, Bill McMillan and the Templetons, departed before the start of 1972 and in came Aussie Paul O'Neil, Alan Mackie and Jim Beaton to the opening side. Mackie was then replaced by Robin Adlington, who had a brief stint before returning in June for a longer spell, and young Jim Beaton was replaced by Norwegian Kjell (Shell) Gimre, who had a short thirteen-match run. Scot Jimmy Gallacher, who had a spell under the wing of Barry Briggs at Swindon in 1971, came in and held his place for a fair chunk of the season.

Jim Beaton secured a place at Berwick where, later in the season, he crashed and suffered serious injury. Jim was on the verge of becoming a real speedway talent but his injury kept him out of the sport until 1975 and held up his longer term return until 1978.

The Tigers side could never be described as settled and the last major upheaval was the departure of George Hunter to Wolverhampton in mid-August. This opened the door for the arrival of another Norwegian, the ill-fated Svein Kaasa.

Twenty-five-year-old Svein was just starting to find his feet in British Speedway when he crashed in heat eleven of the home match versus Swindon on Friday 29 September, receiving fatal injuries. Svein has not been forgotten and each year Glasgow riders have contested the Svein Kaasa Memorial Trophy. Svein's loss was not the only blow suffered by Glasgow as junior rider George Beaton, son of promoter Jimmy and brother of Bobby and Jim, was killed in a road traffic accident just before the season closed.

Tigers had an up and down home season, losing four and drawing two home league fixtures. On the road they picked up a single win at Wimbledon, losing the rest by fairly big margins. What was to be Tigers last ever match at Hampden

Kjell Gimre.

was a big defeat by Sheffield in the second half of a double header that had started well with a win over Oxford. The league season was disjointed by an abandonment and two rain offs. The team finished fourteenth out of eighteen.

True to form, Tigers had an away tie in the Knockout Cup but they were not disgraced by their 41-37 exit at Belle Vue where the powerhouse Aces were racing to an almost unbeaten league record.

On the international front a Scotland Select, with the only non-Scot being Charlie Monk, narrowly lost to England. The only other home international activity was Tigers' win over Swedish touring side Bysarana, but Tigers did embark on a two match tour of Norway at the end of the season, taking a draw and defeat.

The World Championship qualifier went to Bobby Beaton while Peter Collins won the Northern Riders' Championship round. Ivan Mauger retained his Scotianapolis prize and, in a repeat of the 1971 encounter, Mauger also retained the Scottish Open ahead of Jim McMillan.

The highlight of the 1972 season was the qualification of Jim McMillan, albeit at reserve, for the World Final at Wembley. Jim did get an outing and scored a couple of points. It had taken Tigers a long time to join the ranks of the other three main Scottish teams to have a man at Wembley but they did it twenty-three years after Ken Le Breton in 1949.

The winner of the last race at Hampden Park on Friday 13 October 1972 was Reidar Eide and the last man over the line was Ray Wilson.

The Tigers at Coatbridge

Why Tigers moved out of Hampden and Glasgow is not known. Maybe problems over the playing of music and post-meeting practice sessions played a contributory role. The Tigers moved to Cliftonhill Stadium, Coatbridge – which had lain dormant for three seasons – and lost co-promoter Neil McFarlane in the process. However, Neil returned mid-season, resuming the role of team manager.

Charlie Monk moved south and the Coatbridge Tigers signed wee Swede Christer Sjosten to replace him. They brought back Kjell Gimre, added Kiwi Dave Gifford, who had spent 1972 at Wolverhampton, mid-season and gave Jimmy Gallacher a long run in the line-up. Ex-Coatbridge Monarch Alistair Brady was given a reserve berth and Tigers even signed a World Champion in the making – German Egon Muller had two meetings on borrowed equipment but did not produce the results needed at the time. This was a pity, as had Egon been given a run on his own equipment he might have been the saviour Tigers were looking for.

The steeply banked Coatbridge track should have given home advantage, but this was not so as Tigers yet again stuttered at home losing five and drawing one. Oddly enough, the home defeats were not necessarily against the better teams. The by then confirmed league champions, Reading, were defeated (although maybe if their championship had depended on their display at Cliftonhill the result might have been different). On the road Tigers won at Cradley and came within a whisker of taking a result from Belle Vue.

Egon Muller.

Jim McMillan.

Tigers finished second bottom of eighteen teams, their worst performance for many years. The Knockout Cup format changed in 1973 with ties staged over two legs, making the competition a bit more than the luck of the home draw. Tigers' luck was still out, however, as they faced league champions elect Reading. Despite a win at home, the scale of the away defeat meant they went out on aggregate.

The league and cup programme was supplemented by challenge matches which produced three home defeats and only one win. Tigers went international again and returned to Norway at the end of the season. This time they beat a Bergen side and narrowly lost to Sandnes & Jaeren.

The team had a settled core but had problems with riders going off the boil or being unavailable, for meetings here and there. Jim McMillan was again a tower of strength, but despite raising his average, Bobby Beaton did not make the leap to top star as expected.

The match against Reading was Tigers' swansong in the top flight as 1974 was about to bring the second major shock in successive close seasons. Many reasons could be given for the Tigers move to the Second Division, but their relative isolation did not help. Their closest rivals, geographically speaking, were Halifax

Mitch Shirra.

whilst the nearest Second Division tracks were Berwick and Workington.

McMillan, Beaton and Dave Gifford were all meant to go to Hull, but Gifford stayed to lead the charge. Robin Adlington and Jimmy Gallacher were retained and Tigers made a major signing in Brian 'Pogo' Collins, who came back to Scotland after a spell with Wembley and Poole. They signed a couple of Hull assets – Graeme Dawson, who immediately became a favourite and raced the full season, and Eddie Argall, who moved on to Bradford after a short spell out following a broken arm. Scot John Wilson, a regular second-half rider at Hampden and Coatbridge, was also given a team spot.

Like Muller the year before, Tigers had a star in the making and let him go. This time the rider was Mike Ferreira, who raced eleven matches without scoring heavily. Mike came back a few years later to be a big star at Canterbury. Tigers did, however, hang on to young Mitch Shirra, who rode in second-half rides until it was discovered that he was underage.

The Second Division debutants held their own at home, losing only to Berwick. Whilst they had a couple of close-run affairs, the visiting teams were largely despatched south with heavy defeats, the biggest hammering being reserved for Sunderland. It was at the Wearside track that Tigers managed their only away win, although a couple of extra race points at a few venues would have given wins rather than narrow defeats. Tigers 'lost' 41-9 at Canterbury when the team walked out because of what they considered to be a bad decision by the referee.

The Tigers finished mid-table, ninth out of nineteen. In the two-leg Knockout Cup Tigers dispatched Scunthorpe then Stoke before losing to eventual runners-up Eastbourne in the semi-final.

Gifford was top man with an average of 8.82, with Collins on 8.65 and Adlington on 7.59. Jimmy Gallacher, who won the Scotianapolis, was not far behind on 7.30. The first season at the lower level was reasonable and the fans hoped for a rosier 1975.

Promotional changes marked the run-in to 1975 as Neil McFarlane moved out to run Paisley. In came former Berwick manager John Docherty, a move not greatly appreciated by Tigers fans as he was seen as a rival. However, Tigers again had Scottish competition in the New National League and that had to be good for Scottish speedway.

Docherty's Tigers started out without Gifford and Adlington, but Mitch Shirra backed Collins in the heat leader berths. The opening squad included Paul Heller and Billy Rae from southern training schools. Neither stayed long, Heller going out with injury; misfortune was to overhaul a few of the Tigers of 1975. John Wilson, ever present in the previous season, suffered two injuries which kept him out for a while and Jimmy Gallacher broke a leg preventing his upwards progression. The man who built Coatbridge, Doug Templeton, returned but he too suffered injury when running in some decent form.

It was not all doom and gloom as Tigers saw Shirra blossom and Mick McKeon slot in and show a bit of promise before being recalled by Ellesmere Port. Eddie Argall had a decent run and Tigers picked up a youngster called Derek Richardson. Coatbridge, with the toothless Tiger on their race jacket entered the four-valve era and, as might be expected of an unsettled side, slipped down the table. They lost four home league fixtures in a season where it was either a big win or defeat. They picked up wins on the road at Paisley and Weymouth plus a draw at Berwick, but most away trips saw them on the wrong side of big scores.

The Knockout Cup started with a win over Ellesemere Port then defeat by Newcastle. The triangular tornament Scottish Cup was won by Tigers, winning against Paisley at home and losing narrowly at Berwick. Their aggregate scores in the two matches gave them the silverware.

Collins and Gallacher represented Tigers in the inaugural League Best Pairs event but did not progress beyond the heats. Collins upped his average to 9.51 and came within a whisker of winning the New National League Riders' Championship, losing out to Laurie Etheridge after falling in the run-off. Shirra's debut 8.80 showed him to be a hot prospect and ripe for elevation to the top flight, and in 1976 he went to Coventry. Third man Jimmy Gallacher had 7.28 in his

Brian Collins.

injury-reduced season. The list of riders used in 1975 is extremely lengthy but few gave the instant fix needed to boost the team.

The 1976 new National League Tigers saw Collins, Dawson, McKeon, Richardson and Gallacher joined by Aussie Bob Maxfield and 1975 junior find Benny Rourke. Only Richardson was an ever-present, but the list of those who 'also rode' was down to reasonable proportions. Most were covering for injuries with one notable exception.

The peripheral riders included Doug Templeton, who started the season well but faded at home. He ended his riding career the way he had begun, as a Tiger. John Wilson became an 'also rode' but retired shortly thereafter. The enigmatic Maxfield had a spell out due to injury and his temporary replacement, Max Brown, stayed for almost half the season, moving on when the Aussie returned.

The settled side did a wee bit better at home, winning all but two league encounters – they could not hold a rampaging Newcastle side or Workington. Most wins were not big enough for the fans liking. On the road Tigers mauled Paisley and Weymouth again and drew at Peterborough. These were rare bright spots in an otherwise lacklustre series of away results. However, seventh place was the best that would be achieved in the Tigers' Coatbridge era in the lower echelon.

In the Knockout Cup Tigers progressed to face Workington thanks to a win over the Middlesbrough-based Teesside Tigers. Workington won both legs to end Coatbridge's national silverware aspirations.

Coatbridge took part in the inaugural finals day of the Four Team Tournament at King's Lynn. Tigers were runners-up in a section which featured Paisley,

Workington and Newcastle to qualify for the finals day. For some reason Berwick, the most obvious and more local rivals, were in a different qualifying section. The foursome from Coatbridge ended joint last in the semi-final draw behind eventual winners Newcastle, Eastbourne and Boston. In the League Best Pairs Dawson and Collins failed to make it beyond the first round.

The 1977 season was bittersweet for Tigers fans. Gone were the Paisley Lions, who had been unable to beat them, and onto the scene came the revived Edinburgh Monarchs. Lions had raced on a Saturday but Monarchs elected to run on a Friday and clashed with the Coatbridge race night.

Tigers had the sour taste of moving out of Coatbridge after being served roughly two weeks notice, but could enjoy the move to a new track as an alternative to oblivion. Initially there wasn't much change from the side that had ended 1976. Tigers brought in a new Aussie, the flamboyant Merv Janke, who did as well as most rookie Kangaroos. After a short spell Maxfield fell out of favour and left by mid-season and he was effectively replaced by a string of aspiring riders, the best of whom was Nicky Hollingworth, who had a run of eleven matches. The team wasn't helped by the dip in form of almost every rider except for the disillusioned Maxfield.

At Coatbridge the Tigers exited the Knockout Cup with a narrow aggregate defeat by Newcastle and also lost narrowly 38-40 at home to British League Halifax – in both events just a few more race points would have seen them

Benny Rourke.

victorious. They did well at home in the league and won away at Berwick.

The Four Team Tournament was a bit of a disaster as they gathered a paltry 44 in the qualifying series won by Berwick from Middlesbrough and Edinburgh. They showed up a bit better in the Pairs, but did not progress from the qualifying heats. Tigers won the Scottish Best Pairs, thanks to Collins and Rourke.

The last match at Coatbridge was staged on 17 June when champions elect Eastbourne inflicted a big home defeat. The greyhounds that replaced the speedway failed the test of time and went defunct. The stadium is only used for football now.

Glasgow Tigers and the Blantyre Era

Those in the know were aware that the Coatbridge promotion were fixing to run speedway at a new venue in 1977. Fittingly, the track was located in a town which had strong links with speedway in the West of Scotland and had produced its share of Scotland's stars right from the pioneer days, Blantyre. Little did the promotion think it would be needed for league action so quickly.

On moving to Blantyre the decision was made to revert to the name Glasgow, even if Blantyre was as far away from the city as Coatbridge.

The Blantyre opener on Friday 8 July was the start of a new era. The compact track, built inside a dog track, was unusual in that it had bends of different radii and represented a real challenge for riders. The smooth sweep of turns one and two failed to prepare riders for the tight and pointed third and fourth bends. Sweeping the third and fourth was a recipe for ending in the fence or, like Merv

Merv Janke.

Left: Steve Lawson. Right: Derek Richardson.

Janke at the opener, bouncing off it and careering out of control across the centre grass – much to the consternation of the unsuspecting St Andrew's Ambulance member seated in the then long grass on the infield. Mick McKeon, on the other hand, had the place well sussed and his bursts on the third and fourth were a joy to behold.

At Blantyre, Tigers had a reasonable home advantage and only Newcastle took points away from there. On the road they did little, including a poor show in the finals of the Four Team Tournament at King's Lynn.

The tragedy of 1977 was the near fatal injury to Graham Dawson which effectively ended the career of a very well-liked member of the team. The last meeting of 1977 was a benefit for Graham.

Tigers competed for the Scottish Cup, which also proved elusive. For some strange reason, even as holders, they had to qualify for the final. Out of Coatbridge they beat Berwick, but out of Blantyre they could not prevent old rivals Edinburgh taking a narrow aggregate win.

The only sweetener of a traumatic 1977 season was the mid-table position in a season that saw Tigers lose four on their home tracks and win two away at Berwick and perennial favourite Weymouth. A further consolation was the fact that their position made them best Scottish team for the third year in a row. Bert Harkins won the Scottish Open, which had been relegated to a second-half event.

As in seasons past, Tigers let a potentially big fish off the hook. Young Aussie Gary Williams was a second-half regular and never got a team berth. He went to Coventry in 1978 and held a place under his real name – Gary Guglielmi. They had, however, in Charlie McKinna a cub who would grow into a fully blown Tiger.

The Brian Collins transfer east to Edinburgh prompted Tigers to sign Workington's Stephen Lawson. This was one of their best ever moves as he would repay them handsomely until the eve of the 1992 season. Steve joined 1977 regulars Janke, Richardson, Rourke and ex-Paisley and Edinburgh Kiwi Colin Farquarson, Terry Kelly and Mick Newton. The squad, now managed by director David Thomson soon lost captain Kelly, who was replaced by Charlie McKinna. Newton went too as Jim Beaton made a brave return to the sport. Towards the end of the season Tigers added Keith Bloxsome.

Tigers were, yet again, a solid squad with Lawson, Janke and Richardson as heat leaders. The team lost twice at home in the league and picked up a couple of wins, at Scunthorpe and Workington. The draw at Milton Keynes helped them into ninth position out of twenty teams in the league – a placing that was a fair bit above Edinburgh. Their Knockout Cup exploits were ended by Rye House who drew at Blantyre and won at Hoddesdon. Edinburgh qualified from the Four Team Tournament group which included Berwick and Barrow and the Lawson Janke pairing did not go beyond the qualifiers of the Best Pairs.

The display cabinet was not entirely bare. Tigers picked up the Anglo Scottish Cup from Workington and won the Scottish Cup thanks to home and away victories against Edinburgh after beating Berwick in the semi-final. It was a massive change in fortunes as they had suffered huge defeats at both Edinburgh and Berwick in beginning of season challenges. The Scottish Best Pairs was won by Steve Lawson and Andy Reid.

Colin Farquharson.

Glasgow team 1979. From left to right, back row: Jim Beaton Snr, Colin Caffrey, Andy Reid, Charlie McKinna, Keith Bloxsome, Steve Lawson, David Thompson. Front: Jim Beaton Jr, Derek Richardson (on bike), Kenny McKinna.

1979 saw another change in personnel with Andy Reid and Keith Bloxsome added to the squad. When Bloxsome was injured, Tigers added ex-Paisley rider Colin Caffrey to the squad.

Steve Lawson and Merv Janke increased their averages to over 9 points each while Richardson, Charlie McKinna and Beaton also upped their performances. The 'also rode' list was quite lengthy again and this year it included another emerging Tiger, Kenny McKinna. For the first time in years Tigers had a clean league sheet at home with no defeats. On the road they only won at Scunthorpe in a season of many heavy defeats and a few close-run affairs.

Rye House were their Knockout Cup rivals again, and the Rockets dumped the Tigers out of the tournament once again. Hull inflicted a big home defeat in the Inter League Cup, but it gave fans another look at Ivan Mauger and a chance to see top league stars in action.

Third place in the Four Team Tournament qualifiers, ahead of Edinburgh but behind Newcastle and Berwick, meant no place on finals day and the League Best Pairs was another flop. The domestic pairs event was won by Janke and Caffrey.

Tigers retained the Anglo Scottish Cup and the Scottish Cup. This time they were seeded to the final where they defeated Berwick thanks to a magnificent home leg revival of fortunes after a big away defeat. The Inter City Cup was won from Edinburgh. Belle Vue Aces visited Blantyre for a challenge and lost in what

Left: Alan Emerson. Right: Cumbrian Geoff Powell.

was a disappointing show by the top league side.

The 1979 side had all improved from previous showings, but not enough to lift major honours. They did finish in seventh place in a league of seventeen teams, which was a move in the right direction.

Skipper Derek Richardson and Bloxsome moved on to Newcastle before the start of 1980 and Janke moved up a division, linking up with Halifax. Tigers brought in Alan Emerson and gave a chance to Kenny McKinna. Ray Palmer was given a late-season run as a replacement for Colin Caffrey.

Steve Lawson raised his average to 10.17 and scored 15 league maximums in forty league and cup outings. Emerson effectively replaced Janke and the rest stood still except for Kenny McKinna. An ever-present, Kenny weighed in with an average of 5.36 and scored a single maximum.

At home in the league a loss to Oxford and a draw against Crayford were the only blemishes. Away wins at Weymouth and Workington and a draw at Milton Keynes gave them eleventh place out of twenty. This was down from 1979 and for the first time they were below Edinburgh – who also put Tigers out of the Knockout Cup.

Facing Berwick, Middlesbrough and Newcastle in the qualifiers, Tigers won the group to make it to Peterborough but could not push past Rye House or Stoke to qualify for the final. The league Best Pairs was another wash out. The Inter League Cup resulted in a win for visiting Cradley Heath. Tigers lost the Inter City Cup to Edinburgh early in a season that did not feature a Scottish Cup contest.

In a busy league season the only other challenges were a fixture with a Tigers Past team and an international challenge against Red Star from Prague. No individual events were staged and the Best Pairs went to Lawson and Kenny McKinna.

It hardly seemed possible, but Steve Lawson raised his average again in the 1981 season. The small increase to 10.55 and 16 maximums out of thirty-seven matches illustrate just how good he was both home and away.

Charlie McKinna upped his average by 2.4, while brother Kenny moved up to 7.5 and third heat leader spot. Emerson moved on to Newcastle and in came Nigel Close, son of 1950s Motherwell star Derek. Wandering Scot Harry McLean, who spent a lot of time in England, came over from Edinburgh to link up with Tigers and averaged a respectable 6 point average. Andy Reid had an injury disrupted season starting with the opening meeting at Edinburgh and Tigers gave an extended runs to Kiwi Alan Mason and Ray Palmer. Tigers also gave a few outings to Cumbrian Geoff Powell, who would sit on the margins of the Tigers team for so long but would be recognised for his loyal efforts with a testimonial. They also tracked a Scots youngster from Haddington, Willie Myrtle.

The home league record survived intact with close calls when Middlesbrough and Weymouth visited. However, the form on the road was much better and they won at Ellesmere Port, Milton Keynes, Rye House, Stoke, Wolverhampton and Workington. This gave Tigers fifth spot out of nineteen, a couple of points behind Edinburgh.

Their Knockout Cup 'luck' saw them drawn against Middlesbrough and their interests went no further. Their involvement in the Four Team Tournament ended at the qualifiers as Edinburgh and Newcastle made it to the finals and both Glasgow and Berwick did not. A better showing in the league Best Pairs was still not good enough for further progression. There was no Scottish Cup action but Tigers did take the Inter City Cup with a narrow one point advantage on aggregate. Blantyre staged a junior international in August when Young Scotland narrowly beat Young England.

Glasgow were not the only team to use the Blantyre track as a home base in 1981 as the nomadic Berwick Bandits had a spell in residence from 1 August, when they raced Milton Keynes, until 29 August, when they lost to Weymouth. An objection from Mike Parker, then the Edinburgh promoter, set off the chain of events that saw the nomadic Berwick pull out of the league.

The Tigers' 1981 season ended in uncertainty as proposals emerged that the Blantyre Greyhound Stadium, like White City before it, lay on the line of a new road proposal. The last meeting was staged on 18 October when Tigers defeated Bobby Beaton's Buccaneers on a miserable night which kept many fans away. Tigers needed to find a new home for 1982.

The move was probably the shortest in the history of the sport. In April 1982 Tigers literally moved next door into Craighead Park, which was the home of junior football club Blantyre Celtic. The stadium area was constricted but the track was a reasonable shape, even if the spectator facilities were a bit limited. Bizarrely, only the track changed as the riders used the same dressing rooms as before.

The track opened on Friday 30 April when Rye House were the opposition in a challenge match. Steve Wilcock won the opening heat in the first leg of the Silver Helmet Match Race tie against Steve Lawson, who suffered engine failure. Lawson and the Tigers went on, however, to make it a winning start.

Although his average fell a little, Steve Lawson managed to score a massive 520 race points from 36 matches and Kenny McKinna became the second-heat leader on 8.78. Given a full-season's run, Alan Mason upped his average a bit, but Colin Caffrey effectively stood still. Unfortunately, the rest of the lads, including Kym Mauger, son of Ivan, Derek Wilson, Rob Carter and a third McKinna, Martin, did not pull up any trees. Tigers were without Charlie McKinna, who moved up a division to Coventry and Close, who moved sideways to Long Eaton.

Despite the setbacks, Tigers only lost at home twice. Runaway league winners Newcastle and Crayford were the only teams to take league victories in the newly introduced sixteen-heat format. Away from home, Tigers were without a win for the first time in years and only one of the defeats, at Stoke, could be described as narrow.

Glasgow did not compete in the Knockout Cup. The only non-league venture was the Four Team Tournament qualifiers and Tigers finished last in their group behind Edinburgh, Middlesbrough and Newcastle. In the league Best Pairs, history repeated itself as Tigers went out in the first round. At the end of the season Tigers finished eleventh out of nineteen and reclaimed their place as top Scottish side.

No Scottish Cup meetings were staged in 1982 but Tigers raced a couple of end-of-season challenges, one against Berwick and the other against a scratch side featuring Charlie McKinna called The Buccaneers. They had ensured their survival yet again and were ready, thanks to new pay scales, to move ahead into 1983.

Loyal top Tiger Steve Lawson was back for 1983. He had Andy Reid and Kenny McKinna to back him as he started the season. Kenny was a Tiger for eleven matches before moving on to Belle Vue in the top division, which weakened the team. They were joined by a sensational new signing, Jim McMillan, a man who had been a Tigers favourite until the end of 1973. Caffrey, Martin McKinna and Powell were all regulars for Glasgow but the side employed the services of Scottish youngster David Cassells, English lads Miles Evans and David Walsh, and even called Jim Beaton out of retirement to field a seven during the season.

A whole string of riders donned the red and white stripes and appeared for odd meetings for Tigers, ensuring the there was no such thing as a settled side. Injury and illness also played a big role in disrupting the team. Steve Lawson averaged 10 points and McMillan was not far behind but, Andy Reid apart, no

The McKinna brothers. From left to right: Kenny, Charlie and Martin.

Tiger managed an average over 6 and the loss of Kenny McKinna was keenly felt.

The side finished thirteenth out of eighteen in the National League, losing three at home and collecting one solitary draw on the road at Edinburgh. The Knockout Cup campaign started with an aggregate victory over Stoke thanks to a very good win in Glasgow. In the next round Tigers faced Weymouth and the South Coast side won decisively at Craighead Park in the first leg to make the return at Radipole Lane all but a formality – although only a small consolation, the Weymouth side were runners-up in the competition.

The Four Team Tournament was another non-event as Newcastle headed the qualifier from Edinburgh and Tigers' only consolation was that they were better than Berwick. Messrs Lawson and McMillan cruised to the final of the League Best Pairs. The Tigers' team riding was not rewarded as the 3-3 score in the final of the event meant the trophy went the way of Weymouth because Martin Yeates won the race.

The Scottish Cup was not staged, but Tigers did beat Monarchs in a challenge match. In a triangular event early in the season, Berwick won from Edinburgh with Glasgow in last place.

Other events included a Glasgow Tiger Cubs fixture in which they beat a Sheffield side that included Kym Mauger and short-term Tiger John Walmsley. Steve Lawson won a Scottish Open event staged on 11 September from Bobby Beaton and Andy Reid. The junior version was won by Dennis Gallagher. The season ended on 22 October after two successive attempts to meet Edinburgh had been washed out.

The low point of 1983 was the death of twenty-eight-year-old Mike Walsh, who died a few days after being injured on 26 August.

Jim McMillan did not re-sign for 1984 and his departure left a big gap in the ranks which was never filled. Tigers signed Brian Collins, but he did not regain his big scoring mantle. They did, however, rise to eleventh place in a sixteen-team league thanks to the efforts of Lawson, who averaged almost 10.4. He was backed by fellow ever-present Andy Reid (7.64) and third heat leader Collins (6.57). Martin McKinna, Caffrey and Jim Beaton had regular places but Cassells, Tam Baggley, Barry Ayres and Geoff Powell all had spells filling the gaps that appeared in the team and spells in the reserve berth.

The home results were a mixed bag with two defeats, one from league winners Long Eaton and the other from wooden spoonists Edinburgh, and a draw. On their travels, Tigers picked up a draw at Canterbury, a win at Edinburgh, and just missed a result at Arena Essex. The away form was similar to the home efforts – patchy to say the least.

Berwick scored 44 points in both ties in the Knockout Cup to send Tigers packing; yet again, Tigers were deposed by the team that would take runners-up spot. Tigers did not do well enough in the Four Team Tournament to make it to the finals day. They managed third place behind Berwick and Middlesbrough but they were better than local rivals Edinburgh. In the league Best Pairs Messrs Lawson and Reid finished well down the list in an event that now favoured team riding and they failed to qualify for the final.

The Scottish Cup went to Edinburgh after a fraught second leg at Craighead Park was rained off and restaged the following week to close the season. The promotion, keen to give the youngsters a chance, staged a few junior events.

Berwick won the 1984 Scottish Triangle by a long way, but it was Tigers who edged Monarchs for second place by a point. In a challenge match, Tigers lost to a scratch side called the Buccaneers.

After five seasons of superb scoring, the 1985 season would be the first in six years that Steve Lawson would fail to gain a double figure average. Nevertheless, he still scored a massive 450 points in 30 fixtures, setting a average of 9.39. He was, yet again, a solidly dependable regular and his record of missing only two matches since signing in 1978 was unequalled. Sadly, Steve had no real heat leader backing and the squad again lacked a regular one-to-seven line-up as injuries picked off riders for varying lengths of time.

Martin McKinna on 6.59 was second best man in the averages and third best was Lawson's brother-in-law Andy Reid on 5.98. Regulars in the squad were Scots Kenny Brailsford, David Cassells, Jim Beaton and Brian Collins, while Caffrey and Powell also had a fair number of outings. Tigers promotion did try to strengthen the side, but without any luck.

Despite a bright start with a win at Edinburgh followed by a win in the Scottish Triangle home fixture against Monarchs, it is no real surprise that

Tigers did so badly in 1985, both home and away, as the season progressed. Arena Essex took their second draw in two years while Wimbledon also snatched a point. Defeats on the track were posted against Berwick, Birmingham, Eastbourne, Mildenhall, and Stoke while Ellesmere Port won an appeal against the Tigers to take the points. Only once on the road did Tigers score more that 30 match points. Not surprisingly, Tigers were down near the bottom of the pile with seventeenth place out of nineteen teams.

It was their poor away showing against Birmingham that cost them progress in the Knockout Cup, after they narrowly defeated the Midlands side at Craighead Park. The Four Team Tournament qualifiers were a disaster, with Tigers scoring an abysmal four points at Edinburgh in the opening leg. Middlesbrough and Berwick made it to the finals and Edinburgh limped in third. The washed out Glasgow leg was not staged as neither Scottish side was capable of progressing further. Glasgow did not contest the league Best Pairs event.

In the Scottish Cup Tigers were beaten by a big margin at Powderhall and could only manage a draw at Craighead Park, so the cup went east. Despite their bright start in the Scottish Triangle, Berwick's win at Blantyre gave them the trophy.

Jim Beaton was awarded a testimonial and on 11 October a Tigers Past and Present team lost to Shawn Moran's Seven. Jim only scored a single point but he had the privilege of watching the efforts of the stylish maximum-man Moran set a new track record from the back of the field in heat eleven.

Things looked a bit better at the start of 1986, despite the mooted move to Scotstoun Showground that had been suggested in 1985 not coming off. Bobby Beaton was added to the Tigers squad after years away racing at Hull, Newcastle and Edinburgh. Bobby was a genuine second heat leader but he and Steve Lawson, yet again a big scorer and top man, did not have the backing of a third heat leader. Third highest average man Martin McKinna, ever-presents Jackson Irving and Geoff Powell, together with Caffrey were the backbone of the side while Derek Cooper had over twenty appearances. Kym Mauger, Jim Beaton and Kenny Brailsford had a few outings at the tail-end of the team.

Glasgow also had a sponsor, Kishorn Windows, and hoped to parade their new colours on 20 April but rain prevented play from starting. Race rusty in the extreme they opened with a league defeat from Eastbourne. Had Andy Reid seen a bit more action than five fixtures after his mid-season move from Cradley, things might have been a bit better. However, it was not to be and Tigers again languished near the foot of the table, eventually settling for eighteenth place out of twenty teams in the National League. At the end of thirty-eight matches Tigers had lost five at home and won none away.

Eastbourne, Middlesbrough, Peterborough, Rye House and Wimbledon all took both points south and a few teams came mighty close to emulating them, taking Tigers to last-heat deciders. The away form was not as bad as the year before, but at no time did Glasgow feature in a last-heat decider.

The Knockout Cup campaign ended at the first hurdle when they ran into Edinburgh, who soundly defeated Tigers at Powderhall and won at Blantyre a couple of days later. The 1986 Four Team Tournament qualifiers were marked as a failure yet again as they ended last out of the group behind Middlesbrough, Edinburgh and Berwick. As with 1985, Glasgow did not contest the league Best Pairs event.

The Clyde/Forth Trophy or Inter City trophy was a closely contested event points-wise, but almost three months separated the fixtures on the track. Edinburgh took this with a 7 point margin and the Scottish Cup was not contested.

The last meeting at Craighead Park was marked by an astronomical event – a total eclipse of the moon – and Tigers bowed out with a good win over Milton Keynes. Their top two heat leaders, Steve Lawson (average 9.11) and Bobby Beaton (average 8.16), signed off with a full maximum apiece.

Problems arose over the availability of the Craighead Park circuit before the start of the 1987 season. Hopes that a track could be built at a stadium known as Rosebery Park in the south-east of Glasgow, not far from Shawfield, were dashed and other prospective venues fell by the wayside. Tigers were faced with finding a new home and signing a team, all in a very short space of time.

David Thomson assembled a line-up consisting of Lawson, Martin McKinna, Jackson Irving, Powell, Cooper, Michael Irving, with Caffrey at number eight, and faced Berwick in their opening fixture. The delays to Rosebery Park being available were seen as short term, but the team needed a home. The solution was moving the team to race at Workington and the Tigers moved into Derwent Park, hoping to entice the Cumbrian fans and a travelling support from Glasgow in sufficient numbers to tide them over.

Their first fixture was staged on Friday 1 May with a big win over Boston thanks to paid maximums for Bobby Beaton and new signing Gordon Whittaker.

The distance between the promotion and the track was a major stumbling block and track preparation staff could not manage to put in the hours, which often created problems. Sometimes track staff and fans were delayed by traffic problems. On one occasion the referee failed to show and timekeeper Ian McFarquhar had to stand in only to abandon the meeting when rain arrived at heat one. Three other rain-offs did not help their situation. There is also the tale of a locally-hired slurry tanker, obtained to water the track, depositing a liberal coating of the smelly contents remaining from its previous load.

The Glasgow name was dropped after the meeting of 27 July. The change to Workington did not bring much better luck as the opening fixture was rained off and for the meeting of 7 August the track preparation was delayed and late watering could not counter the dust. The referee brought this meeting to a premature halt after heat nine. The side raced as Workington until mid-September when they were expelled from the league. The last match was staged on Sunday 13 September when Wimbledon returned south with both

1987 Glasgow Tigers. From left to right: Gordon Whittaker, Derek Cooper, Geoff Powell, Martin McKinna, Jackson Irving, Steve Lawson (on bike).

points. Two days later the management committee expelled Tigers from the league, leaving promoters Jim Beaton, David Thomson and Eric Ross without a track.

For the record, the Glasgow/Workington Tigers team raced ten home fixtures, losing six and drawing another. On the road they raced thirteen, losing almost all by big margins. Steve Lawson was, yet again, top man. He had a little backing from Gordon Whittaker but the rest of the regulars never fitted the heat leader bill. Bobby Beaton, injured in a crash at Workington, saw action in only five matches and his loss was quite a blow. Regulars in the tail-end were Martin McKinna, Irving, Cooper and Geoff Powell. A number of juniors helped make up the seven during the season, but none scored very heavily.

As the Glasgow Kishorn Windows Tigers they raced in the Knockout Cup, losing both legs to arch-rivals Edinburgh. They also raced in the Four Team Tournament qualifiers, but the misery was continued as Berwick and Middlesbrough cruised to the finals while Edinburgh also piled up a three-figure score in third place. For the third year in a row, Tigers had no one to cheer on in the league Best Pairs. The Scottish Cup did not take place.

It was a valiant attempt to keep the Tigers alive and it is a pity that such a brave venture did not get the reward it deserved. However, the salvation of the

Tigers and a rebirth in their home city was just a winter away. 1988 was to make up for the lows of 1987.

The Stay at Shawfield

Shawfield Stadium, split half and half between Glasgow and Rutherglen, had been the home of greyhound racing and Clyde Football Club for many years. It had been the subject of several redevelopment proposals, which had been repulsed, and the owners were looking to boost their income.

Glasgow Speedway needed a home and Shawfield needed lodgers. There was scope for football and speedway to co-exist provided the issue of the football pitch corner areas could be resolved. A suitable track was pegged out but Clyde FC were reluctant to accept any sharing and finally walked away from the stadium. As a result the track was fitted inside the greyhound track and it had longish straights and wide but fairly tightly banked turns. The track was 363 yards, exactly the same length as Old Meadowbank. The pits were hidden out of sight of the track behind the tote board. The stadium offered good seating and bar accommodation and plenty of covered standing round the track. Unfortunately, the area available for viewing was reduced over the years as areas of the terracing were closed off to keep down maintenance costs.

The first meeting was staged on Friday 15 April when the Radio Clyde sponsored Tigers defeated Edinburgh to win the Convener's Trophy match 50-46. Steve Lawson won the opening heat.

Their opening league fixtures went the way of the visitors, Poole and Hackney respectively. They would suffer another defeat and take draws, but away from home they beat Middlesbrough Rye House and Long Eaton to finish tenth out of sixteen.

Comeback man Kenny McKinna dropped down a league and showed his class with an average of 10.05, despite a brief interruption due to injury. Steve Lawson was better than Kenny at Shawfield but his away performances pulled his average down to 8.69. Third man was David Blackburn on 7.33. The remainder of the squad was not so settled except for new Aussie Shane Bowes, who had a decent season despite suffering an injury mid-season. Phil Jeffrey, Martin McKinna, Geoff Powell, Gordon Whittaker and Wayne Ross all had spells in the side but none had an unbroken run due to various reasons. Tigers had hoped to track Bobby Beaton, but he only rode in one league fixture.

In the Knockout Cup, Tigers lost home and away to Berwick. They made it to the final of the Four Team Tournament, following Middlesbrough but leading Edinburgh and Berwick. At the finals they struck an all-time low in the first stage with Lawson scoring their solitary point. In the league Best Pairs they did not progress beyond the heats. Kenny McKinna was third in the League Riders' Championship, losing a run off to Mark Loram. The Scottish Cup was washed out both home and away and not restaged until 1989.

Steve Lawson had his testimonial and on 20 May the Tigers took on Les

1988 Glasgow Tigers. From left to right: Phil Jeffrey, Jackson Irving, Kenny McKinna, Steve Lawson, Wayne Ross, Shane Bowes, Martin McKinna. Kneeling: Dick Barrie. With trophy: Councillor Jennings.

Collins All-Stars as the big event of the year. Steve also became the top rider in Scotland, claiming the Scottish Open Riders' Championship, which was staged at Powderhall.

The season closed on a bit of a downer as two of the vital cogs in the wheel that set up Shawfield, Dick Barrie and Neil Grant, moved out of the promotion. They would be replaced for 1989 by yet another returnee, Neil McFarlane.

The 1989 Radio Clyde Tigers was a much more settled side with the three McKinna boys, Lawson, Bowes, Jeffrey and Powell lining up for most of the matches. Charlie came to Shawfield and Blackburn moved in return to Berwick. Kenny McKinna was again top Tiger with an average of 9.71, thanks to a home average of 11.21. He was almost unbeatable at home but his away form dipped a bit. Second top Tiger Lawson raised his average a little and Bowes became third best on 6.30, a little adrift of a heat leader average.

In the league a single home defeat when Jeffrey was injured was compensated for by a win at Newcastle and they earned a halfway spot in the table, ninth out of eighteen. The Knockout Cup trail stopped when Eastbourne put them out, drawing at Shawfield and winning at Arlington. The

Four Team Tournament faltered in the qualifiers as they ended last behind Berwick, Middlesbrough, and Edinburgh and, yet again, the Best Pairs involvement ended in the qualifiers. Improving one place, Kenny McKinna took runners-up spot in the League Riders' Championship.

At the start of the 1989 season the 1988 Scottish Cup was secured by Edinburgh, winning at both Powderhall and Shawfield. The 1989 version staged in August was also a win for Edinburgh on aggregate and the Autumn Trophy also went east. Tigers narrowly lost a challenge match with top league Belle Vue.

On the individual front, Blackburn won the Grand National qualifier and the Svein Kaasa Trophy was won by Todd Wiltshire.

The Radio Clyde Tigers started 1990 with a squad of nine riders, adding new Aussie Jason Lyons and Sean Courtney to the McKinnas, Lawson, Bowes, Jeffrey and Powell. Jason had his bad days – for example he wrecked two bikes in one meeting – but on others he scored heavily. After two seasons of playing second fiddle to Kenny McKinna, Steve Lawson edged ahead again with Bowes the third heat leader. Charlie McKinna, Courtney and Jeffrey were sound second strings and Lyons did well, moving into the team after a spell at reserve. Kenny was again the main man at Shawfield, but away his form pulled him down.

The promotion opened with a special meeting to herald the Glasgow's

Shane Bowes in front.

A fine action shot of Charlie McKinna.

staging of the Special Olympiad. Ronnie Correy, Gary Hicks and Rick Miller appeared with Tigers men in a Stars *v.* Stripes contest.

The solid side lost three home league contests but won away at Arena Essex, Edinburgh, Long Eaton, Milton Keynes, Newcastle and Rye House to take fourth spot in the seventeen-team league table. Tigers felt hard done by on some of their away visits. They complained bitterly about poor refereeing at a couple of venues, but all it did was cost McFarlane a fine or two.

The league contest did not end with the league matches as the top nine teams contested the National Series. Tigers faced Middlesbrough and Berwick in the qualifier and progressed to meet Wimbledon and Stoke, teams which had won at Shawfield in the league, in the final. A good second place in the first round at Wimbledon was followed by wins at Stoke and, at Shawfield on 27 October, Tigers won their home round, scoring enough points to win The National Series on aggregate. Their Knockout Cup aspirations foundered on the rock of Ipswich Witches.

Glasgow won the Four Team Tournament qualifiers from Berwick, Edinburgh and Newcastle but failed to progress from the semis on finals day. The league Best Pairs event was staged at Shawfield but the fancied Glasgow duo failed to make the semi-finals in an event won by Hackney's Andy Galvin and Steve Schofield.

Tigers dominated the Scottish Three Team Tournament, winning all three rounds to head Edinburgh and Berwick. They won the season's opening challenge against Edinburgh on aggregate and also won the Scottish Cup on aggregate. In an early season challenge they beat Danish touring team

Tigers in 1990. From left to right, back row: Jim McMillan (team manager), Kenny McKinna, Geoff Powell, Steve Lawson, James Grieves, Charlie McKinna. Front row: Sean Courtney, Jason Lyons, Phil Jeffrey, Shane Bowes.

Kulsvierne by a narrow margin.

The Glasgow management staged their second testimonial event in 1990. This time it was the Cumbrian, 'Big Leggy' himself, Geoff Powell who was the beneficiary. This was a well deserved reward for all his efforts as a dependable rider who was always there when he was needed. Tigers faced a side dubbed Heroes – essentially an Edinburgh side with a couple of Glasgow men.

All in all, 1990 was a successful season and promoters McBride, McFarlane and Logan were well pleased with the efforts of the team managed by Jim McMillan.

In 1991 controls over the strength of teams caused problems. Tigers signed Edinburgh Aussie Mick Powell at the start of the season and had to drop Charlie McKinna to meet team limits. Powell was injured early season and was replaced briefly by juniors before Tigers brought in new Aussie Brian Nixon.

Martin McKinna was dropped as Tigers shuffled the side and before long the McKinna era at Glasgow was over. Kenny had a falling out with the promotion and moved out to complete the season at Middlesbrough. Mark Courtney, brother of Sean, was signed as a replacement.

The Tigers promotion staged a testimonial for Martin McKinna on 14 July, thereby marking his ten years' contribution to the red and white stripes. The three McKinnas were in a McKinna Select which went down 34-43 to Tigers – scored Martin 0, Charlie 1 and Kenny 9.

The season started with the Gold Cup mini-tournament and, under Neil McFarlane, Tigers lost two home and all their away fixtures. In the Sunbrite League they won all but one at home and away at Long Eaton, Middlesbrough, Rye House and Milton Keynes to steadily climb the table to finish second to Arena Essex. Top Tiger in 1991 was Shane Bowes ahead of Steve Lawson, who headed the league and Knockout Cup averages, and Jason Lyons. The settled side was a major asset to the team.

The Knockout Cup saw Tigers easily eliminate Milton Keynes and narrowly beat Newcastle to qualify for the final against Arena Essex. This started with an anti-climax of a call off as Tigers led 32-16. The Arena leg was also a victim of the weather. A narrow 46-44 win at Shawfield seemed to see the trophy set to go south but Tigers, with a display of true grit, matched the score at Arena, setting the stage for a restaging of the final.

In the restaging, Arena won 60-30 in Essex and Tigers could only pull back 10 at home. Arena took the league and cup double, but it would be Glasgow's turn in the two years time. Tigers' Four Team Tournament hopes again faltered in the qualifiers.

Jason Lyons qualified for the World Under 21 final staged at Coventry in October and made it to the rostrum in third place. The Easter Trophy went Edinburgh on aggregate by a narrow 2 point margin but Tigers won the Scottish Cup thanks to wins away and at home where the action was televised. In the inter-league BSPA Cup they lost to Reading at Shawfield.

Glasgow provided the venue for a Sunbrite Inter-Nations Championship event. The first staging was rained off after a few heats but it was restaged in October. England replaced Great Britain and raced against Sweden and Australia. 1990 World Champion Per Jonsson led his Swedish side to victory in the match and the series. England were runners-up on the night and Australia, who included Tigers favourite Jason Lyons, were last.

A challenge match won by the visiting Hungarian touring side in April gave the promotion a look at the visitors. They were impressed by Robert Nagy (pronounced Naaj) and Robert Csillik (Shilik) and would sign them before the start of the 1992 season. Ironically, Steve Lawson had his worst night at Shawfield and struggled to score 4.

The new promoter for 1992, Douglas Hopes, brought big changes. The Hungarians were joined by Dane Tim Korneliussen and Neil Collins. Juniors James Grieves, Stuart Coleman and Jason Straughan all had runs in the Gold Cup. The opening of the season saw Tigers lose at Edinburgh in the Spring Trophy, suffer a couple of wash outs then lose to Berwick at home in the Gold Cup. Radio Clyde Tigers lost two home and all their away fixtures, finishing in last place in the mini league.

For the Homefire League, Csillik was dropped in favour of Mick Powell as Shane Bowes came back and Mark 'Buzz' Burrows replaced Korneliussen. Later in the season, Tigers signed Dane Jesper Olsen to replace Burrows, with the previously mentioned juniors also being given occasional outings.

Nagy became top Tiger followed by Bowes and then Neil Collins. Steve Lawson dropped down to fourth man but still had a respectable near 8 point average. It was not a bad way to end a long and illustrious career with Glasgow.

Tigers finished third in the league of eleven teams. They were unbeaten at home but lost a point when the BSPA awarded a point each to Glasgow and Rye House for a fixture not contested on the track because of rain offs, and took away wins at Stoke and Exeter. A draw at Mildenhall was expunged from the records after the Fen Tigers closed.

Tigers went out of the Knockout Cup at the hands of Edinburgh, who won both legs. In the Four Team Tournament, Tigers qualified for the finals which were won by home side Peterborough. Tigers did better in the BSPA Cup, defeating top league Cradley at Shawfield in a last-heat decider, won by Nagy from Alan Grahame, Bowes and Billy Hamill, but they failed to beat Ipswich at Shawfield in the next round.

Edinburgh lifted the Scottish Cup with home and away wins and then took the Spring Trophy. Glasgow won the Scottish Three Team Tournament, contested with Berwick and Edinburgh, by winning the Edinburgh and Glasgow rounds

Robert Nagy in action.

and finishing runners-up at Berwick. Tigers raced a late season challenge against a side that included former favourite and Belle Vue Ace, Jason Lyons.

Robert Nagy and Shane Bowes qualified for the League Riders' Championship, which was won by Nagy after a run-off with Mick Poole of Peterborough. Nagy was awarded a place in the First Division Riders' Championship and did well to score 7 points. At one point, Nagy was just five rides away from a place in the World Final, but finished just adrift of the qualifying bunch. It was the best a Scottish-based rider had done in the premier event for many years and was a creditable effort.

Glasgow broke new ground staging a sidecar speedway international in August but the experiment was not to be repeated.

The 1993 season dawned without Steve Lawson, who had decided to hang up his leathers. With hindsight it is a pity that Steve was not to become part of what must be looked upon as the glory years after holding the team together, often single-handedly, for so long.

Tigers had new sponsorship from quarrying company Alfred McAlpine and new men in the red and white were Nigel Crabtree, David Walsh and Anthony Barlow; Crabtree and Walsh were to become vital cogs in the Glasgow machine. James Grieves became eighth man while Stewart McDonald came over to the Tigers from Edinburgh mid-season. David Nagel and Scot Stuart Coleman, a trier all they way, both had outings for the squad. The British League Second Division featured eight-man teams, and matches were raced over eighteen heats. The riders in the last three heats were determined by the points they scored in heats one to fifteen.

This was Tigers' season. It was a league only year, with no minor mini-league events, and each team raced two home and two away fixtures. Tigers won all their home fixtures. Most were runaway wins with few teams stopping Tigers gathering 70 points or more in matches where a maximum score would have been 90-18. Away from home, Tigers drew at Newcastle, won once at Rye House and twice at each of Middlesbrough, Exeter, and Oxford. In addition to match points, bonus points were awarded for aggregate wins in league encounters. Glasgow added 19 bonus points out of the 20 on offer to their haul of 55 match points.

Tigers started their league campaign with the draw at Newcastle and then won home against Rye House, away at Middlesbrough and then at Exeter. They then won at home over deadly rivals Edinburgh and Sheffield in successive weeks before running into the Panthers at Peterborough, who brought their unbeaten run to an end. Swindon made it two defeats in a row.

Back home, Glasgow steadied the ship with a narrow win over Middlesbrough then, after a wee break, continued on their way to the title by dispatching Long Eaton at Shawfield. Rye House sent Tigers home pointless but they bounced back to defeat Exeter at Shawfield before another defeat on the road, this time at Long Eaton.

A break in league action in late June was followed by a big defeat of Peterborough to take match points and a bonus. The away Knockout Cup win at

Middlesbrough buoyed them up to take a win at Oxford, despite the very late arrival of David Walsh. David scored a single point which had little bearing on the result.

Glasgow started July with a large Shawfield win over Oxford followed by big Shawfield defeat of Sheffield and a Fairs Friday going over of Rye House, despite an early match exit for David Walsh who collided with Martin Goodwin. Tigers' July roll continued with a win at Rye House followed by another win at Exeter and a home win against Newcastle.

Unfortunately, the run came to an end again with visits to Peterborough and Swindon which proved fruitless as far as the match points were concerned, but the margin of defeat set them up for more bonus points.

August started with a defeat at Sheffield, a home win against Exeter and an away defeat at Edinburgh. Oxford were the next league victims, firstly at Shawfield then at Cowley before arch-rivals Peterborough then Middlesbrough were sent packing on the wrong end of big scores.

The run-in to the championship started in September and Newcastle offered little resistance at Shawfield in the afternoon, but could not quite keep up the form for the return at Brough Park in the evening. The trip to Edinburgh at the end of the week produced another defeat but the bonus point was secured as the Tigers piled up 70 points against Monarchs at Shawfield in the return. They sat poised to win the coveted trophy for the first time in their history.

The win over Middlesbrough gave Tigers the points they needed, but they had to wait a day for Peterborough to dispatch Long Eaton at Alwalton to make sure. On 24 September 1993 Tigers became champions. Their strength in depth was the secret and they were carefully steered in the right direction by their astute team manager Ian Steel.

The home league season was wrapped up with a win over Long Eaton, who gave Tigers their first heavy defeat away from home a few days later. Tigers wrapped up their league campaign at Sheffield on 18 October with a defeat. The excuse for the Long Eaton defeat was that Tigers had Knockout Cup business on their minds.

The Knockout Cup was also annexed as they put out Middlesbrough early in the season before the rush of fixtures towards the end of the season when they pushed out Peterborough before beating Swindon in the final. Tigers got the perfect start to the final by taking a draw at Blunsdon. This set them up for the return at Shawfield where they managed to give their fans their first Knockout Cup to add to their league and Scottish Cup silverware.

The team efforts were spearheaded by Nagy, who pushed his average to 10.37 and he was supported by Bowes on nearly 9 and Crabtree on nearly 8.25. Walsh chipped in with almost 8 and Mick Powell boosted his average to nearly 7.5.

They did not clean up on all fronts though, as they were not good enough to qualify for the Four Team Tournament finals, finishing behind Newcastle and Edinburgh and ahead of Middlesbrough. On the individual front, Nagy

1993 League and Knockout winners celebrate with Glasgow's Lord Provost. From left to right: Neil McFarlane, David Walsh, Nigel Crabtree, Doug Hopes, Stewart McDonald, Bob Innes, David Nagel, Shane Bowes, Jesper Olsen, James Grieves. Kneeling: Anthony Barlow, Mick Powell.

failed to retain his League Riders' Championship. Tigers did, however, provide the winners of the Farewell Pairs event, Mick Powell and James Grieves.

The old enemy, Edinburgh, were the defeated by similar score home and away in the Scottish Cup but Tigers bit off more than they could chew in a challenge fixture with Belle Vue. They also raced First Division Poole Pirates at Wimbourne Road in July but, despite guest Tony Langdon, were outclassed.

The Tigers of 1994 must have known that the double of 1993 would be hard act to follow, but they set about their task with relish, opening with a win over Middlesbrough in a free admission event called the Charity Challenge. They did the double over Edinburgh in the Easter Trophy, but Belle Vue proved just too tough a test.

The league campaign started with a big win at Sheffield followed by repeat dose at Shawfield. The unbeaten record remained intact as they put Oxford out of the Knockout Cup with a bigger win at Oxford than they recorded on their own Shawfield strip. Back to league action and the unbeaten run was extended by a win at Middlesbrough, despite the injury to Olsen, which was followed by a going over for Edinburgh. This featured a big 18 point maximum by David Walsh as

Dave Walsh in action.

Tigers again used a rider replacement for Mick Powell and Sean Courtney as a replacement for Olsen. The unbeaten league record was stretched to five with a big win over Peterborough as Tony Langdon was the perfect guest and Walsh again earned a bulging pay packet with another 18 point full house.

A massive win at Oxford was followed by yet another big home win over Middlesbrough, featuring the return of Powell. This purple patch took Tigers to the middle of May looking odds on to be champions again. The second half of May continued in the same vein with a big win at under strength Edinburgh, a home win over Swindon and an away win at Exeter.

Unfortunately, heat thirteen proved unlucky at the County Ground and Nagy, attempting an overtake, fell and sustained a shoulder injury. Without Nagy and Olsen and with guest Mikael Teurnberg the unbeaten run came to an end on 27 May at Peterborough. Had Walsh not fallen in his opening race and had the track had been a bit slicker, the result might have been different. Olsen came back for the win over Oxford at Shawfield but his bike packed up at the start of heat one and so did he.

The Swindon leg of the Knockout Cup was washed out but Glasgow posted a big lead in what should have been the second leg tie. Back to league action and Tigers, without Nagy, defeated Exeter at home; this time Crabtree took

18 without reply and Powell was paid for a similar score. Nagy was back for the big win over Sheffield with Powell, Walsh and Grieves (paid) taking 15 point maximums. Tigers' run continued with a win at Middlesbrough, made all the more remarkable as they did it without Nagy, who was injured in the opening heat. Using rider replacement the return was another big win for Glasgow. A far-from-fit Nagy returned for the Newcastle match out of necessity as Olsen was being rested and rider replacement was being used for Grieves. Despite concerns about the strength of the side they won handsomely, even with Nagy's below-par 3 point score but the return at Brough Park, without Nagy but with Grieves, was lost and the bonus went to Diamonds after Mark Thorpe beat Crabtree in a run-off.

With 39 points in the bag after only eighteen meetings things were looking good, A draw at Long Eaton without Nagy was followed by a surprise defeat at the lowly Sheffield with him. After their mid-July departure from the Fours, Tigers bounced back to win at Oxford and secure their place in Knockout Cup semis with an aggregate win over Swindon. An enforced break due to rain and the Fours at Peterborough possibly contributed to the narrow defeat at Exeter on the 8 August, but the following week started with a sound home win over Oxford.

Swindon showed their mettle at Shawfield on 21 August, taking Tigers to their first last-heat decider – Walsh and Powell taking a 5-1 to end it 51-45. This was not the only shock for Tigers fans as Long Eaton, albeit with more league fixtures under their belt, headed the table on points. The top of the table clash at Long Eaton the next week went the way of the Invaders, and, after a wash out at Shawfield, Tigers made a fruitless trip to Newcastle and another defeat.

Glasgow dug into their reserves and, without Powell who had broken his collarbone guesting at Oxford, took a narrow win at Swindon after Crabtree and Walsh scored a last heat 5-1. The following night at home, using Peter Carr as a guest, Long Eaton were relieved of three points, 2 for the win and 1 for the bonus. Long Eaton were still top but the form guide was still pointing Tigers' way.

Knockout Cup action again intervened and the home tie against the Panthers was a bit tight for comfort at 54-42. The second leg was rained off, giving Tigers time to rest before their league double header against Newcastle and Exeter. Nagy was back by this time and the side, without Powell, completed their progress to the final with a narrow 50-45 defeat at Peterborough. As late as heat twelve Tigers' had their noses in front, effectively snuffing out Panthers' challenge.

A league visit to Swindon on 24 September saw the points go south but they bounced back to beat Peterborough in the league to climb back to the top with four fixtures to go. The return at Alwalton, with Powell but without Nagy and Crabtree, was fruitless but on Sunday 9 October, without Nagy, Glasgow clinched a 51-45 win over nearest rivals Long Eaton to take three points and their second league title.

The all-Scottish Knockout Cup final was given a big build up and both sets of supporters looked forward to the encounter. The groundwork for the Tigers' win was set by a narrow 4 point defeat at Powderhall. A solid showing at Shawfield in the second leg the day after clinched it for Tigers by the end of heat thirteen. The aggregate 101-91 gave Tigers the back-to-back double, the first for a Scottish side, and Tigers and all connected with them were delighted.

Their last League fixture was at Powderhall on 21 October, when local rivals Edinburgh gained revenge for their aggregate Cup defeat the week before. Overall though, things did not go smoothly as they suffered from injuries that would have sunk many other teams. What Tigers might have done had they had a full strength side is mind-boggling. In addition to the 53 league points they added 14 bonus points out of a possible 18.

Nigel Crabtree, who had a great testimonial year, and David Walsh were the main planks in the platform. The main support came from Nagy and Powell when they were in action between injury spells. Sean Courtney made a significant contribution when he returned to replace Dane Jesper Olsen, who spent the second half of the season out because of injury. The valuable contribution of James Grieves and Stewart McDonald should not be overlooked as they gave the tail that league-winning edge.

The season closed with Mick Powell and James Grieves lifting the Farewell Best Pairs Trophy.

Things did not all go Tigers' way in 1994. The Four Team Tournament was, yet again, a disaster. In the qualifiers they finished third behind Long Eaton and Edinburgh but ahead of Newcastle and Middlesbrough in a five-team section. Although they equalled their league Best Pairs record when Crabtree and Walsh finished as runners-up, Crabtree and Nagy didn't pull up any trees in the League Riders' Championship.

The Scottish Cup was clinched at Shawfield after a big win at Edinburgh helped secure the silverware to add to the Easter Trophy. There was no individual action but Nagy and Stewart McDonald won the Farewell Best Pairs from other Tigers duos.

Big changes were afoot for 1995. The two leagues amalgamated and Glasgow were up against the big boys in a newly named Premier League. With Weir Toyota as sponsors, the Tigers acquired American Charlie 'Dukie' Ermolenko, but lost Crabtree and Nagy.

The likelihood of winning the league in the company of the big teams was small, but when the dust had settled they showed a clean sheet at home and recorded a win at Middlesbrough and a draw at Hull. Tigers also picked up 14 bonus points out of 20, including some from the big boys, boosting them to seventh place in the league.

Walsh, Ermolenko and Bowes were the top players, receiving sound support from the exciting-to-watch Olsen, Grieves and Courtney. Mick Powell's early season injury pegged back his scoring and probably pulled down Tigers' potential finishing position. Tigers used guests or rider replacement to cover rather than drafting in a youngster at the tail.

The Knockout Cup was surrendered as well. Glasgow beat Middlesbrough home and away, but despite running Cradley close in the next round they lost

Charlie 'Dukie' Ermolenko.

by a small aggregate difference. Tigers' progress in the Four Team Tournament followed the usual pattern, with an exit at the qualifiers.

The Scottish Cup fixtures were separated by a couple of months. Tigers took a big lead to Powderhall in September which was enough to regain the trophy. They also collected the Spring Trophy with wins away and at home.

In a bold move, the Tigers promotion staged an all-star City of Glasgow International Trophy which was partly sponsored by the local council. World Champions Hans Nielsen and Sam Ermolenko, Charlie's brother, took part but after the dust had settled it was Yank Ronnie Correy who collected the big prize cheque after beating Chris Louis, ex-Tigers favourite Jason Lyons and Nielsen. The meeting attracted a big crowd.

The promotion was having financial difficulties, however, and in the mid-season a cash crisis was averted when the stadium owner agreed to drop the rental fees. By the end of the season the problems had mounted up and the Glasgow fans were stunned to hear that the Tigers were going out of business.

The end of 1995 also brought crisis to Edinburgh with the eviction of the Monarchs from Powderhall, a plight worsened by the refusal of planning permission for a replacement track at Armadale. The problem of one track with no team and one team with no track was solved by Edinburgh moving to Glasgow and running as the Scottish Monarchs. This was resented by many in the Tigers' ranks and a lot of the regulars boycotted Shawfield for 1996.

The boycott had a knock-on effect in 1997 when the Tigers returned under the reins of the stadium owners and Neil McFarlane, who travelled up from his Manchester base on a weekly basis. Many fans had probably got out of the Sunday speedway habit and did not come back. The new Tigers started well, taking the Easter Trophy with home and away wins, but the official competitions did not bring too much joy.

Tigers' side included a mixture of new and old. Mick Powell captained the side with Neil Collins, Stewart McDonald and Sean Courtney, who were all former Tigers, together with youngsters Will Beveridge and Grant MacDonald. The six-man side changed little over the season and Collins was top heat leader with 9.09. Mick Powell averaged 8.61 and Stewart McDonald 7.58. The season opened with the Premier League Cup mini-league. They lost to Newcastle and Edinburgh at home and won nothing on the road, thereby failing to progress to the semi-finals.

The team finished sixth out of fourteen in the British Premier League. At home they lost twice, Edinburgh and Long Eaton taking points, and their trips away produced draws at Stoke and Berwick and a win at Oxford. The additional bonus points gave Glasgow a place in the end of season play-offs but they were eliminated by Edinburgh, who won at both Shawfield and Armadale.

Progress in the Four Team Tournament ended in the qualifiers. Tigers finished behind Edinburgh, Berwick, and Newcastle while in the league Best

Left: Sean Courtney. Right: Kaj Laukkanen.

Pairs they also failed to progress beyond the qualifiers. Monarchs also took the Scottish Cup on aggregate.

Question marks were set against the 1998 season as the '97 promotion was reluctant to continue. The 1997 season had suffered from a number of rained-off meetings, which did nothing to help swell crowd numbers.

Undaunted, a group of fans gathered together and ex-Tiger Jack 'Red' Monteith came forward to co-ordinate a committee that successfully fought to keep the Tigers on the track.

The saviour of the Tigers turned up in the shape of bowling alley owner Brian Sands, a self-confessed admirer of the big rivals, and Tigers were back in action. The Tigers faithful did their bit as well chipping £20,000 into the pot. Tigers also managed to obtain sponsors with 96.3 Qfm radio backing them.

The line-up changed with the additions of Swede Daniel 'Dalle' Andersson, Zimbabwean David Steen and Brian Turner to a seven-man side. Andersson did not perform as hoped as a heat leader, but he was not helped by a spell on the sidelines. The promotion acted to strengthen the team and, in late August, Tigers signed Finnish rider Kaj Laukkanen, who rattled in big scores home and away. Top Tiger Mick Powell was injured mid-September and Glasgow rode out the season replacing him with guests.

The Premier League Cup produced an unbeaten run at home and a draw at Edinburgh. On the track they recorded a win at Stoke and Tigers thought they had done enough to qualify for the next round. Problems with the Stoke promotion resulted in the Loomer Road result being expunged from the records, much to the annoyance of the Glasgow promotion and the fans, who felt robbed by officialdom. The promotion took their concerns to a tribunal and won their appeal but it was to no avail and Tigers exited this competition.

Premier League action saw a loss at home to Peterborough and couple of close calls away, the Tigers actually winning at Stoke and Berwick. Their efforts were good enough to win them seventh place out of thirteen teams and a place in the play-offs for the Young Shield. Tigers took a narrow advantage in their tie against Reading but could not best the Isle of Wight Islanders in the semi-finals.

Another poor showing in the Four Team Tournament qualifiers saw Glasgow in third place behind Edinburgh and Newcastle and ahead of Berwick. Glasgow took no part in the league Best Pairs. Edinburgh won the Spring Trophy on aggregate and the Scottish Cup was not contested.

The Tigers promotion had been working towards providing training facilities to rival the operations at Linlithgow during 1998. In a surprise move they secured a lease for the home of the Glasgow Giants, Saracen Park, which had been a greyhound track since about 1956.

Various rumours circulated the city about the proposed venture but, after all the dust had settled, it was clear that Tigers' meeting at Shawfield on 18 October 1998 had brought down the curtain on another era. At the time of writing, Shawfield remains in use as a greyhound circuit.

Ashfield for the Tigers

The Tigers promotion worked against the clock to build a new track at Saracen Park in time for the 1999 season. Much credit must go to the crew under the direction of Bob Sneddon and track-building skills of Alan 'Doc' Bridgett, for producing – or in the opinion of some, reproducing – a great racing circuit.

The return to Ashfield, some forty-six years after it had closed, came on Sunday 25 April, when the 96.3 Qfm Tigers met Newcastle Diamonds in a Premier National Trophy qualifying round event. It had been touch and go with delays, but after the track had been officially opened by Norrie Isbister, Diamonds' Robert Eriksson flew round to win the very first race.

The second heat lasted no more than a lap or so when young reserve Scott Courtney hit the fence and fell. He required hospital treatment and, on its way out of the stadium, the ambulance snagged on the replaced pits gate rail, pulling down the wall pillars, one of which landed on a parked car. This all resulted in a long delay and when racing did resume, Tigers were beaten.

The Premier National Trophy mini-league saw Tigers lose another at home and all but one of their away fixtures (at Berwick) even though the starting line-up of Powell, Beveridge, new signing Paul 'Banger' Bentley, Turner, Sean Courtney, Stuart Coleman and Scott Courtney had only one change when Jittendra Duffill filled the younger Courtney's place.

The National Trophy line-up exited the Knockout Cup thanks to home and

Left: Mick Powell. Right: Paul Bentley.

Left: Will Beveridge. Right: Les Collins.

away defeats by Reading Racers. It was in the home leg of the competition that Bentley was injured in a freak accident which sidelined him for about six weeks, but this did not blunt his scoring ability when he came back.

Tigers moved quickly and signed German-based Argentinean Emiliano Sanchez, who had a bright debut but was inconsistent. Things were not going well enough for the promotion and further strengthening was required. The man they signed in the hope of boosting their fortunes was the experienced Les Collins who had, in 1986, helped pull Edinburgh out of one of the their deepest ruts. Whilst some fans had reservations, largely because of Les' links with Monarchs, he would become as popular at Glasgow as he had been at Powderhall with his controlled bursts from the back.

Les was a sensation, scoring a string of double figures and showing his new found Glasgow fans that speedway is not all about winning from the gate. Only twice in official fixtures did Les drop below double figures.

The return of Bentley in August caused a headache for the promotion. In order to keep within the team points limit, someone had to go and the unthinkable was thought – then carried out. Long-term Tiger and star man at Shawfield, Mick Powell, who was having a wee bit of an up and down season, was axed in order to keep Collins and Bentley. It was not a happy situation and many fans disagreed with this course of action.

In the Premier League the Tigers lost three at home to Reading with the original squad, to Sheffield with the transitional squad and to Newport with the finalised septet. They finished in twelfth place out of thirteen, their worst Premier League showing, and failed to qualify for the Young Shield.

In the Four Team Tournament their high-scoring third place behind Edinburgh and Newcastle, but ahead of Berwick gave them a place at finals day. However, they did not progress. The league Best Pairs saw Beveridge and Sean Courtney manfully score 18, but it only gave them last place.

Edinburgh collected the 1999 Scottish Cup and the promotion had to fork out cash to a charity when Tigers were defeated on aggregate by Workington. The Ashfield Classic was the closing big name meeting which was won by Carl Stonehewer, from James Grieves and Emiliano Sanchez. Robert Nagy, former Tigers' favourite was injured in a pre-meeting parade crash and Jason Lyons failed to appear due to flight problems.

In November 1999, pioneer Norrie Isbister passed away after a short illness at the ripe old age of ninety-three. It was fitting that his ashes were scattered on the Ashfield track, an appropriate final resting place for someone who loved the sport and Ashfield so dearly. The new millennium season opened with a memorial meeting for Norrie, won by ex-Tiger Jesper Olsen.

New Allied Vehicles Tigers in 2000 were James Grieves, who had been a Tiger in the past and whose move to Glasgow was viewed with annoyance by his 1999 club Edinburgh, Dane Richard Juul, and Aidan Collins, the son of Les Collins. They used a string of youngsters at reserve early and late season. Tigers settled with Scott Courtney, who was joined by his dad, Mark, to make Glasgow the first side to track two father and son combinations. Mark's brother, Sean, retired to make way and was rewarded with a testimonial meeting in July.

Juul disappointed, however, and by mid-June was replaced by young Aussie

Left: James Grieves. Right: Mark Courtney.

Emiliano Sanchez.

Russell 'Rusty' Harrison. Injury problems for Sanchez, Scott Courtney and Grieves did not help the Tigers' cause. At the end of the season the ever-dependable thriller Les Collins was the top scorer on an average of 8.57 while Grieves' injury problems contributed to his average falling to 8.19.

The Premier Trophy saw Tigers finish near the bottom of the Northern section, losing two at home to Hull and Workington and winning none away. In the Premier League, Tigers finished in ninth spot out of fourteen, just missing out on a Young Shield place. When the dust had settled the records show that they had lost four at home, three on the track, to Hull, Newport, and Swindon and one, against Sheffield, was awarded to the visitors by the Speedway Control Board. Tigers also drew at home to Exeter. On their travels they won at Newcastle and Reading and drew at Workington. They picked up 5 bonus points out of 13.

The match versus Sheffield was abandoned by the referee when no licensed replacement could be found to take the place of the starting marshall, who had been fined and banned from the meeting following an alleged altercation with a rider. This was the second controversy to hit Glasgow as the referee reported promoter Brian Sands to the Speedway Control Board over an incident with rider Andre Compton, who was guesting for Newport. Sands was fined a substantial sum which remained unpaid for some time, placing doubt over Glasgow's future. The fine was, however, paid by well-wishers, allowing Tigers to take to the track in the following season.

In the Knockout Cup they were eliminated by Exeter. Glasgow did not have a place in the Four Team Tournament finals and did not contest the League Best Pairs. The Scottish Cup went to Edinburgh, who won both legs. The match at

Ashfield produced fireworks with Grieves being fined for an incident which followed Edinburgh's Eriksson's exclusion for unseating the Glasgow man. The Spring Challenge also went to Edinburgh, who clinched the trophy thanks to a draw at Ashfield.

In the early season they raced and lost to Young Sweden, a meeting which starred visiting Andreas Bergstrom, who set a new track record. Yet again the Glasgow promotion paid out after losing the Charity Challenge to Workington.

The Ashfield Classic went to the popular Les Collins, who won the final thanks to an uncharacteristically superb start, from the more fancied Michael Coles and Carl Stonehewer.

James Grieves ended an eventful season with a testimonial meeting in which a Grieves Select, including reigning World Champion Mark Loram, defeated a Wolverhampton side.

The Ashfield track played host to a Conference League team in 2000. Homeless Linlithgow Lightning and Ashfield Giants merged, under the promotion of Edinburgh promoter John Campbell and managership of Linlithgow's Alan Robertson, to become Lightning Ashfield Giants.

They raced eight home meetings at Saracen Park, mostly on Monday nights, losing to Mildenhall, Boston, Newport and Somerset and winning none away. Their ninth home match was raced at Armadale and it is notable as this fixture produced the team's only maximums of the season. Ever-presents Derek Sneddon and Robert McNeil scored a full 21 points and 13 paid 15 respectively.

Had the Giants been able to track their strongest septet for every meeting they would have probably been up near the top. As it was, their line-up was never the same two meetings running, including a double header in Glasgow, and it is not surprising they did not do better. However, they did give a lot of lads and a lass (Charly Kirtland) their chance of competitive league racing and that cannot be a bad thing.

At the time of writing, Glasgow Tigers are looking forward to the 2001 season. Brian Sands stepped down in early February, selling his controlling interest to Alan Dick, chief executive of Partick Thistle Football Club, and Stewart Dickson, a local businessman.

Four
Ashfield

'The White Ghost' Ken Le Breton.

Duri ng the winter of 1948, Bill Manson reported in the *Daily Record* of the possible move of the Newcastle team to Glasgow and that the move was being met with the approval of the promoting parties.

This move did take place, with Middlesbrough closing down and their team moving to Newcastle. The 1948 Newcastle side moved over the border to Saracen Park, which is situated in Hawthorn Street in the Possilpark area of Glasgow, almost due north of the city centre and just a short way from the main Edinburgh-to-Glasgow Queen Street railway line. It was while travelling by train that Ian Hoskins spotted the stadium that was home to the Ashfield Juniors football team. After visiting the site he talked to the stadium owners about the possibilities of building a speedway track around the existing football pitch. Ashfield Football Club's reaction was positive, and after talking to Johnnie Hoskins the Newcastle move was put into action.

Planning permission was granted and work started on 19 February to construct a track and safety fence. The work was contracted out to Messrs George Wimpey (Builders) who carried out all the necessary tasks required for the opening on 19 April 1949.

Ashfield Speedway Limited had four directors: Ian Batchelor, Johnnie S. Hoskins, Norrie Isbister and Tom Gentleman. Johnnie Hoskins and Norrie Isbister were to take over the day-to-day running of the Ashfield Speedway Club, with Norrie, who was a pioneer rider from the Nelson and Celtic Park era of 1928, carrying out the clerk of the course and managerial duties.

The team were to be known as the Giants, their colours being blue with a large

Alex Grant (left) and Gruff Garland.

Merv Harding (left) and Eric Liddell.

white 'G' embossed on the front. The riders were mainly the 1948 Newcastle team, namely Ken Le Breton, Maurice and Rol Stobart, Alec Grant, Keith Gurtner and Norman Evans, who was to captain the side. The newcomers included an unknown Aussie Mervyn (Merv) Harding, who arrived in this country along with Jack Young (who was to have a glittering career with Edinburgh). They arrived in early 1949 to prepare for what they hoped would be a place in a league side for the new season. Merv had little or no previous experience and had to chance his luck. He approached Johnnie Hoskins and, asking for a trial, said 'I want to ride for the Giants, I have a good machine, and paid my own fare from Australia'. Hoskins replied, ' If you can hold a place in the Giants team for three months, I'll pay £100 towards your fare, but if you don't make it you'd better get yourself a good-size feed and start swimming back to Australia'.

Not only did Merv get his £100, but he went on to play a supporting role to Ken Le Breton in the Ashfield team. Merv rode in pillar-box red leathers, and inherited the nickname 'Indian' or 'Plaster Nose' (due to the plaster he wore across the bridge of his nose). Twenty-two-year-old Merv also christened his bike 'Cowboy Kate'. Other newcomers were Gruff Garland, who came into the side with a wealth of experience travelling across the Clyde from near neighbours Tigers. Willie Wilson, who was to become known as 'Wasp' due to his striped jersey, was to become a regular team member after coming into the side for the second match. Willie was spotted riding in the second half at White City (Glasgow) by

Norrie Isbister, who gave him his chance by throwing him in at the deep end.

The big day arrived on 19 April 1949 when 9,707 spectators witnessed the opening of the Saracen Park track by The Lord Provost of Glasgow, Sir Hector McNeil, before the meeting against Walthamstow Wolves in a league encounter. Another guest at that opening ceremony was Lt-Col. Brook, chairman of the Speedway Control Board. The Giants made the perfect home debut with a win 48-36 over the Wolves, and Ken Le Breton became an instant hero with an untroubled maximum and the track record of 68.4 seconds.

Manager Norrie Isbister was another who was glad that the opening night had gone without a hitch, stating later 'that after eight weeks he was looking forward to a full night's sleep'. This was not the first time that the Giants had taken to the track as a team, as their season had opened with three away fixtures. The first was at Edinburgh on 2 April, where they had the misfortune to lose their captain Norman Evans, who damaged his left knee in the opening heat. It was an injury that was to keep him out of the team for a number of weeks. On the plus side of this opening 57-27 defeat was the form of 'Ghost' Ken Le Breton, who scored 10 points (Ken rode in white leathers, hence the 'Ghost' tag). Fellow Aussie Merv Harding also showed Johnnie Hoskins that he was here to stay with a well-taken 7 points.

The second League encounter against Southampton on 12 April turned out to be another misadventure when Ken Le Breton missed the meeting due to transport difficulties, and Rol Stobart also failed to turn up – but in his case it was not his fault as the train which was transporting most of the team failed to stop at

Winner of Ashfield World Championship Round, Ken Le Breton (right).

Little Boy Blue – Keith Gurtner.

Carlisle! The Control Board, in their wisdom, were to fine the Ashfield promotion £50 for not fielding a full side. Ken Le Breton did not escape, suffering a £10 fine for his non-appearance.

Changes were made to the side for this fixture, as out went Maurice Stobart, Jack Martin and Peter Lloyd, and in came Keith Gurtner for his debut. Keith was another colourful character who raced in blue leathers and was the original 'Little Boy Blue'. Keith was a twenty-eight-year-old who hailed from the quaintly named town of Wagga Wagga (pronounced Wogga Wogga) in New South Wales. Others were new rookie Willie Wilson, along with veteran Gruff Garland. The Giants had to borrow Johnny Bradford and Bert Croucher from Southampton to complete the team, but to no avail as Southampton ran out easy winners 50-34. Another heavy defeat at Sheffield, 52-31 on 14 April, meant that the Giants had not found the strong start they were looking for.

Tuesday 26 April at Saracen Park saw the first local derby with near neighbours Glasgow Tigers take place, Tigers winning 46-35 in front of a 13,113 crowd. The meeting finished with a bizarre incident in the final heat when Alec Grant was disqualified after passing Buck Ryan on the last lap, causing Ryan to fall. Grant was excluded and, with Rol Stobart already fallen, the heat was declared a 3-0 result with Norman Lindsay the winner.

Out of the eight League meetings, five at home and three on the road in May, the Giants only emerged victorious on three occasions. They won twice at home against Cradley Heath and Coventry, and at Coventry on 14 May they recorded their only away win of the season with a 45-38 victory. Norman Evans was back in the side, and his 10 point return made all the difference in supporting the three

Aussies, Ken Le Breton, Merv Harding and Keith Gurtner, who had held the team together up to that point.

Crowd figures were on the increase, and 13,958 spectators witnessed yet another home defeat when the Edinburgh Monarchs plundered the league points on 14 June. However, wins against Newcastle and Norwich in the final two weeks of June helped raise the team spirit as they moved into second half of the season.

On 5 July Ashfield held a round of the World Championship, which included Wembley's Freddie Williams among other top First Division stars. With such a high-class field of riders the racing was fast, but lacked incident. A very large crowd of 17,657 witnessed a night on which the track record tumbled in just about every race. The existing time of 66.6 was beaten no less than twelve times, with the home hero Ken Le Breton not only winning the round with an unbeaten 15 points but also securing the new track record, his new time being 64.8 seconds.

The Tigers again crossed over the River Clyde to Saracen Park on 19 July, but this time they returned home after suffering a 51-33 defeat. The biggest crowd of the season, 18,117, watched as the Giants ripped into their city rivals to reap ample revenge for that early season defeat. The three Aussies, Ken Le Breton, Merv Harding and Keith Gurtner, led the way with only Keith dropping a point in his final outing. The following week, on 26 July, it was Edinburgh who were making a return visit, but again it was the mighty Monarchs who returned home with a 45-39 win.

August came and went with more indecisive performances. Wins against Fleetwood and Coventry were interrupted by heavy defeats at the hands of Norwich and Southampton at Saracen Park. Again the Giants had no luck on their travels, suffering defeat in all their three league encounters. One bright spot was that Ken Le Breton did enough at Wembley and Belle Vue in his final World Championship qualifying rounds to reach the final, which would be held at Wembley on 22 September. This was quite a feat by Ken, as he would be Division Two's only representative on the big night.

The mighty Bristol side were the visitors to Saracen Park on 6 September, and were expected to return home with the league points in the bag. The Giants had other ideas and in a classic encounter the Bulldogs were held to a draw.

Following this, on 13 September, First Division Harringay were the visitors in the second leg of a challenge match against a side labelled Scotland. 17,000 spectators again witnessed a classic encounter. The Scots included Ken Le Breton and Jack Young alongside true Scot Gordon McGregor, and together they held Harringay to a draw. In the first leg at Harringay, however, the First Division men had done enough to win on aggregate 100-68.

Newcastle were the visitors to Saracen Park on 20 September, but it was a tragic end to a great speedway career when the Giants captain Norman Evans was involved in a bizarre accident. The events all started in heat one of the meeting when Keith Gurtner and Ernie Brecknell, who were having a neck and neck battle for first place, locked together as they crossed the finish line and crashed through the first bend fence into the crowd. Meanwhile Norman Evans, who saw what had happened, turned onto the centre green which was shrouded in darkness. He did this to avoid the crash in front of him, but failed to see a track employee John Goroven who was running to help the accident victims. John and Norman clashed and this resulted in both taking an ambulance ride to hospital. Thankfully, John was not too badly injured, but Norman suffered a knee injury which resulted in him having to retire from speedway.

Altogether eleven spectators received medical attention at the track, but none needed further treatment. Amazingly, Keith Gurtner was able to return despite a leg injury and take his place in the meeting, scoring 10 paid 11 from his four races in a relatively easy 51-33 win for the Giants.

In that same week, a novice rider from Ashington, Northumberland, thirty-two-year-old Robert Langdown, was having a trial at the Ashfield circuit when he crashed suffering a broken leg. 22 September was Ken Le Breton's big night at Wembley when he took his place among the speedway elite. He made his World Championship bow with a 4-point haul, a third in his first race was followed with a last place. Another three thirds left him in thirteenth as Tommy Price of Wembley became champion.

The Ashfield Giants closed their league campaign with meetings against Cradley Heath on 1 October and Sheffield on the 4 October. Both ended in defeat, relegating them to the lower reaches of the final league table. The Giants finished next to bottom with Coventry holding the cellar position.

The season closed in 1949 with four challenge matches, the first of those being Scotland *v*. Holland in a Charity Challenge which was attended by Lord Provost Mr Victor Warren. Sadly, the match turned out to be a runaway win for the Scots, 62-22. It may have been a poor year result-wise for the Giants, but on the plus side crowd figures held at a steady 11,000-12,000, which was to cause the authorities some concern. Because of this, essential work had to be carried out on the terraces before the 1950 season could get underway.

Ken Le Breton seemed to make a habit of winning second-half trophy finals at Saracen Park, but the most unusual trophy he ever won must have been a breastplate and helmet in the final of the Knight of Speed contest in the second half of the Southampton match on 10 May, when Ken got the helmet stuck on his head. Phil Bishop of Southampton made to help him remove it, but actually pushed it on even harder!

1950 saw the Giants climb off the bottom of the Division Two League table. They were to finish eleventh out of fifteen teams, but still lost five times at home with only three successful ventures away.

Ken Le Breton was back to lead the side, but at times seemed to lose his sparkle due to the amount of open bookings he was taking on all over the country. He dipped out of the World Championship, failing to progress from the third round ties. Merv Harding on the other hand made further progress both on the team and individual front. Merv reached the Championship rounds in his quest for glory, but failed to amass enough points to reach the final.

Keith Gurtner, Alec Grant and an ever-improving Willie Wilson were back, but it was the lower end of the side which seemed to cause the most concern. Veteran leg-trailer Bob Lovell was recruited in late April and provided some stability, and, after a number of riders had come and gone, local man John 'Larry' Lazarus claimed a regular spot along with Londoner Ed Noakes. In July, Eric Liddell made way for a new signing from Wimbledon, Bruce Semmens, who proved an instant hit with some big scores, slotting in as the third heat leader.

The 1950 season started with the Kemsley Shield Northern Trophy, which was organised on a mini-league format. There were eight teams in the league, and the Giants came close to winning their first piece of silverware. In the end they had to settle for the runners-up position, the trophy ending up with Halifax.

Two home defeats against eventual winners Halifax, 42-41, and Edinburgh 51-33 surely cost the Giants the title. What made the defeat against the Monarchs more galling is that on 13 May the Giants had done what should have been the hard part of the job, winning at Old Meadowbank 44-38, and this was only three days after taking the points off city rivals Tigers at White City 43-41. Their other away win came at Newcastle on 24 April.

In the National Trophy the Giants reached the Division Two final, and again it was Halifax who spoilt the party, Ashfield finishing as runners-up. On their way

Left: Bruce Semmens. Right: Ashfield Andy.

to the final, the Giants performed a few miracles, having to pull back some big deficits from the away legs – 13 points down to Cradley Heath in their first round first leg on 29 May, they did enough the next night at Saracen Park, despite losing Alex Grant in a heat seven crash, to progress to the second round with a 108-107 aggregate win.

They met Sheffield in the second round on 9 June and went down 57-51, leaving themselves a good chance in the second leg, which took place at Saracen Park on 20 June. If they thought it was going to be plain sailing, however, Sheffield had other ideas and they made the Giants work for the 114-101 aggregate win.

Walthamstow were the opponents in the semi-final on 26 June, and in the first leg in London they left themselves a mountain to climb when the Wolves amassed a 25-point lead to take to Ashfield on 4 July. For the second leg, Bruce Semmens had come into the side and was involved in a controversial incident in heat sixteen, which was re-run after Bruce had reared at the start. In the re-run, Merv Harding and Bruce raced home for a 5-1, but it was then announced that Bruce had been excluded for bumping and the race was awarded 3-3. Bruce was unbeaten in his other outings and with Ken Le Breton along with Merv Harding also unbeaten by an opponent, the Giants scraped into the final by one point, winning 108-107 on aggregate.

They met Halifax in the final with the first leg being held at Saracen Park, where they won 58-50 on 11 July, but found the Dukes in a determined mood at the Shay, going down 64-43 in the second leg.

In the league the Giants were on a winning streak at home until they met Norwich on 5 September, going down to a 38-45 defeat. Then on 19 September, Fleetwood were the visitors to Saracen Park and left with a 49-35 victory. Keith Gurtner was missing for this match, having suffered a head injury at Newcastle the day before.

The final two home meetings both ended in defeat, as the Glasgow Tigers romped to a 10 point victory on 10 October and then the next week Cradley Heath won the re-run fixture, the original being rain affected three weeks previously. Cradley's 49-35 victory was made easier as Ken Le Breton was missing, being on his way home to Australia. On their travels the Giants were successful on three occasions, winning at Fleetwood, Plymouth and against bogey team Halifax 48-36 on 13 September.

Crowd figures were on a par with 1949, with the meeting against Edinburgh on 1 August drawing 19,377. In fact, when Edinburgh were visitors to Saracen Park they always seemed to boost the crowd with their travelling support, as shown when 18,241 witnessed the North Shield encounter in May.

On 15 August a challenge match took place between Jack Parker's Seven and Jack Young's Seven. Jack Young's Seven won this encounter 49-35, but it was the Champion of Champions Match Race, which preceded the main match, between Parker and Young that caused the most interest. Norrie Isbister claimed that these match races, both won by Jack Young, were the best he had ever witnessed, with

Jack Young being presented with the Champion of Champions trophy by Bailie McAslan with Norrie Isbister, Johnnie Hoskins and Jack Parker looking on.

nothing between either rider for four laps. Jack Young was always a popular visitor to Ashfield, and it was Jack who won the World Championship qualifying round there on 25 July.

On Monday 28 August a BBC Scottish Home Service transmission went out at 8.25 p.m. It lasted thirty-five minutes and featured Johnnie Hoskins, Norrie Isbister, Ken Le Breton, Willie Wilson and Gordon McGregor, amongst others. Johnnie Kelly introduced the show which traced speedway from its roots in West Maitland in 1923 through to the present day (1950). Interviews were based on a fictitious meeting between the Giants and Meadowbank Monarchs. The title of the broadcast was *Round and Round They Go* and it was devised by Bill Craig and John Law. The programme was produced by Archie Lee.

Overall it was a good campaign for the Giants, apart from that end-of-season lapse, and they could only look to 1951 for further improvement.

Norrie Isbister stated that it was the worst day of his life when he received a telegram on the 8 January 1951 with only five words on it. It read 'Ken Passed Away Saturday – Joan'. Ken Le Breton was a key member in the second test match for Australia *v.* England at the Sydney Sports Ground on Friday 5 January and had scored 7 plus 5 bonus going into his last race, heat eighteen. Partnering Ken was

Jack Gates, while the riders for England were Eddie Rigg and Bob Fletcher. Jackie Gates led the race from Fletcher and Rigg, with Ken bringing up the rear. Going into the final bend Rigg went wide. Ken was also taking the outside course and cut into the rear of Rigg's machine. Rigg managed to pull out and fell, but Ken's bike locked and he drove straight into the safety fence.

There was nothing anyone could do, and Ken died the next day in the St Vincent's hospital in Sydney of severe head injuries, including a fractured skull. He also had a punctured lung. His funeral was held on Tuesday 9 January at Woronora Crematorium. The pall-bearers were riders from the two test sides, and the cortege of fifty-five cars had a police escort to the crematorium.

Norrie Isbister went on 'I will never forget the scenes when the news came through in January 1951 that Ken had been killed. I was sitting in the office at Ashfield when the ambulance man came in. He said "Have you seen what it's like outside?", I said, "No, I've been here since early on". I went out to look, and the place was packed outside Ashfield. Such scenes, there were women and girls weeping ... Ken was a god to these people. He was known as the White Ghost, but he was a god.'

'Ken lived for two things, and I don't know in which order – his wife Joan and speedway, or speedway and his wife. You always found him in the evening in the

Ken (right) in action in Australia.

Ken with wife Joan and Norrie Isbister.

workshop, working on his machine. He was a good guy, a good thinking guy.'

Would Ashfield survive without Francis James 'Ken' Le Breton? Would there be life without 'The Ghost' in 1951? To make matters that bit harder for the Ashfield promotion, Keith Gurtner departed. 'Little Boy Blue' wended his way a few miles along the road to join Motherwell who had entered the Second Division in 1951.

Into the Ashfield side came Jack Gates from Wembley and Ron Phillips, an Aussie signed from Edinburgh for £100. Bruce Semmens and Merv Harding, along with the ever faithful Willie Wilson, were back to lead the side, but as before the Giants had troubles down in the reserve department and had three different number sevens in three meetings. Larry Lazarus held the number eight berth for much of the season with odd spells in the team and odd spells out with injury. Ed Noakes, Eric Liddell and the aforementioned Ron Phillips all had turns at reserve, as did new Aussie Chum Taylor and Bob Lovell, who stayed until late August. Cyril Cooper, Ron Johnson, who saw out the season from mid-August onwards, and Dick Howard, who had a single outing at the end of the season, also rode for the Giants. They also used ex-Sheffield Aussie Jack Bibby for a brief spell at reserve. Chum Taylor moved on to Cardiff in Division Three and became a great hit.

Ashfield's season got off to a bad start in the North Shield with only two wins at Saracen Park. Newcastle and then Edinburgh both left win big wins under their

Ashfield squad 1951.

belts. Then, on 15 May, city rivals the Tigers stole the points, winning 44-40. Away from home, Giants were successful at Motherwell with a 45-39 win over their near neighbours and finished next to bottom of the North Shield table.

In the National Trophy they progressed though to the next round after disposing of Liverpool, winning 116-100 on aggregate. Against Cradley Heath in the first leg of the second round at Saracen Park, they built up a good lead of 71-37, but at Dudley Wood in the second leg on 11 June the Giants let it slip when their only race winner was Willie Wilson, going down and out of the National Trophy 83-25 on the night and 120-96 on aggregate. In the Scottish Cup they also dipped out at the first hurdle against Edinburgh, being beaten in both the home and away legs, 134-81 on aggregate.

Their early League performances are barely worth mentioning, as they won only two matches from their first eight encounters, and at that point they were firmly established at the foot of the table. However, from mid-July they lost only two fixtures at Saracen Park, with Edinburgh continuing their sequence of Ashfield wins on 4 September 44-40 and then to Liverpool on 25 September, where they again went down 44-40.

On the road they did pick up wins at Fleetwood, Motherwell and Cradley Heath to lift themselves to a respectable eighth place in the table, a remarkable recovery after starting in such an inauspicious manner.

Bruce Semmens was the top man in 1951, but at times he lacked consistency. Bruce was a bit of a character, described by some as a lovable rogue. He was an accomplished pilot and flew his own plane from down south for home meetings. He would buzz the Ashfield stadium, this being the signal for Johnnie Hoskins to have him picked up at the airport and delivered to the meeting.

Crowd levels were down on previous seasons, although the Scotland *v.* England test match on 3 July, which ended in a 59-49 win for Scotland, attracted 20,688 paying spectators. A crowd of 13,000 watched the American touring team take a heavy defeat 51-33 on 22 May and 17,198 turned out to watch Larry Lazarus win the Ken Le Breton Trophy on 6 October.

The Scottish Junior Championship closed the 1951 season on 16 October, with Edinburgh's Harry Darling winning after a run-off with Nivvie McCreadie.

Merv Harding moved on to New Cross for the 1952 season, having made it clear that he would like a move down south at the end of the 1951 campaign. In exchange, Don Gray came in the opposite direction, but did not hit the heights of the colourful Merv.

Willie Wilson, Cyril Cooper, Ron Phillips and ever-improving Larry Lazarus were back, along with the unpredictable Bruce Semmens, who was made club captain for 1952. As in years gone by, the reserve position was filled with many

Larry Lazarus, winner of the first Ken Le Breton Trophy.

faces – Jim Blythe had an extended run, as did Dick Howard before moving into the top six. Veteran Wilf Jay joined the Giants in June and did a reasonable job until he broke his arm at Wolverhampton in August, while Norman Hargreaves was acquired from Belle Vue at the tail-end of June and soon moved into the main body of the team after a spell at reserve. After Wilf Jay was injured, a young local Scottish rider called Jimmy Tannock took his chance to hold onto the reserve spot until the end of the season.

The Second Division had been reduced to twelve teams in 1952, and the Giants finished in seventh spot. Their League form was much the same as the previous season, starting with a 42-42 draw at Saracen Park on 8 April, then travelling to Coventry on 12 April to pull off a good 43-41 win over the Bees, with Bruce Semmens scoring a full 12 point maximum.

Up until the end of July they had a good run with some convincing displays, losing only to near neighbours Motherwell on 10 May when Derek Close led his side to a convincing win 51-32, and then to the Tigers, when their City rivals inflicted a 48-36 defeat.

In the second half of the season, from August onwards, Poole, Cradley Heath and Leicester all left Saracen Park with the league points in the bag. Away from home, apart from their win at Coventry, victory came at Motherwell on 25 June 45-39 and at the same venue 44-39 on 9 September. Their only other success on the road was at Oxford, where they drew 42-42 on 28 August.

In the Scottish Cup the Giants disposed of Motherwell 120-94 on aggregate, winning both legs to reach the final against city rivals Tigers, but after losing their home leg 58-50 were crushed 75-33 in the White City five days later. They had also bowed out of the National Trophy to the Tigers who, after winning at Saracen Park 56-52, finished the job at White City 65-43 for a aggregate 112-95.

Ashfield's round of the World Championship came on the 19 July. It was won by Belle Vue's Ron Johnston with a score of 14. The best Giant on the night was Bruce Semmens with 11, and Cyril Cooper with 10.

Crowd figures were falling off as the season wore on. The Scotland *v.* England international was held on 5 August. The old enemy won 55-51 and the event drew the largest crowd of the season, 14,899. Whereas the first meeting against Coventry had pulled in 8,500, the Cradley Heath defeat in September attracted only 3,966 spectators. Television and other entertainments were blamed for crowds falling throughout the land, but the loss of Ken Le Breton and departure of Merv Harding and Keith Gurtner may have played their part, although 10,596 paying customers witnessed Tommy Miller win the Ken Le Breton Trophy meeting, which was the final event of the season.

Back on 2 April 1949 the Giants opened with a 57-27 defeat at Edinburgh. Less than four years later, on 11 October 1952 at the same Old Meadowbank venue, they rode their last league meeting, suffering another defeat 61-23. 'If we are compelled to leave the league' Johnnie Hoskins told the supporters at the final meeting at Ashfield in 1952, 'We will bring up the stars and stage novice meetings in an attempt to build up an all-Scottish team for 1954.'

Willie Wilson and Bob Mark (Edinburgh) fight it out.

In January 1953 it was announced that Ashfield were out of the league, and Sheffield were in for 1953 season, but before the campaign had started, Sheffield had withdrawn their entry without turning a wheel. Johnnie Hoskins was to take a back seat, moving on to run Belle Vue in 1953, and Norrie Isbister was to take charge at Ashfield after they were granted a licence to run open and challenge matches.

This meant that the team members would move on to pastures new. Willie Wilson went to Belle Vue for a reported £1,500, Larry Lazarus to Glasgow Tigers and Ron Phillips, along with the up-and-coming Jimmy Tannock, went to Motherwell. A total of nine meetings were completed, with another on 28 July being abandoned due to heavy rain. There was one rain-off on 14 July when an Ex-Giants *v.* Scottish Select was the victim.

The 1953 season started on 9 June with a meeting involving individual competitions for both junior and senior riders. Bob Lindsay won the junior and Harold Fairhurst the senior trophies. Norrie tried to involve those riders who had served the Giants over the years with Wilson's Wasps *v.* McGregor's Clan, or Harding's Red Devils *v.* Campbell's Dandies, but crowd levels had now dipped to an all time low. Just 5,159 attended the Scotland *v.* Dominions on 23 June, then only just over 3,000 for the return of Merv Harding for the Red Devils meeting on 7 July. In this meeting, Merv Harding crashed on the first lap of the first heat and that was the last time he visited the track. In this same meeting, ex-Giant Cyril Cooper failed to arrive due to a car breakdown.

There was a long break between the Best Pairs meeting of 4 August and the Ken

Glasgow's Tommy Miller – twice winner of the Ken Le Breton Trophy.

Le Breton Trophy meeting on 29 September. Crowds had tailed off, with just over 2,500 turning up for this final event. The Ken Le Breton Trophy, which was retained by Tommy Miller, marked the end of an era, and at the end of the meeting the promotion handed over the track licence to the ACU steward.

Two final meetings were run at the stadium, both featuring midget cars only on 6 and 13 October. Thereafter the Saracen Park Stadium fell silent to the sound of speedway until 1999, when the Giants great rivals, the Tigers, moved in.

Five

Motherwell

A fine action study of Bluey Scott.

The steel-making town in the Clyde Valley in Scotland's Black County first saw speedway in 1930 at a track in the town's Airbles Road. The track staged a few meetings in September and October, featuring the White City lads known collectively as 'The Blantyre Crowd'. They advertised a match between Blantyre and Glasgow for the last Saturday in October, assuring the readers, probably misleadingly, that 'This meeting will run irrespective of the weather'.

Nothing is known of any 1931 action, but in 1932 the Lanarkshire Speedway Club opened a track on the same site. At least four meetings were staged, again featuring The Blantyre Crowd and some newcomers. The site was redeveloped as a greyhound stadium which became operational in July 1932, suggesting that speedway had fizzled out by early June.

The Post War Era

The success of the three other tracks in Scotland acted as a catalyst for the reintroduction of speedway to Motherwell. The venue had been a derelict coal bing which had been restored to provide the land for a joint speedway and greyhound stadium. Known as The Stadium, the track was built from scratch with speedway in mind and the bends were capable of accommodating six cars side by side.

The first meeting was staged on Friday 14 July 1950, when the Lanarkshire Eagles side, comprising Glasgow Tigers men like Tommy Miller and Junior Bainbridge, together with Tommy Bateman of Sheffield, defeated Newcastle. Two

Glasgow's Junior Bainbridge with Noel Watson.

The 1951 Motherwell 'Eagles'.

men who would become great Eagles stars, Derek Close and Gordon McGregor, were in the opposing line-ups. Lots of fans turned out but, more importantly, they came back for the rest of the season in ever growing numbers. The good folk who lived in the town's Milton Street had never seen the like of this before.

The main task for Eagles was building up a team, and they soon had Noel Watson and Clive Gressor on their books. Gressor was injured mid-season but wee Aussie Watson came on in leaps and bounds as the season progressed, making Ashfield rue parting with him. Will Lowther also became an Eagles fixture.

The team varied from week to week, normally drawing upon riders from Newcastle and other southern tracks rather than using riders from the Scottish teams. They had a season facing a mixture of club and select sides, put together to form attractive lines-ups. Eagles lost to weakened sides from Cradley Heath 49-33, a Glasgow Tigers Select 47-37 and Edinburgh Monarchs 51-33, but beat Sheffield 43-41 and Ashfield 50-34.

Jack Young won the Gala Cup in July with Merv Harding taking second and Don Wilkinson third. The other non-team event was the closing fixture, a best pairs, won by Eagles duo Noel Watson and Will Lowther. The individual star of the pairs was Son Mitchell, but partner Don Wilkinson had a poor (for him) Motherwell meeting and they finished third.

The Lanarkshire Eagles – not to be confused with the local motorcycle club known as the Motherwell Eagles – were admitted to the Second Division of the National League in 1951. They secured Gordon McGregor from Tigers, Danny

Bluey Scott.

Lee from Edinburgh, Bill Baird from Ashfield and added Stan Bradbury, Scottish junior Bob Lindsay and a new Aussie, Bluey (Eric) Scott, who was recommended by Jack Young, to Watson and Lowther.

The opening fixture at The Stadium was against the Swedish Lions, who included Bertil Carlsson, Stig Pramberg and Sune Karlsson. The Eagles, using guests Merv Harding and Chum Taylor from Ashfield, won 48-36. The Swedes had been treated to a slap-up lunch in the afternoon of the match, but when racing began the Eagles bared their talons.

Eagles also won their opening North Shield event against Fleetwood 47-37, going on to beat Glasgow Tigers in what was their first official Scottish derby 46-35 and then narrowly beat Newcastle. They then lost at home to fellow Scottish sides Ashfield and Edinburgh. Away from home, the Eagles took defeats everywhere but Fleetwood, where they recorded their first ever away win on 2 May. The team changed with the introduction of Joe Crowther, another ex-Tigers stalwart, while the loss through injury of Bradbury, Lee and Scott saw Harry Andrews and Malcolm Riddell slotted in at the reserve berths.

In early May, Halifax Dukes threw Motherwell out of the National Trophy with sound defeats at both The Shay and The Stadium (79-29 and 39-69 respectively). The start of the league saw the Eagles go down 32-52 at Leicester and 24-60 at Halifax. Despite adding Bill Dalton and the arrival of Aussie Keith Gurtner at the start of the league campaign, the tale of woe continued with an exit from the

Scottish Cup at the hands of Glasgow Tigers. The only consolation was that their display at White City, a 57-51 defeat, was better than that at The Stadium, which was a 61-47 defeat.

The side struggled on until early June, when the promotion pulled off a big signing which boosted the Eagles' fortunes. They secured the services of Derek Close from ailing Newcastle – but promptly lost to the Geordies at home on Close's debut evening. However, the following night they rocked the Scottish speedway establishment by winning 48-36 at Old Meadowbank in Edinburgh against what was, admittedly, a weakened Monarchs side.

This steadied the Eagles and they performed much better for the rest of the season. They won away from home at Stoke, Newcastle and, more importantly, at the White City home of Glasgow Tigers, but had the odd glitch or two at home with a narrow defeats by Ashfield and Edinburgh and a thumping by Liverpool. However, by and large, they held their own.

The club collected a bit of silverware in the shape of the Lanarkshire Cup after beating Ashfield in the first round and Glasgow Tigers in the final. Both matches in this tournament were staged at The Stadium. The team that travelled to Ireland suffered a defeat at Chapelizod in Dublin but defeated their American touring team guests, who spent the season operating out of Dublin's Shelbourne Park stadium.

All in all the side did well enough for their opening season in the League, with

Joe Crowther welcomes Derek Close to the team.

a line-up that was a mixture of rising stars, veteran second strings and journeymen-reserves-cum-second strings. They finished a respectable seventh place in the Second Division ahead of Ashfield and Glasgow. On the individual front the big trophy event was the Skelly Trophy, sponsored by the local motor dealer. This went to Tommy Miller, while home favourites McGregor and Close both collected 12. Earlier in the year, McGregor had won the Motherwell round of the World Championship with 14 points. Gordon made it to the First Division round but did not progress further.

Bill Dalton dropped out of the side for the start of the 1952 and Eagles drafted in young Scottish find Scott Hall, gave Bluey Scott a bigger role and settled down to the business of the Second Division of the National League. They had big wins against Liverpool, Stoke and Yarmouth in quick succession, they then repulsed Poole and Coventry before winning at Oxford, only coming back to earth with a home defeat from Glasgow Tigers.

Eagles bounced back to beat Oxford and Coventry at The Stadium and things looked good for a run in the National Trophy. Opponents Coventry had other ideas, however, and a big 61-47 win in the Steel Town was countered by a 71-36 defeat at Brandon. Other trophies which slipped away from the Eagles were the Lanarkshire Cup, which went to the Tigers and the Scottish Cup, which saw them take a first-round exit at home thanks to home and away defeats by the Giants – 46-61 at Motherwell and 48-59 in Glasgow.

Veteran Joe Crowther dropped to reserve then lost his place to Bob Lindsay

Edinburgh's Roy Bester leading Bluey Scott (outside) and Derek Close.

Gordon McGregor, Stan Bradbury and Derek Close.

right at the end of May. The side looked capable of winning at home but did not have much chance of success away. The home defeat by Ashfield in the Scottish Cup was followed by a win over Cradley. Defeats by Tigers and the Ashfield Giants and a draw against Monarchs in rapid succession was not popular with the fans. A win against Liverpool at home and a win at Oxford seemed to steady the ship, and it was followed by wins over Oxford and Yarmouth.

Eagles did not allow this to lull them into a sense of false security and they added Johnnie Green to their side as a direct replacement for the unsettled Keith Gurtner. Gurtner was a swap for Green, who had come from Edinburgh. Unfortunately, the Giants took the shine off Green's debut by winning the league encounter 44-39, Eagles feeling the loss of Gurtner quite acutely. The side stuttered to the end of the season and eighth place in the Second Division, making them the worst placed of the four Scottish sides.

The home high spot of 1952 was the hotly contested Scotland *v*. England fixture, which was won by the home side 56-52 after they had trailed for much of the match. England used a number of First Division men and it was Eagle Close who came good towards the end and helped clinch it. This meeting attracted the biggest ever crowd in Scotland, with 35,000 paying customers.

A high spot was the World Final appearance at Wembley of Derek Close, one of the few Second Division men to appear in the event. Derek managed fourteenth place with 4 points which was a great showing in the illustrious company, Scottish clubs Ashfield (with Ken Le Breton), Edinburgh (Jack Young) and Motherwell (Derek Close) setting a never-to-be-bettered record.

The 1953 Motherwell Eagles.

On the individual front Tommy Miller won the World Championship round with a maximum while Close scored 11 in an international event. Swedes Stig Pramberg and Briger Forsberg and American Ernie Roccio featured in this meeting. The Skelly Trophy went to a run-off won by Edinburgh's Don Cuppleditch from Glasgow's Ken McKinlay and Derek Close, after they ended level on points. A Novice Championship, staged when the team was away, was won by 'Cowboy' Bob Sharp of Glasgow.

Without Ashfield, the Scottish Second Division contingent in 1953 was reduced to three. The Eagles added ex-Giants Ron Phillips and Jimmy Tannock to their squad with Lowther retiring, Bob Lindsay moving on to Edinburgh and Stan Bradbury also moving on.

Eagles started with a big win against Coventry and a narrow defeat at Leicester and things looked good. However, the Monarchs came and blew their world apart, winning 45-39 at The Stadium. A narrow defeat at Coventry and a big home win against Stoke the following week steadied the ship but the form was up and down until the end of May – this month brought in some silverware again as they won back the Lanarkshire Cup from the Tigers.

Into June and the Tigers took the league points in a hotly contested encounter, but this was only a temporary setback, Eagles heavily defeating Yarmouth and

Stoke in quick succession. The loss of Close in July was initially made good by promoting a reserve and bringing in junior Jock Pryde. However, instead of sticking with Jock they signed Guy Allott, who stayed until the end of the season. They also added ex-Ashfield man Cyril Cooper, who displaced fellow ex-Giant Jimmy Tannock. A few close calls and some big defeats away, except at Coventry where they won 46-38, saw the season draw to a close with the Motherwell side yet again the poorest of the Scottish teams.

For the first time in their history the Eagles progressed beyond the first round of the National Trophy as they put out Third Division Swindon 124-92 on aggregate – the 'Robins' won 62-46 at Blunsdon but went down 78-30 at The Stadium. The next round against Poole proved an easier hurdle than expected and Eagles dispatched the Pirates 119-97 on aggregate, their powerful 73-35 display at home winning the tie.

The reward for defeating Poole was a crack at First Division Harringay, a side which featured Spilt Waterman and Jackie Biggs. These two star men had been on the World Championship rostrum. Eagles managed a respectable 63-45 win in Scotland but disaster struck in the second leg at Harringay Stadium in Green Lanes. Not only were they defeated by a massive 85-23, but they lost Derek Close because of a serious head injury in what was (in the terms of the tie at that stage) a meaningless heat at the end of the match.

The cup form stayed with them in the coronation year special event, the Queen's Cup. This was a single-match competition and, thanks to an away win at

Jimmy Tannock.

Coventry, they progressed to the next round. This saw the Eagles narrowly defeat Poole at The Stadium in Motherwell 55-53, with Noel Watson and Ron Phillips the last heat 4-2 heroes. The Queen's Cup semi-final was, however, over two legs and Edinburgh Monarchs won both of them to end Eagles' cup run.

The Eagles did gain their revenge for this as they put Monarchs out of the Scottish Cup, winning 112-104 on aggregate thanks to a good 57-51 display at Old Meadowbank. The final was against Glasgow Tigers and they lost on aggregate by winning 58-50 at The Stadium but losing 65-43 at White City.

Ron Mountford of Birmingham won the World Championship round from Swedes Stig Pramberg and Briger Forsberg. Tommy Miller retained the Skelly Trophy, with Ron Phillips best Eagle on 12. The annual novice event was elevated to the status of Scottish Junior Championship and was won by Glasgow's Arthur Malm, after team-mate Stuart Irvine blew a perfect run up until then with a fifth race fall.

Problems with pay talks delayed the start of the 1954 season. A bit of a cloud hung over The Stadium as the wee Aussie Noel Watson, a real rising star who had been with them since almost the start, had been killed in his home country during the winter. On the up side, the Eagles had Derek Close back and the promotion had pulled off the signing coup of the year by securing the services of Glasgow's 'Atomic' Tommy Miller. The downside was an unhappy Gordon McGregor, who wanted away down south to pursue his career. McGregor's transfer request was turned down flat by the ambitious Motherwell promotion.

Eagles started with a narrow home defeat by Coventry. They then lost a close

Arthur Malm with Larry Lazarus.

Action from Ashfield v. Motherwell.

match at Edinburgh before embarking on an eleven-match North Shield and Second Division unbeaten run, home and away. It was 15 July before they suffered a league defeat when Oxford Cheetahs pulled them up at Cowley.

By now Tommy Miller was, like McGregor, wanting to leave and his form dipped alarmingly. He got his wish in early August after Eagles had raced Bristol. Ironically, Eagles first away match after the transfer was at Miller's new home track, Coventry, and Tommy bagged a maximum against his old team-mates. In the meantime, both Glasgow and Edinburgh had closed. Eagles had signed Larry Lazarus from Tigers, who edged out Scott Hall, and acquired the services of Doug Templeton, who moved into reserve after Miller left.

The loss of Miller was partly compensated for by a return to form of Gordon McGregor, but whilst their home form stayed with them, the Eagles were not so good on the road. They acquired ex-Monarchs man Bob Fletcher in the run in to the end of the campaign. The league fixtures were never completed, however, because of a wet end to the season. The missing match versus Leicester had been washed out after eight heats and a futile attempt to stage heat nine.

The Eagles went out of the National Trophy to Rayleigh Rockets in a tie that went to the penultimate of thirty-six heats – Eagles won 64-44 at The Stadium and lost 65-43 at The Weir; Rockets had the tie won in heat 17 when a 5-1 gave them 64 points, although Miller and Close made an effort and took a 5-1 in the last race. The Eagles ended up with their worst league display in their history, finishing up second bottom despite not losing a home league match. What was to be the last league match was raced on 8 October, with Eagles winning 45-39 over

Ipswich Witches.

Derek Close did well enough in the Second Division round of the World Championship to progress to the First Division round, but a sound 10 at Belle Vue was followed by 6 at West Ham and out he went of the tournament. Derek won the World Championship event at Motherwell from team-mate Miller, while Green tied with Edinburgh's Dick Campbell for third. A few weeks earlier, Campbell had scooped the Skelly Trophy from Miller and Close. Motherwell men won the top three spots in the Scottish Junior Championship with Scott Hall winning from Doug Templeton and Jimmy Tannock.

The demise of the other three Scottish promotions and the contraction of the sport elsewhere did not bode well for Motherwell. Despite a wish to run a team in the Second Division of 1955, they were effectively pushed out into the cold as the teams south of the border did not fancy a long trip north for a single match. Plans for an August 1955 revival came to nothing and the track lay unused by the bikes for three years.

In 1957 Ian Hoskins decided to try out a revival at The Stadium. He set up training sessions during the winter of 1957 and the spring of 1958 with a view to running competitive meetings using Scottish-based riders.

He signed up the Templeton brothers, Doug and Willie, Middlesbrough man Freddie Greenwell, ex-Tigers junior Jack 'Red' Monteith, ex-Monarch Jock Scott, ex-Eagle Jimmy Tannock and his greatest discovery, a young Fife grass tracker, George Hunter. The Golden Eagles raced a series of matches against English

The 1958 'Eagles'. From left to right, back row: Red Monteith, Freddie Greenwell, Willie Templeton, Jimmy Tannock, George Hunter. Front row: Dougie Templeton, Gordon Mitchell.

Motherwell programme from 1958.

junior sides, starting with Belle Vue Babes, followed by Coventry, Bradford, Leicester and, finally, the side that had closed down the 1954 season, Ipswich.

Gordon Mitchell replaced Jock Scott and the Golden Eagles, who would become the Edinburgh Monarchs a couple of years on, completed their brief season unbeaten. Doug Templeton was the star man of the venture with Willie Templeton and Greenwell the other heat leaders. It would be at Edinburgh that George Hunter would prove to be the major Motherwell find of all time.

Speedway never returned to The Stadium in its original form. The venue was abandoned and, at a later date, demolished. Some time later it was redeveloped as a trotting track. Speedway did return to the site of the original speedway and greyhound venue, but in a redeveloped stadium in 1972. The owners wanted to capitalise on the potential of the venue for motor sports and they launched an ambitious effort to introduce long-track speedway racing in Scotland. A total of three meetings were staged featuring big name speedway stars, who used conventional speedway bikes rather than the high-speed specialist long-track bikes. Unfortunately, this did not draw the massive crowds expected.

A small track was cut out on the centre green and the new Golden Eagles lost one fixture to the rain before staging their one and only meeting. In this fixture they managed to defeat a side from Middlesbrough, then known as Teesside Tigers. The Golden Eagles featured Scottish riders, including Tom Blackwood, Allan Mackie and George Wells, along with other guests. The meeting did not draw much of a crowd and the promotion did not stage any more events. There ended the Steel Town's interest in speedway.

The Motherwell team raced one last away fixture at Barrow, borrowing a couple of guests including John Jackson from Crewe who scored a maximum. Ironically perhaps, the Golden Eagles lost to the team known as the Happy Faces.

Six

Linlithgow

Blair Scott leads Neil Hewitt.

On 26 June 1994 Alan Robertson's dream came true when Linlithgow took to the track in the second leg of a challenge against Iwade and in front of a decent crowd. The new Linlithgow side got off to a good start, winning 42-35, but lost out on aggregate due to the fact that they had gone down in Kent 51-26 in their first official team match on 30 May.

Alan Robertson had been a junior, racing in the Edinburgh second half during the 1980s, but with the lack of track time many of those young riders soon drifted away from the sport. Consequently, Alan decided to place a notice on his tyre depot in Linlithgow which read 'Wanted, any type of land to build a speedway track'. An answer came from a farmer, Robert Cameron, who had just moved into the area. Robert told Alan that there was a field available at his farm (Myrehead). Alan went and found that the field was like a swamp, but this did not deter him as he and his band of helpers succeeded in draining the site, laying a raceable surface and moving hundreds of tyres into place to form a safety wall.

By May 1989 the track was ready for the first bikes to try it out, and that honour fell to Aussie Mick Powell who, wearing just a pair of fancy shorts, bare feet plus a crash helmet, jumped on a bike and flew round as though he was in a World Final. When he returned, and was asked what it was like, he replied 'Well, it's quite deep in a few places and you will have to watch it. The first bend is really deep and scary.'

So from mid-1989 through to early 1994 the small circuit was used as a training ground for novice riders to learn their craft. Two of those young lads

The Linlithgow track, with the home side on parade at the opening meeting against Iwade.

Left: Mick Powell, the first man on the Linlithgow track. Right: Stewart McDonald.

who made good were James Grieves, who went onto greater things with Glasgow, and Stewart McDonald, who got his chance with Edinburgh. Les Collins and Brian Collins have held training schools at Linlithgow amongst others, and in 1989 it was filmed by TV, when *Reporting Scotland* did a feature based around Debbie Arneil, a young lady who was giving the sport a try at that time.

Unofficial meetings did take place in those early days. Many were essentially just fun days, but with the formation of a Third Division in 1994, Alan was keen to get involved. Work started to make the track suitable for league racing. Planning permission was granted and the old track was virtually demolished, then rebuilt with a proper safety fence, and a new track was laid which measured 214 metres.

Heathersfield Stadium, as it was to be known, was so named because of a mistake on Mike Hunter's part. While publicising the circuit Mike named the venue as Heathersfield, when it should have been Heatherfield. From that report the 's' stayed in and Heathersfield was born. The Linlithgow team rode their first few meetings without a nickname. The local newspaper ran a competition with a prize of a season ticket to the person who would come up with a winning moniker. The winner was David Raeburn of Linlithgow, who came up with the name Lightning.

Geoff Powell, a former Glasgow second string, came into the side for the start of the league campaign. Being over six foot tall, Geoff was known as 'Big Leggy' due to his unique riding style. He had joined the Lightning for the

1994 Lightning. From left to right: Grant Blackie, Stuart Coleman, Paul Gould, Geoff Powell, Colin Mackie (team manager), Paul Taylor, Raymond Fosbury, Anthony Boyd, Alan Robertson, Brian Mercer (on bike).

challenge against an Edinburgh Select on 17 July, and his races with Mark 'Buzz' Burrows had to be seen to be believed. Also in that meeting, another youngster in the Edinburgh side caught the eye. His name was Neil Hewitt, and he did enough to go straight into the Linlithgow team for their opening league meeting at Heathersfield against Mildenhall.

The Lightning won that encounter convincingly 52-26, with both Geoff Powell and Paul Gould undefeated, but it was Neil Hewitt who made such an impact on his debut with a 11 paid 12 maximum from his four races. In that first year of Division Three racing the Lightning finished in fourth place out of six. They won four of their five home meetings and only lost out to the champions, Berwick. They failed to win on the road, but were close on a few occasions, going down 38-39 at Buxton, then 38-40 at Mildenhall. Geoff Powell led from the front, finishing with a home average of 11.43 (9.40 overall). He was ably supported by Paul Gould (8.72) and Peter Scully, a young Edinburgh asset (6.50).

The racing was interesting, and, at times, a bit unpredictable. The new division had entertainers aplenty, and Linlithgow had one of best in the league. Stuart Coleman had been around for a few years, trying to break though the Glasgow second half. It was Stuart who gave everyone the fright of their lives when, after winning his first three races against Buxton on 14 August, in his final race, heat twelve, he crashed straight through and over the fence on the first bend. It looked bad, but when help arrived expecting the worst they found Stuart in the field opposite. He had cleared the perimeter fence and escaped with nothing more that bruising. He was none too pleased to find out he had been excluded not just for being the cause of the stoppage, but for leaving the stadium! While lying in the field, curious cows came over to see what all the commotion was, then stood looking over the fence to watch the rest of the meeting. This was to become a regular sight at Heathersfield.

The 1995 season opened well enough with a huge 59-35 win over Buxton in a challenge, with Stewart McDonald, a former Edinburgh Monarch, scoring a marvellous 20 points from the reserve berth! In the renamed British Academy League the Lightning started with defeats at Buxton and Mildenhall before redeeming themselves with a 58-38 win over Cleveland at Heathersfield.

However, dark clouds were just round the corner when Alan Robertson announced that league racing was going to cease during July, while proposals to solve problems caused by spiralling running costs, not only at Heathersfield but throughout the league were thrashed out.

Alan said, 'We're supposed to be training up riders and giving them experience to join the big boys, but we're getting hammered financially.' He went on 'It's costing us the same to hire Speedway Control Board personnel as it does the big leagues and that's not on. Even the insurance cover is the same as the big teams and it was costing us something like £2,000 to stage a meeting'.

Left: Alan Robertson. Right: Barry Campbell.

Left: Fifteen-year-old Blair Scott. Right: Stuart Coleman.

During July an Under 16 championship did take place, with Barry Campbell winning from a young David Howe. Barry was a regular at Powderhall when, in the second half of the Monarchs' meetings, he went out in demonstration races with another hopeful, Blair Scott. David Howe went on to glory with Peterborough in both the Premier and Elite leagues.

On 5 August the Lightning were back in action at Berwick and were thrashed 71-24. This was to be Geoff Powell's last meeting for Linlithgow, Geoff moving on to Mildenhall. Cleveland youngster Brian Turner moved in to support Linlithgow and top scored with 8 points.

After a long break the Lightning did get back to league action, but not before a fun day was held at Heatherfield on 26 August as part of the Les Collins testimonial. This was an unusual meeting with two teams of fifteen members, raced over thirty heats, which was won by the 'Whites' over the 'Reds' 103-73. The team managers were Mike Faria (Whites) and Les Collins (Reds).

The first league meeting on resumption was away at Stoke on 31 August and, with Geoff Powell now out of the Lightning side, Alan Robertson decided to give Barry Campbell, now of racing age, his chance at reserve. Barry did not let the side down by top scoring with a 12 point return from his full quota of seven races as the Lightning went down 63-33.

In the Linlithgow Riders' Championship at Heathersfield on 9 September, Barry Campbell was again looking sharp, winning his first two heats, but at the finish of the second race he clipped the fence and had to withdraw from the meeting. Stewart McDonald – who had started the season with the Lightning, but since got his chance with Middlesbrough – won the meeting.

The Linlithgow side failed to win another match in the league to finish second from bottom position, sixth out of seven. The match against Stoke at Heathersfield on 29 October failed to take place when the Stoke side didn't to turn up. The Lightning gained the match points and Alan Robertson did amazingly well to put on a show for the public, finding enough riders to run a challenge match – Thunder *v.* Lightning, with the Lightning running out 49-44 winners. Their home match against Sittingbourne was also a strange affair, since it was staged on the same day as their away fixture. The Lightning were on the losing end in both matches.

After all the turmoil of 1995, the league again had a change of name. It was now to be known as the Conference League in 1996.

Alan Robertson decided to enter a mainly young and inexperienced side, with Barry Campbell (sixteen years old) and Brian Turner (seventeen) from the previous season being joined by Blair Scott, who had created the existing track record 52.1 seconds in 1995. Blair was just fifteen years old and was to become a star in the Conference League.

Grant MacDonald (sixteen), a Cradley Heath asset from Barrow, was another who was to improve over the year. Neil Hewitt was now established in the Lightning side as was Peter Scully. Elder statesmen Brian Mercer and Stuart Coleman were to act as coaches to the younger members of the side.

Brian Turner.

Grant MacDonald (centre).

The first signs of 1996 being a good year came on 7 April when a qualifying round for the British Under 21 took place at Heathersfield, with Barry Campbell and Blair Scott tied on 14 points each. After a run-off it was Blair who took the honours, becoming one of the youngest, if not the youngest, winner of an official meeting.

The first league opponents were Buxton who were beaten 42-35 at Heathersfield, with the youngsters all scoring well. Brian Turner (10), Barry Campbell (10) and Grant MacDonald (7) all did well, but Blair Scott fell after winning his first race and had to withdraw from the meeting. Defeats followed at Swindon with Blair Scott back in the side and top scoring with 11 points. Then the next day, 27 May on the Isle of Wight, they went down by the narrow margin of 2 points with Barry Campbell (13) and Blair (11) again to the fore.

Mildenhall were well beaten at Heathersfield at the start of June before the Lightning set out on the road again. Despite being Peter Scully absent due to work commitments, and a nightmare journey due to a traffic hold-up on the M25, the Linlithgow side pulled together at Arena-Essex on 7 June with Grant MacDonald (13) this time heading the score chart in a 43-33 win. The next day at Mildenhall, Blair Scott, with a paid 18 point maximum, led the side to a 44-34 win to put the Lightning on top of the league.

Before their next home meeting against Berwick, Neil Hewitt had broken his left collarbone in a nasty crash at Shawfield (Glasgow), but with another rider from the Heathersfield production line David Stokes, a sixteen-year-old from Glasgow coming into the side, the Lightning kept their top of the table position with another convincing win.

The next week, on 23 June, the team had a rest from the league, and a challenge took place between the Linlithgow 'Scots' and Linlithgow 'English', with the English winning this encounter. It was back to league action on 30 June at Buxton which resulted in a 38-40 defeat. Peter Scully had not been at his best up to this point, but with the help of Edinburgh's Mike Faria, the American was to put Peter back on track with fewer mechanical problems and an improved on-track attitude. It was to be a new, near unbeatable Peter from here on in and without doubt it could be said that Peter was to become just about the most consistent rider in the Conference League.

Peter started by winning the Linlithgow Riders' Championship on 7 July. He led the Lightning to a first-leg home win over Buxton in the Knockout Cup, then on an unbeaten away run in the league with wins over Peterbrough, Reading and Sheffield in July.

In August, the Linlithgow bandwagon, under the management of Glaswegian Colin Mackie, just kept on rolling. Defeats of Ryde (Isle of Wight) and Sheffield at Heathersfield were followed by away wins at Sittingbourne and Eastbourne before an enthralling meeting in Devon against Exeter on 26 August brought the run to a halt with a 39-38 defeat.

On 1 September at Buxton, a 39-39 draw put the Lightning into the Knockout Cup final, when their opponents would be Mildenhall. It was back to winning ways in the league with wins over Arena-Essex and Peterbrough, at Heathersfield.

The following month was a big one in the history of Linlithgow. On the weekend of the 5 and 6 October they first met Sittingbourne on the Saturday

Peter Scully.

The exciting style of Peter Scully.

in the league, winning 54-22. This showed the strength in depth of the Lightning squad as they were without Blair Scott, who was injured at Arena-Essex the night before, and Stuart Coleman, who had broken a collarbone in the previous week. Peter Scully also stood down for the Sittingbourne encounter to give Iain Milne a outing.

The next day Sittingbourne again went down in a second league match 54-24, following the first leg of the Knockout Cup final against Mildenhall. Needless to say it was a full Linlithgow side, including the injured Blair Scott (who could be forgiven for an unusually low score of 4 points). However, it was Blair who, at a crucial point in the meeting, pulled off one of the best races of the day by beating top Tiger Geoff Powell. Peter Scully (15), Barry Campbell (11 and 4), Grant MacDonald (8 and 1) and Brian Turner (8) paved the way to a 20-point lead from the first leg.

A busload of enthusiastic supporters made the journey to Mildenhall on the 12 October for the second leg of the Knockout Cup final. Despite Blair Scott still suffering from his injuries, he played a big part by winning his first two races. Peter Scully and Barry Campbell led the way with 10 each as the Lightning won their first major trophy with a well-earned draw. The league title was won on the 20 October when they met and defeated Eastbourne over two matches at Heathersfield. This left their final league match at Berwick a non-event, which was just as well since they went down to a big defeat 50-27 after losing Brian Turner after a first heat crash.

The next day would be the last time the majority of the successful 1996 side would be seen together when the Farewell Pairs was won by Blair Scott and Paul Gould, who was making a comeback after a year out, with a combined 21 points.

After such a successful season it was inevitable that the team would be split up as Barry Campbell and Blair Scott both joined Edinburgh, while Peter Scully (Hull), Brian Turner (Newcastle) and Grant MacDonald (Glasgow) also moved up a division. Stuart Coleman and Brian Mercer had both decided to retire, Neil Hewitt had signed for Edinburgh, but was loaned back to lead the 1997 re-named Lathallan Lightning, who were now racing in what would be known as the British Amateur League (the fourth name change for the lower league).

Apart from Neil, Iain Milne and David Stokes, who had both made a few outings for the Lightning in 1996, were all to get their chance to shine in 1997. Other new names were Steven McAllister, a fifteen year old from Glasgow who had been a regular in demonstrations at Heathersfield since 1994, and Ross Brady, a junior moto-cross champion aged fifteen from West Lothian. Ross's father, Alister, was a former Edinburgh Monarch at Coatbridge back in 1969, then a stalwart with Berwick in the 1970s. Mark MacIlkenny was another from Glasgow to get his chance as the season progressed. Paul Taylor, another former Edinburgh junior who had been part of the Linlithgow teams

Double winners. From left to right, back row: Robert McNeil, Alan Robertson, Iain Milne, Barry Campbell, Brian Turner, Blair Scott, Colin Mackie. Front row: Grant MacDonald, Neil Hewitt, Brian Mercer, Peter Scully, Stuart Coleman.

Neil Hewitt.

of 1994 and '95 rode again in 1997.

The season opened at Ryde (Isle of Wight) on 31 March with a 59-19 trashing, Neil Hewitt scoring 11 of the 19 points. This was to set the pattern for the rest of the 1997 season in which the Lightning only won five of their league matches to finish in the lower reaches of the league table. Amazingly, one of those wins came on their travels, on 31 July at Ipswich against the Anglian Angels 43-34.

On the individual front the season started well for Neil Hewitt with unbeaten 18 point maximums at Heathersfield against Berwick and Mildenhall before missing meetings due to being promoted into the Edinburgh line-up. While racing at Armadale against Skegness on 30 May, in heat ten he crashed and as a result of this accident has been confined to a wheelchair ever since due to serious back injuries. The loss of Neil was a massive blow to the Linlithgow promotion. People rallied round Neil and with the help of so many riders and officials a successful fundraiser was held at Heathersfield on 14 June.

Ross Brady always looked as though he was a rider just waiting to burst to the fore, but the tight Heatherfield circuit just did not seem to suit his all-out style. There was a mutual parting of the ways as Ross moved to the bigger Peterborough track where he was to become a big hit. Jonathan Swales, a twenty-two-year-old from North Yorkshire, topped the averages with 9.81 from his ten matches, Jonathan proving to be a reliable replacement for Neil Hewitt. A total of twenty riders were used over the season, including 1996

Linlithgow stars Blair Scott, Barry Campbell, Brian Turner and Peter Scully. Stuart Coleman came back for one meeting and was unbeaten in his three outings against the M4 Raven Sprockets at Reading on 16 August. The only other youngster to really shine was Paul Taylor, who averaged 7.31 from 23 meetings. Paul held the side together on many occasions throughout what was a poor season.

In 1998 Alan Robertson, after at first agreeing to run in the Conference League, (following another change of name for the league) suddenly, and for various reasons, withdrew. A season of open meetings took place instead; getting back to grass roots speedway was Alan's intention. Ian Grant, a master goldsmith, made a magnificent helmet trophy which was awarded to the rider winning the competition – which lasted throughout the season. The winning rider received a unique gold medal as the helmet could not be won outright.

The riders were in the main from the North of England with Newcastle's Steven Jones, who had a few outings for the Lightning in 1997, finishing as the runaway winner, taking first place in the three qualifying rounds, then winning the final on 15 November.

Other meetings which took place were a three-team tournament on 2 August, and the Linlithgow Riders' Championship which Jonathan Swales won with 13 points on 6 September.

1999, and the Linlithgow Lightning were back under the Chairmanship of

Ross Brady.

Left: Jonathan Swales. Right: Golden Helmet winner David McAllan.

Edinburgh promoter John Campbell in the British Conference League but, with a very young side, favourable results were again hard to come by as the Lightning finished bottom of the table.

Jonathan Swales led by example with an 8.48 average from all twelve league matches. David McAllan, the Edinburgh reserve, rode in five meetings for 9.33, with the rest of the side being made up with new young talent.

Scott Courtney, the son of Glasgow's Mark Courtney, had some great meetings, his best being against St Austell – his pass on Seemond Stephens will long be remembered. Sadly injury and machine problems seemed to hold him back.

Former Berwick rider from the 1980s Rob Grant was a regular by the side of his fifteen-year-old son Rob junior and it was young Rob who was to become the new hero with some terrific races for a newcomer. Rob finished with a 7.23 average. 9 in his second meeting at Rye House was followed by a broken collarbone which kept him out of the side in July. He returned for the home match against Rye House on 7 August and his 10 points in one of their few wins showed his fighting spirit.

Ryan Milburn, another who looked as though he might go places, broke both his legs at Heathersfield on 24 July against Newport. Up till then he had shown that he could be a big scorer at this level with 10 against Ashfield in a challenge, then 14 in the Gold Helmet qualifier. Another new boy starting to make his mark was Derek Sneddon, who again showed that if he was mounted on good equipment, he would progress further.

The Lightning went out of the Knockout Cup to Buxton losing heavily at

Heathersfield 23-67, then 51-39 at Buxton where Jonathan Swales scored a magnificent 19 points and Jamie Birkinshaw 15 in one of his few meeting for the Lightning.

David McAllan won the Heatherfield Club Championship with a 15 point maximum, the Heathersfield Gold Helmet final, before making it a full house of open meetings at Heathersfield he became the Linlithgow Riders' Champion.

Glory did come to Linlithgow in the shape of the Conference League Riders' Champion. Jonathan Swales lifted the title at Mildenhall, with Linlithgow's other representative Scott Courtney finishing in third place.

It was known that this would be the final year at Heathersfield as the farmer who owned the land had sold up. So on 24 October a Farewell to Heatherfield meeting was held to raise funds in the hope that a new venue could be found. The largest crowd ever at Heathersfield watched Les Collins race to a maximum, but it was not enough for his team the Midlands to win the four team tournament. That honour went to the Easterners who scored 28 points

Ian Grant (left) with Gold Helmet medal winner Steven Jones.

The opening 2000 Lightning Ashfield 'Giants'. From left to right, back row: Rusty Harrison, Christian Henry, Gary Flint, Steven McAllister. Front row: Rob Grant, Robert McNeil, Derek Sneddon.

with James Grieves on 11.

With no track, the Lightning riders moved to Ashfield to become the 'Giants' for 2000. The former Linlithgow riders Derek Sneddon and Rob Grant progressed such that they are now part of the Premier League, Rob with Newcastle and Derek with Edinburgh. Another who made slower progress, Robert McNeil, came good in 2000 and got his chance with Glasgow.

So Alan Robertson's dream did come true when so many young riders moved on to bigger and better things. The only hope now is that Alan can find another venue, or the conveyor belt will stop running.

Seven

The Short-lived Venues

Pioneer rider Frank Varey mounted on a water-cooled Scott.

There are a number of tracks which have operated in Scotland that have flourished for a very short time, some lasting as little as one or two meetings. Whilst they do not merit a full chapter each, they are worthy of coverage for the sake of the completeness of the history of speedway racing in Scotland.

GLASGOW NELSON

The first of the short-lived venues was Glasgow Nelson or, to give it its full title, the Olympic Stadium. This 486-yard long circuit was Scotland's first track and staged five meetings in 1928 and a further one or two in 1932.

GLASGOW CELTIC PARK

Celtic Park in Glasgow was a quarter-miler and staged twelve meetings between April and July 1928.

GLASGOW CARNTYNE

Also in Glasgow, Carntyne opened to stage two meetings in 1928 and another four in 1930. Carntyne operated in 1930 when, after track construction costs of a reputed £6,000 had been expended on an 'Australian-style' shale surface, four meetings were staged in the space of ten days in mid to late May. Poor crowds watched a mixture of local lads and riders associated with the Sheffield and Cardiff tracks stage meetings based on the old-fashioned Handicap and Scratch race format.

THRILLS OF DIRT TRACK MOTOR CYCLE RACE.

race in progress at the opening meeting of the Scottish Dirt Track Motor-Cycle Races on the Nelson Grounds, Glasgow, yesterday when the racers were watched by a large foster crowd

Action from the first meeting in Scotland at Glasgow Nelson.

Left: Glasgow Nelson programme. Right: Hamilton Showground programme cover.

Star visitors were Clem Beckett and Charles 'Tiger' Sanderson, from Sheffield and Newcastle respectively. The star home men were Richard 'Buggie' Fleeman and Frank 'Broncho' Bianchi and they were supported by a host of Scottish lads who had raced at the rival White City venue. The loss of the leading Scottish Carntyne star, Jimmie Pinkerton, in the opening meeting was a blow as he would have been a draw card. A notice in the press on the morning of what would have been the fifth meeting announced a temporary closure for some undisclosed problem. Despite suggestions that the track would be used in 1947, to the best of our knowledge speedway was never staged again at this now demolished venue. Proposals for 1947 appear never to have materialised.

BROXBURN SPORTS PARK

The pioneer Broxburn track did not even get the length of staging a meeting. This 436-yard track was the pioneer shale track built using waste retorted oil shale used to surface the modern day Scottish venues.

In 1929, an impromptu race between Drew McQueen and Sam Reid at a motorcycle club event lasted two laps before Reid fell.

GLASGOW GOVAN

A company called A & A Autos, a training school for chauffeurs, built a track in Helen Street, Govan in 1930. How long this lasted is not known, nor is there any information about who used it.

MOTHERWELL AIRBLES ROAD

A dirt track on a site in Airbles Road, Motherwell was organised by the 'Blantyre Crowd' in late 1930 and in early 1932. The 1930 venture was known as Paragon Speedway.

EDINBURGH STENHOUSE STADIUM

An attempt at reviving the sport in Scotland in 1935 was made at Stenhouse Stadium in the west of Edinburgh. A demonstration event was staged on the trotting track but appears to have failed to progress further due to the reluctance of the stadium owners to spend money on building a proper safety fence. Proposals to stage speedway at Stenhouse Stadium in the late 1940s never progressed beyond the application to the Speedway Control Board.

EDINBURGH GYLE

In the winters of 1968/69 and 1969/70, Ian Beattie ran a training track on the infield of the Gyle Trotting Track, which was located in the Glasgow Road on what is now the site of the Royal Scot Hotel. The track was used by local riders and helped discover Andy Meldrum, who went on to bigger and better things with Berwick.

AYR DAM PARK

The Stobart Brothers, Maurice and Rol, dabbled in promoting speedway in 1937 at a few venues including the Border town of Carlisle. They staged two meetings at Dam Park in Ayr on Scotland's Clyde Coast in July and August 1937.

Using northern-based riders and a couple of Scots, including Willie Durward who had raced at White City, the Stobarts staged an open meeting and one which featured a team event between Workington and Lancaster. The great Scottish road racer Jimmy Guthrie was honorary clerk of the course at the first meeting.

The anticipated holiday crowds failed to appear. Those who used to flock to the Clyde Coast obviously didn't want to spend a night out at the speedway. A revival of the sport at Ayr in the 1970s failed to get going after John Docherty had secured planning permission to use the Whitletts Greyhound Stadium.

HAMILTON SHOW GROUNDS

From 1947 to 1951 and from 1953 to 1955, the Lanarkshire Agricultural Society staged speedway racing at their Hamilton Palace Grounds show ground. Despite the programmes describing it as grass speedway, the track was formed on the ubiquitous red shale football grounds with makeshift fencing and starting arrangements. Scratch teams called variously Hamilton, Bothwell and Glasgow and consisting of a range of riders from star names to novices entertained the crowds of farmers. The highlight was the second-half Hamilton Trophy contested by the four top scorers in the match. No event was staged in 1952 due an outbreak of foot and mouth disease.

BOTHWELL

The track at Bothwell lay in a rural location between Bellshill and Uddingston and was used for training purposes. It opened in 1949 and lasted until late in 1950. The track helped launch the careers of a number of Scottish riders, its most famous old boy being Tommy Miller. The track was operated by club members who, as well as paying their subscriptions, had to work on the track to earn the right to practice. The track had a team known as The Bulls and they raced challenge events against other training schools such as Newtongrange and High Beech.

CHAPELHALL

Situated on the south side of the rapidly expanding town which lies south of Airdrie, the Chapelhall track was built in an old iron works. It followed on from the Bothwell track and used the safety fence transported from its predecessor. The venue opened in 1951 but it is not known when it was abandoned.

NEWTONGRANGE

Newtongrange lies a few miles south of Edinburgh. The former mining company village football stadium was known as Victoria Park and provided the venue for the Scottish Speedway Club to build its training track. The track was about a quarter mile per lap and was used by east coast novices, but the stars of Edinburgh Monarchs often used it for pre season practice sessions. The training track team was known as the Newtongrange Rockets. Opened in 1950, the track continued until it was closed down by the authorities for showering the next door bowling green with clouds of cinder dust.

The Taylor family, who operated Berwick Speedway, reopened Newtongrange hoping to draw in the Speedway starved Edinburgh Monarchs fans in 1970. However, the Newtongrange 'Saints', composed of Second Division racers and juniors, did not attract the crowds and after only eight of a proposed ten meetings were staged, one of which was postponed due to rain, they closed the doors.

The Saints opened on 27 May against Berwick, with a narrow win 39-37, and of seven completed meetings they won three, lost three and the last, on 15 July against King's Lynn 'Starlets', ended in a draw. Two further meetings were to be the Commonwealth Invitation Trophy (22 July) and against Peterborough (29 July), but with support failing to materialise they were never run. A further attempt to tempt Edinburgh fans into Midlothian was made in 1973. Despite the team operating as the Edinburgh Monarchs, the venture lasted only a few meetings. It was not a good start for the Monarchs as their opening meeting, on 30 May against Teeside, fell foul of the weather. Only four further meetings were to take place, the final meeting being against Barrow on 27 June. All four meetings ended in defeat for the doomed Monarchs. Like Cowdenbeath, the track was taken over for stock-car racing but this closed also, and the site was redeveloped for housing in the 1990s.

EDINBURGH CRAIGMILLAR PARK TROTTING TRACK

The now demolished stadium was used for unofficial training purposes by junior riders at various times in the 1950s, 1960s and 1970s.

Left: Cowdenbeath programme. Right: Motherwell 1972 programme.

COWDENBEATH

The former coal mining town in Fife has the honour of being Scotland's most northerly speedway track. The Hoskins family opened the track in Central Park, which is the local football stadium and home of the team known as The Blue Brazil. The track had a brick wall safety fence and was the short-lived home in 1965 of the Fife Lions. The scratch home team composed of Edinburgh and Glasgow contract men raced challenge matches, some against the teams from the most northerly English tracks. Riders could be racing for the Lions one week and against them the next. One of the eight meetings staged at Cowdenbeath was a World Championship qualifying round, Newcastle's Russ Dent winning with an unbeaten 15 points.

Altogether eight meetings took place in that short season, the first on 5 May against Colonial Tigers which was won by the Lions 44-33. The final meeting was against The Rest of Scotland on 17 July, in which the Lions signed off with a 42-35 win.

Following the demise of the organised meetings, the track was used for training purposes until early 1966 and it helped bring on riders like Brian Collins and Jim McMillan. The track is now known as The Racewall and stages stock-car racing.

BREICH

The small village of Breich now lies in West Lothian but in the late 1960s it was part of the sprawling Midlothian. The training track was constructed on a disused coal bing a short distance to the south east of the village and was used for a short spell by novices from Scotland's Central Belt.

MOTHERWELL K&K RACEWAY

The site of The Stadium in Motherwell was redeveloped as a trotting track and the owners saw a possibility of reintroducing motor and motorcycle sports. The trotting track was used to stage three long track events in 1972, some featuring star riders such as Barry Briggs, Bernie Persson and Reidar Eide. A smaller circuit was cut out in the central green area, which was some way distant from the spectator area. Only one meeting, using Second Division riders and juniors, was staged and the Golden Eagles never flew again.

PAISLEY

Glasgow's Neil MacFarlane teamed up with Birmingham co-promoter Joe Thurley to introduce speedway to the former cotton town of Paisley. To the south of the River Clyde and the west of Glasgow, the Paisley promotion sought to capitalise on the large population within the locality which included the famous Hillman factory at nearby Linwood. The track was situated in the St Mirren Football Club stadium, which is situated in the town's Love Street, and the Paisley Lions were entered into the Second Division on the British League of 1975.

The opening meeting on 5 April was against Thurley's other team, Birmingham, in a challenge, with the Lions running out winners 41-37 in front of an encouraging crowd of 6,000. Birmingham went on to win the league that year from Newcastle, but at Love Street both those sides ended up on the wrong side of a defeat.

Newcastle were visitors on 16 August, where two league points were vital to their league title hopes. But controversy reared it ugly head as early as heat one. In a race which was re-run no fewer than four times, Paisley's Sid Sheldrick was excluded for a tape offence and his replacement was reserve Geoff Snider. Then the fun started when Newcastle's Tom Owen had a coming together with both the Paisley riders in quick succession as he came from the back of the field. This, controversially and unusually, earned Tom an exclusion from the whole meeting.

Newcastle then lodged a protest with the referee Crawford Logan regarding the track conditions, to no avail. They then protested as to the width of the track, claiming that it did not meet the SCB rules. They persuaded Mr Logan to vacate his box and visit the part of the track which was causing all the fuss.

As the argument raged on, the Paisley promotion then produced a measuring tape, and measuring commenced. The result was recorded by the referee as being within the specifications and, although not happy with the result, the Newcastle side resumed the battle only to go down 46-30.

The tale didn't end there, the story goes, as the measuring tape had been doctored when a chunk had been removed in the pits before being handed over to the referee. With darkness falling, it seems the home promotion may have got off the hook!

Birmingham went on to take the league title, with Newcastle ending up in the runners up spot, but Birmingham themselves were well beaten 45-33 in the final league encounter of the season at Love Street.

The Lions finished in fifteenth spot in the league out of twenty teams. The lack of an out and out top rider saw them lose at home on five occasions and they went out of the Knockout Cup to Workington 79-76 on aggregate. Top Lion in 1975 was Sid Sheldrick with an 8.00 average, Mick Fullerton was next on 7.20. On 8 August the Lions defeated a West German Select side 55-22, Glasgow's Brian Collins won the Festival of Paisley trophy on 14 May, while Mick Sheldrick took the Championship of Strathclyde with 14 points on 30 August. The Festival of Paisley Trophy meeting on 14 May was televised, but still attracted the biggest crowd of the season – a reported 14,873. It was later admitted by the promotion that there was only 3,000 paying customers, the rest having received free tickets for the night! Two of the First Division top stars featured in the meeting, Ivan Mauger and Scott Autrey, met in three match races, with Mauger winning 2-1. 1976 saw the Lions slide down the league table, finishing in sixteenth spot out of eighteen teams. --They introduced some new faces with Colin Farquarson topping the averages with 8.22, but Sid Sheldrick slipped down the ranks in 1976 from 8.00 to 6.30.

A Scottish youngster who made rapid strides was Colin Caffrey, who from his thirteen meetings secured a respectable 3.16 average in his first season. Again at Love Street they lost five times and failed to open their account on the road, suffering 60-18 thrashings on consecutive nights in July at Teeside (Middlesbrough) and Peterborough, and went out of the Knockout Cup at the first hurdle to Ellesmere Port, going down 88-68 on aggregate. Tom Owen won the Championship of Strathclyde on 7 August with an unbeaten 15 points. Colin Caffrey won the Scottish Youth Championship, with the same unbeaten score on 18 September. Promoter Joe Thurley confirmed that poor crowd figures in 1976 put the club in doubt for 1977. But during the close season leading into 1977 it was announced the club would be running. Sadly, those reports proved incorrect and the doors were closed on Love Street just two weeks before the 1977 season got underway.

DARVEL

The Craig brothers were both farmers and junior speedway riders who raced in second-half events at Scottish tracks of the late 1970s. They had a disused coal bing on their farm which they used to form a training track. The venue was only used for training purposes.

OTHER MISCELLANEOUS TRACKS

There are reports of various private training tracks which flourished briefly. Reports suggest that Ashfield's Willie Wilson had his own track at Beith in Ayrshire, while Bob Lindsay of Motherwell and Edinburgh had a circuit near Dundonald in Ayrshire. There are reports of a one off meeting at a trotting circuit at Roman Camp near Livingston in West Lothian. In the winter of 1967/68, East Lothian County Council tried to attract the homeless Edinburgh Monarchs to Prestongrange, Prestonpans near the site of an informal short-lived training track. Speedway bikes have been given an airing in public at Dundee's Dens Park and at Stirling Albion's Annfield Stadium, but neither could be described as racing events.